LEGACIES OF THE SWORD

LEGACIES OF THE SWORD

The Kashima-Shinryū and Samurai Martial Culture

KARL F. FRIDAY
with Seki Humitake

UNIVERSITY OF HAWAI'I PRESS, HONOLULU

02 01 00 99 98 97   5 4 3 2 1

Library of Congress Cataloging-in-Publication Data
Friday, Karl F.
Legacies of the Sword: the Kashima-Shinryū and samurai martial
culture/Karl F. Friday, with Seki Humitake.
p. cm.
Includes bibliographical references and index.
ISBN 0–8248–1847–4 (alk. paper). -- ISBN 0–8248–1879–2 (pbk. :
alk. paper)
1. Martial arts--Japan--History. I. Seki, Fumitake, 1937–
II. Title
GV1100.77.A2F75 1997
796.8' 15--dc20   96–33624
CIP

University of Hawai'i Press books are printed on acid-free
paper and meet the guidelines for permanence and durability
of the Council on Library Resources

Book design by Kenneth Miyamoto

CONTENTS

LIST OF ILLUSTRATIONS

Figures

Plates

(Plates follow p. 108)

FOREWORD

MY ANCESTORS were samurai, descendants of the Fujiwara and retainers of the Kashima Grand Shrine. My father, Seki Masaji, was a professor of medicine at Okayama University and a holder of the Senior Third Rank in the old imperial court hierarchy. I am a marine biologist by profession, and oddly enough, it was my pursuit of this very modern calling that led me back to the vocational arts of my ancestors.

I spent the summer of 1959—my junior year at the University of Tokyo—interning at the Miyazaki Prefecture Fisheries Experimental Station in the town of Urashiro, near Nobeoka in Kyushu. One evening, while watching the dancers at a local celebration, I was struck by the feeling that the leaps, the movements of the hands, and the other actions of the dance had a vaguely martial character to them. This set me to thinking about the number and variety of ways in which our lives are touched upon by the arts of war, and after further reflection I began to see these arts as embracing something central and basic to human existence.

When I returned to Tokyo, following the end of my internship, I had already decided to take up the study of martial art, and set about searching for a suitable teacher. I looked around for nearly six months before learning of a school operated by Kunii Zen'ya, the eighteenth generation headmaster of the Kashima-Shinryū, in the Takinokawa district of Tokyo's Kita ward. This discovery reminded me of something my father had told me years earlier: that our own family had once practiced a style of swordsmanship called the Shinryū ("New School"), an offshoot of this same Kashima-Shinryū. It may, in fact, have been this ancestral relationship that eventually persuaded Kunii to agree to instruct me. Nevertheless, at first he was considerably less than enthusiastic about the idea.

The first thing that caught my eye upon my arrival at Kunii's residence was an imposing two-line signboard reading "Kashima-Shinryū Martial Art, Kunii School." I slid open the wood-and-paper door to look inside at a newly remodeled training hall permeated with the smell of fresh cedar. When I announced myself, a young woman's face appeared from the darkened room beyond the training hall. I explained my interest in becoming a student, adding that I was especially interested in learning *sōjutsu*, the art of the spear, but the young woman told me that Kunii Zen'ya was out, and that I would have to come back some other time. As I turned to leave, she noticed my student uniform, and asked if I was from the University of Tokyo. I was puzzled at the time by the question, and even more puzzled by the look on her face when I answered yes.

When I returned, around three o'clock the following afternoon, the training hall was bright with electric lights and several men were seated around a table, eating and drinking. None of them was particularly big, but each seemed somehow very formidable. As I stepped into the entryway, they all turned at once to look at me. I explained that I was the one who had come by the day before to ask about admission. At this, a man built rather like a dumpling ordered me to come in. As I drew closer, I recognized him from photographs I had seen earlier as Kunii Zen'ya. The photograph had given me the impression that he was a giant, but in actuality he was quite small in stature, although his eyes glowed like those of a tiger.

Kunii, still seated, glanced sideways at me and growled, "So you want to learn sōjutsu, eh?" Another gentleman seated at the table—mustached and appearing ultraright wing—added something about how unusual an interest this was. At this, the others at the table launched into a bubbling discussion of the art of the spear. As they spoke, they continued to munch on the sushi laid out on the table, spraying bits of foamy saliva from their mouths. Completely excluded from both the conversation and the sushi, I sat and listened politely until early evening. At the time I knew nothing of the subject and understood little of the discussion, which, peppered with jargon, sounded mostly like gibberish. Still, I remember thinking that it seemed to be an interesting exchange.

Suddenly Kunii stood, ordered me to come with him, and strode to a rack of practice weapons on one wall of the training hall. Selecting a nine-foot practice spear, he deftly demonstrated two or three thrusts at the air, handed the weapon to me, directed me to practice, and returned to his seat. Now I was in trouble. I hadn't had time to really absorb anything, but having no choice in the matter, I attempted to imitate his posture and his actions as best I could. Even I knew I looked ridiculous. For a short time the group around the table watched me quietly, but they soon returned to their conversation, ignoring me once again. I continued to practice until my arm began to hurt, and then stopped for a short break, but no one said anything to me; instead they went on with their discussion of martial art. I resumed practicing the thrust Kunii had shown me.

After a little short of an hour of alternately practicing and resting, during which time I was resolutely ignored, I saw Kunii stand once more. He crossed over to the weapons rack, selected another practice spear for himself, and turned to me, ordering me to stab at him. Almost without thinking I thrust my spear at him in the manner I had been practicing. Kunii responded with a thrust of his own that sent my weapon flying off to the side and left the point of his an inch away from my chest. I was too stunned to move. "Okay," he said. "Do that again." Struggling to recover my composure, I tried once more, this time more powerfully, but the result was the same. We repeated this sequence several more times until Kunii declared, "That ought to be enough for today," returned his spear to the rack, and went back to the table.

Throughout this exercise, the group at the table had been watching silently. I was at a loss as to what I should do next until Kunii barked at me to put the spear away and sit down next to him. Terrified, I did as I was told. A moment later the young woman I had met the previous afternoon reappeared and placed a teacup in front of me.

As I sipped my tea, the group resumed talking, only to be interrupted by the sound of a clock hung on one pillar in the hall chiming ten o'clock. Apologizing that I had early classes that next morning, I rose and started toward the door. Kunii accompanied me to the entrance and watched as I bowed and announced that I would be back the next day. When I raised my head, I was startled to see him grinning broadly—he looked so different that he seemed another person entirely.

The young woman, as it turned out, was Kunii's eldest daughter, Michiko. Several years later she recounted to me her version of the events of my first day in the school. After my first visit, she explained, her father had returned, accompanied by a group of his students, all members of an ultranationalist, right-wing organization. Informed that a University of Tokyo student had come by to ask about admission, Kunii had winked at his entourage and declared his intention to see to it that if I did make a second visit, I would not make a third. The reason behind this somewhat cruel idea was the extreme, politically inspired animosity that Kunii and his companions held for University of Tokyo students. In the opinion prevailing among the right wing at the time, University of Tokyo students, having been in the forefront of the demonstrations against the renewal of the U.S.-Japan Mutual Security Agreement, were all out to destroy Japan and deserved to be obliterated. Kunii himself had recently declared that, if he could but get his hands on a machine gun, he would march down to the University of Tokyo campus and kill every student he saw. And then I showed up at his own training hall in my student uniform!

Michiko later told me that on many occasions in subsequent months, when she watched me enduring severe training sessions, she had wanted to take me aside and explain what her father was trying to do. All things considered, it's good that she didn't, for had I known I almost certainly would have fled the school. Now that I think back on it, I remember noticing at the time that my instruction was considerably harsher and more rugged than that of the other students. Fortunately, optimist that I am, I mistakenly concluded that my teacher must have singled me out for unusually rigorous training because he saw some special talent in me. And so, far from being discouraged, I was delighted by the exceptional treatment and applied myself all the harder.

Some time after, I learned that the Kunii family's ties to right-wing politics ran very deep. During the late nineteenth century, large numbers of anti-shogunal, anti-Western activists and guerillas came to the Kunii home for martial art training. Kunii Zen'ya's predecessor, Kunii Eizo, taught the famous Maruyama Sakuraō, and Zen'ya himself had a close relationship with such prewar right-wing activists as Imaizumi Teisuke, Ashizu Kōjirō, and Tōyama Mitsuru. Given this sort of family history and personal background, it is hard to imagine how my teacher could not have developed the sort of worldview that he did.

In any event, Kunii's original attitude toward me did not continue indefinitely. One day, all of a sudden, the oppressiveness was gone from his instruction, and he began to describe me in public as his most trusted student. I remained Kunii's personal student until his death on August 17, 1966. A little less than two years earlier he had honored me by naming me his successor as headmaster of the Kashima-Shinryū.

This was only a few years after I had begun my training, but by then I had filled out to 275 pounds, and had developed a physical confidence in myself that told me I would not lose a fight to anyone. Nevertheless, I felt a wide gap between my own level of expertise and that of my teacher, who to me was divinely gifted. Such feelings of unreadiness magnified the problems of facing the discipline of martial art for the first time without a teacher. Although I could not avoid being weighed down by them, I responded with renewed dedication to Kunii's legacy: training, teaching, meditating, and studying the texts Kunii and earlier Kashima-Shinryū masters had left behind.

During the early 1970s, I wrote a series of articles for the magazine *Kashima bunka*, analyzing and explaining Kashima-Shinryū concepts and principles from a scientific point of view. I later consolidated them, along with additional material on the school's history and organizational structure, into book form to produce a reference for my students and for others who might follow me in the pursuit of this tradition. On November 2, 1981, a copy of this work, *Nihon budō no engen: Kashima-Shinryū*, was presented at Court to the late Shōwa emperor, who, I was honored to learn, expressed considerable pleasure at receiving it.

In the twenty years that have passed since my book appeared, the Kashima-Shinryū has become a worldwide organization. It is, therefore, altogether fitting that the Kashima-Shinryū, the wellspring of Japanese martial art, be the focus of a study that seeks to introduce the history, philosophy, and structure of classical Japanese martial art to Western audiences. I admire Dr. Karl Friday for his efforts in making this sophisticated philosophical material understandable to every thinker or scholar in the world. It is my hope that this book might prove useful to those who seek to understand the arts to which my ancestors and I have dedicated much of our lives.

SEKI HUMITAKE
Nineteenth-Generation Headmaster, Kashima-Shinryū
(Professor of Microbiology, University of Tsukuba)

PREFACE

THIS PROJECT, the result of more than fifteen years of fieldwork and research, has evolved through many stages. It began in 1979 when I set out to translate the book *(Nihon budō no engen: Kashima-Shinryū)* that Seki Humitake, the nineteenth-generation headmaster of the Kashima-Shinryū, had published three years earlier. After a few drafts, it became apparent that simple translation would not be enough; substantial additions and adjustments would be necessary to make the book accessible to Western readers; and so I moved from translator to co-author.

Eventually, however, I realized that the book I really wanted to write differed from the one Dr. Seki had produced not just in format, but in fundamental conceptualization. For Dr. Seki's book is essentially a primer and a reference work showcasing the documents and curriculum of the Kashima-Shinryū, principally to practitioners and aficionados of martial art. But my objective was to use the school and its arts as a lens through which to focus a somewhat more ambitious cultural study: an exploration of one martial art school undertaken as a tool for illuminating the evolution and internal dynamics of the classical martial arts in general, primarily for historians and others interested in samurai history, culture, and thought.

Accordingly, I set aside my earlier work and began afresh, taking the project into yet another incarnation. In this resulting study I have drawn heavily on Dr. Seki's material, and even more heavily on his continued advice and encouragement, to produce a very different kind of book. I have also been favored with suggestions and recommendations from many other friends and colleagues, but responsibility for any blunders of fact, analysis, or conclusion rests completely with me.

The unsung hero of this project is Will Bodiford, who was—among other things—responsible for getting me involved with the

Kashima-Shinryū in the first place. It was Will that discovered the Kashima-Shinryū Club at the University of Tsukuba, where the two of us were studying as exchange students in 1978, and who talked me into joining this group with him. In the years since, he has been my friend, fellow student, training partner, and more recently, fellow teacher, scholar, and administrator. He has also backed and encouraged me in this project from the beginning, offering innumerable valuable suggestions about possible topics to include or sources to explore, and wading through more than one early draft of the manuscript to provide me with much-needed critiques.

I would also like to thank Paul Varley for his advice and suggestions on revising the manuscript; Cappy Hurst, for goading me into writing on the martial arts in the first place and for sharing with me the drafts of his own book on the subject; Patricia Crosby and Cheri Dunn of the University of Hawai'i Press, and copy editor Lee Motteler for their time and efforts in polishing the manuscript and bringing it to publication; Sakaguchi Ikuo, who produced the line drawings of forms and techniques; my wife, Chie, who designed those illustrations and who, as always, acted throughout as a patient listener and sounding board for my ideas; the Kunii family, who shared essential documents and photographs with me; Tanaka Kichizō and Chiyako, who helped me decipher the calligraphy of some crucial, handwritten documents; Jeff Stancil, one of my early—and one of my best—Kashima-Shinryū students, whose departure owing to perceived religious conflicts forced me to clarify my thoughts on the relationship between classical Japanese fighting arts and Japanese religious traditions; and the dozens of Kashima-Shinryū teachers, *senpai, kohai*, and students who have helped me forge whatever understanding I have acquired of this venerable and complex art.

This project has also benefited from the direct and indirect financial support of several institutions. Most important among these is the University of Georgia Senior Faculty Research Grant, which provided funds for a research assistant, as well as for supplies and writing time. In addition, much of the archival research and fieldwork that underlies the study was completed in Japan, alongside research on other projects funded by the Japanese Ministry of Education (Monbushō), the Japan Foundation, and the Social Science Research Council. I gratefully acknowledge the contributions of all.

LEGACIES OF THE SWORD

1.
Introduction

When one looks at the birds and the beasts, one sees that those
with teeth bite, those with claws grab, and those with stingers
sting. This is not taught; it is the way of nature.
—*RYŪ NO MAKI*

The arm, indeed, is rather bestial than human: the weapon is,
speaking generally, human, not bestial.
—SIR RICHARD F. BURTON

YAMAGA SOKŌ, the seventeenth-century samurai philosopher, was
troubled by the continued, privileged existence of a warrior class in
a society that no longer knew war. "The samurai," he wrote,

> eats food without growing it, uses utensils without manufacturing
> them, and profits without buying or selling. What is the justification for
> this? . . . [The samurai] does not cultivate, does not manufacture, and
> does not engage in trade, but it cannot be that he has no function at all.[1]

For Yamaga, the answer lay in identifying warriors with a higher
purpose: The samurai were no longer to be mere fighting men, they
were to serve as exemplars of moral virtue and symbols of the nation
as a whole.

Modern audiences, Japanese and foreign alike, have taken
Yamaga's identification to heart. One would, in fact, be hard pressed
to find a more pervasive symbol of Japan than the samurai. Prewar
propaganda, wartime memories of "banzai charges," five decades of
samurai movies, and thousands of jūdō and karate studios all over
the world have fixed the equation of Japanese with warrior culture
as firmly in the public mind as the association of the cowboy with
the United States. Indeed, it is a rare journalist or novelist who can
resist the temptation to portray contemporary Japanese business-
men as latter-day samurai clad in suits instead of *hakama* and bearing briefcases instead of swords.[2]

Scholars too have embraced Yamaga's conclusions and have extensively researched the institutional role warriors played in shaping

1

Japanese history, as well as the repercussions of warrior ethics and aesthetics on Japanese culture. The samurai have been studied in depth as landowners, feudal lords, governing bureaucrats, diplomats, litterateurs, philosophers, tea masters, and even painters.

And yet through all this, academic authors—in the West at least—have forgotten an equally important part of Yamaga's dictum: "Within his heart [the samurai] keeps to the ways of peace, but without he keeps his weapons ready for use."[3] They have lost sight of the fact that even the samurai of the peaceful early modern era never ceased to see themselves as warriors. Curiously, Western scholars and educators are generally far less familiar with the samurai in their original—and ostensibly primary—vocation as fighting men and masters of arms than with their other roles, in spite of the fact that samurai *bugei* (the military disciplines, or more popularly, the martial arts) have long been a respected topic of research among Japanese academics.

In their neglect of samurai martial training, scholars have missed out on an important opportunity. For while the samurai themselves are long gone, abolished in the late nineteenth century, the organizations through which they acquired their military skills—as well as many of their key values and convictions—are not. Several dozen bugei schools, or *ryūha*, continue in existence today, providing researchers with a fascinating window into the samurai past.

A key concern for these classical schools, and a cardinal point separating them from some modern cognate martial disciplines such as kendō or jūdō, is the insistence of the former on preserving the authenticity of their training and fighting methods. Students today learn, or believe they learn, the selfsame arts of sword, spear, and glaive that the samurai practiced. The traditional ryūha almost universally reject rules and modifications of technique or equipment that would allow safe practice of their arts as competitive sports. For them, maintaining combative reality and practicality is an essential component of the learning process: When this sense of realism and danger is removed, with it vanishes the unique frame of mind it produces. And without this, they believe, the bugei become indistinguishable from nonmartial sports and other forms of exercise.

No ryūha in the past century has embraced this dictum more tenaciously than the Kashima-Shinryū. Founded in the late fifteenth century and rooted in a legacy that traces back to the very beginnings of the Japanese military tradition, the Kashima-Shinryū is one of the oldest samurai training organizations in Japan. It is also one of the most vigorous: The current (nineteenth-generation) headmaster presides over more than a dozen branch schools and clubs—including several in Europe and North America—with a collective membership numbering in the hundreds of students.

Much of the Kashima-Shinryū's success in preserving the vitality of its art stems from the efforts of Kunii Zen'ya, the school's headmaster from 1914 until his death in 1966. Dubbed "the modern [Miyamoto] Musashi" and "the last sword-saint" by postwar journalists, Kunii became a legend in the Japanese martial art community.[4] Throughout his life he challenged any and all whom he believed to have besmirched the integrity of the Kashima-Shinryū or the traditional bugei to defend their opinions in trials by combat.

In one colorful incident occurring in the middle 1920s, he plunged unbidden into the ring during a series of exhibition matches between Japanese jūdō players and a French boxer, angry because the event had been billed as a test of Japanese versus Western martial art—and angrier still that the jūdō players had proven unable to best the foreigner. After knocking the boxer unconscious with a single strike to the head, Kunii turned to face a French naval officer who, with drawn pistol, was rushing to his countryman's defense. Drawing a knife from his belt, Kunii charged the officer, fully expecting to be shot, but hoping to take his assailant with him. To his surprise, the Frenchman stopped short, threw his pistol at Kunii, turned, and ran. On another occasion, in a duel of psychic energy, Kunii challenged and defeated a Greek Orthodox exorcist whom he believed to have impugned the efficacy of Shintō spiritual practices. On others, he took on kendō masters, sumō champions, jūdō players, wrestlers, ninja, and scores of others adept with virtually every manner of weapon in the traditional Japanese arsenal.[5]

Moreover, Kunii, who himself never lost and never turned down a challenge, made *taryū jiai*—all out, no-holds-barred matches with practitioners of other styles—an integral part of the training and promotion process for his advanced students. Thus Seki Humitake, the current headmaster, is also undefeated in dozens of contests of this nature, against headmasters and other representatives of various arts and schools.

But if proficiency in combat were the only benefit, there would be little reason to study arts like those of the Kashima-Shinryū, inasmuch as few people today have frequent recourse to overt physical conflict, and fewer still to combat with sword or spear. The bugei, however, are held to foster fighting skills not just for their own sake, but as a means to a more sublime end: the completion, the fulfillment of one's human potential.

Cultures and peoples as diverse as the Romans, the Apache, the ancient Polynesians, the Aztecs, the Bedouins, the Zulu, and modern Europeans have venerated and ennobled the warrior and his calling, but nowhere has the cult of the fighting arts reached the level of refinement and sophistication it has in Japan. Only in Japan did martial training appropriate the status—as well as the forms, the vocabulary, the teaching methods, and even the ultimate goals— of the fine arts. Only in Japan did the study of the bugei come to be viewed as a parallel, coequal endeavor to that of music, painting, calligraphy, drama, the tea ceremony, and other high cultural pursuits. And only in Japan have premodern fighting arts retained their vitality and their identity into modern times.

Today, classical bugei like the Kashima-Shinryū are bits of living history, abiding, indelible expressions of the culture of the samurai who forged them and who dominated Japan politically, economically, and culturally for nearly half the nation's recorded history.

The seeds for this warrior class came from a shift in imperial court military policy that began in the middle decades of the eighth century and picked up momentum in the ninth.[6] For a quarter of a millennium the members of this new order obediently fought the court's battles for it, until Minamoto Yoritomo laid the foundations for warrior rule in Japan with his creation of a military government, or shogunate, in the eastern village of Kamakura at the end of the twelfth century. The Kamakura shogunate was in essence a government within a government, exercising authority delegated to it by the imperial court in Kyoto (at the time called Heian-kyō). Under its successor regime, established in 1336 in the Muromachi district of Kyoto, however, warriors not only dominated the countryside, but overshadowed the imperial court as well.[7]

By the late 1400s, while both the court and the shogunate remained nominally in authority, real power in Japan had devolved to a few score feudal barons called daimyō, whose authority rested first and foremost on their ability to hold lands by military force. There followed a century and a half of nearly continuous warfare as daimyō contested with one another and with those below them to maintain and expand their domains.[8]

This Sengoku (literally, "country at war") age ended in the late 1500s, when the successive efforts of three men—Oda Nobunaga

(1534–1582), Toyotomi Hideyoshi (1536–1598), and Tokugawa Ieyasu (1542–1616)—eliminated many of the smaller daimyō and unified the rest into a nationwide coalition. In 1603 Ieyasu assumed the title of shōgun and established Japan's third military regime. The new polity was a kind of centralized feudalism, under which most of the country remained divided into great domains ruled by hereditary daimyō who were in turn closely watched and regulated by the shogunate.[9]

The Tokugawa regime kept the peace in Japan for the better part of three centuries, before at last succumbing to a combination of foreign pressure, evolution of the nation's social and economic structure, and decay of the government itself. In 1868, combined armies from two domains in southwestern Japan forced the resignation of the last shōgun and declared a restoration of all powers of governance to the emperor. This event, known as the Meiji Restoration after the calendar era (1868–1912), marked the beginning of the end for the samurai as a class. Over the next decade they were stripped first of their monopoly over military service, and then, one by one, of the rest of their badges and privileges of status: their special hairstyle, their way of dress, their exclusive right to surnames, their hereditary stipends, and the right to wear swords in public. By the 1890s Japan was a modernized, industrialized nation ruled by a constitutional government and defended by a westernized conscript army and navy.[10] The samurai had passed into history.

But the fighting arts they had shaped and reshaped during their millennium-long existence continued to develop. Many traditional ryūha—the Kashima-Shinryū among them—carried on much as they had during the Tokugawa period. Others disappeared entirely, while still others restructured and redefined themselves in forms they deemed more appropriate to the new age.[11]

The uniqueness of the Japanese warrior arts as historical and cultural phenomena raises problems for English speakers searching for suitable terminology by which to label them. Taken in its original sense, the phrase "martial arts" fits the bill rather nicely, but in contemporary American usage, this term has collected some rather unfortunate connotations. Leaving aside its popular association with kick-boxing, tournament karate, and Chinese action movies, "the martial arts" has largely become shorthand for "the East Asian martial arts," a construct that inappropriately lumps Japanese samurai disciplines together with Chinese, Korean, and Okinawan boxing methods and warrior arts, implying an underlying similarity among what are really very different practices.[12]

To be sure, all such "martial arts," as forms of single combat, share some commonality of function—but then, so do Chinese *t'ai chi ch'uan* and U.S. Air Force fighter tactics. They also, as arts developed in neighboring countries through which individuals—and armies—regularly traveled back and forth, show some degree of cross influence and even some common vocabulary. But the historical circumstances under which these various arts evolved, the purposes they served, and the statuses they assumed in their respective cultures diverged in fundamental ways.

Chinese, Korean and Okinawan boxing arts represent an independent tradition from the battlefield disciplines developed by Chinese and Korean armies. The latter were warrior arts in the strict sense of the term, but the former had multiple, overlapping personalities: part self-defense, part competitive sport, part performance art, and part regimen for promoting physiological health and longevity. The traditional warrior arts became extinct when modern weapons rendered swords, spears, and halberds obsolete, but the boxing forms survive and prosper. Japan, however, had no counterpart to Chinese boxing—at least not until modern times. The bugei practiced in Japan today descend directly from arts developed for the battlefield. Furthermore, until modern times the Japanese fighting arts were more or less the exclusive property of the samurai, the ruling class throughout the period in which the disciplines matured. Chinese, Okinawan, and Korean boxing forms, by contrast, were created by tradesmen, peasants, ascetics, entertainers, monks, rebels, bandits, and other political have-nots. And, as we shall see later in this study, the special character and status of the Japanese bugei emerged precisely because of their ancestry and parentage.

If *martial arts*, then, is a less than totally satisfactory term, what might one ask do the Japanese themselves call their traditional military disciplines? Unfortunately, the answer to this question depends on the period under scrutiny. Historically, the samurai employed at least four words that are still in common use today, as well as others that are not; the meaning and popularity of each varied with the times.

The two oldest terms are "bugei," which I have already introduced, and "*byōhō*," more commonly pronounced "*heihō*" in modern usage. Both appear in Japanese written records as far back as the turn of the eighth century.[13] The early meanings of the two words overlapped to a considerable extent, but by the Tokugawa period, "hyōhō" had narrowed considerably, from a general term to one of several alternative names for swordsmanship. "Bugei," in the meantime, had become a generic term for samurai fighting arts.[14] Today, "heihō" simply means "strategy" in general usage, while scholars and practitioners of traditional swordsmanship and related arts apply it in more restricted fashion to designate the principles around which a school's approach to combat is constructed (see the discussion in chapter 4).

Two other words closely related to "bugei"—*"budō"* and *"bujutsu"*—also came into fashion during the medieval and early modern periods.* Pre-Meiji sources use "bugei" and "bujutsu" interchangeably, but "budō" sometimes carried special connotations. Literally, "the martial path," or "the warrior's way," "budō" appeared in print for the first time in a text compiled in the thirteenth century.[15] Its meaning seems to have been rather ambiguous until the Tokugawa period, when it came to designate what modern authors often anachronistically call *bushidō*—that is, the code of conduct, rather than the military arts, of the warrior class.[16] Nineteenth-century scholar and philosopher Aizawa Yasushi's definition is typical of his age:

> The arts of the sword, spear, bow and saddle are the bugei; to know etiquette and honor, to preserve the way of the gentleman, to strive for frugality, and thus become a bulwark of the state, is budō.[17]

Among modern authorities in Japan the terms "bugei," "budō," and "bujutsu" have acquired a more or less conventional usage that, for convenience, I have adopted for the present study. "Bujutsu" describes the various Japanese martial disciplines in their original function as arts of war; "budō" denotes the process by which the study of bujutsu becomes a means to self-development and self-realization; and "bugei" is a general term for the traditional Japanese military arts, embracing both bujutsu and budō. It should be stressed, however, that this usage is modern, not traditional; projecting it

---

*While the debate over the demarcation of and appropriate nomenclature for periods of Japanese history continues, most authorities today style the interval between Minamoto Yoritomo's creation of the Kamakura shogunate in the late twelfth century and Oda Nobunaga's rise in the late sixteenth the *medieval period;* and the rest of the sixteenth, seventeenth, eighteenth, and nineteenth centuries, up to the fall of the Tokugawa shogunate, the *early modern age.*

backward into Tokugawa times, as Western literature on Japanese martial art often does, is anachronous.*

Errors of this sort persist in Western writings due in large measure to the insularity of both the audience and the authors. The overwhelming majority of the literature on Japanese martial art has been directed at practitioners and other aficionados, and penned by journalists, martial art teachers, and others without formal academic training in premodern Japanese culture or history. Not surprisingly then, most English-language books and articles on the topic have relied almost exclusively on *other* English-language martial art books and articles, supplemented by survey histories.[18] Thus, mistakes and misinformation tend to circulate and recirculate largely because those with the wherewithal to correct them—the community of experts versed in Japanese history and thought, and trained to read primary sources—have generally viewed the bugei with little more than bemused condescension.

This lack of academic regard is unfortunate, and more than a little odd, when one considers that interest in Japanese or other martial arts has served many students as a springboard to wider study of things Japanese.† More importantly, the bugei were an integral ele-

---

*Western literature on the bugei often asserts that during the Tokugawa period, bugei masters began replacing the suffix "-jutsu," meaning "art" or "skill," with "-dō," meaning "way," in the names of their disciplines, to distinguish the sublime from the purely technical applications and purposes of martial art. Thus *kenjutsu*, "the art of swordsmanship," became *kendō*, "the way of the sword"; *bujutsu*, "the martial skills," became *budō*, "the martial way"; and so on (the late Donn F. Draeger seems to have been the originator of this thesis; see, for example, *Classical Budō*, 31–40). But, as the discussion in the main text demonstrates, the historical record does not support this conclusion. Meiji period educators, like jūdō pioneer Kanō Jigorō, did differentiate "-jutsu" and "-dō" in precisely this fashion, but their forebears did not. In the Tokugawa period, "budō" had far broader connotations than it does today, the nomenclature applied to various disciplines betrayed no discernible systemization (swordsmanship, for example was called kenjutsu, kendō, *kenpō, hyōhō, tōjutsu, tōhō, gekken, gekishi no jutsu*, and various other appellations, without distinction of form or content), and numerous sources from the period use "bugei" or "bujutsu" in ways that clearly imply a construct with moral, spiritual, or social components, as well as technical ones. (Tominaga, *Kendō gohyakunen shi*, 18–20.)

†Judging from questions, conversations, and choices for term paper topics over the years, I would estimate that at least a quarter to a third of the college students enrolling in my premodern history courses are drawn there largely by an interest in the samurai and/or the bugei. Conversations with colleagues suggest that my experience has been fairly typical.

ment of samurai culture and remain a formidable piece of Japanese culture today.

The English-language literature on the traditional bugei includes how-to manuals, biographies of master swordsmen, translations and commentaries on classic texts, and broadly synthesizing historical or analytical studies. Much of this work suffers from historical naïveté, flawed by errors of fact or conception, but most is useful in one way or another and some is quite excellent. Even the best, however, suffers from limitations imposed by the sheer diversity of the bugei.

Simply put, there is no such thing as a typical or representative martial art ryūha. To varying degrees, each of the more than 700 schools that scholars have identified is unique in terms of organizational structure and history, strategy, philosophy, and technique. Anyone attempting to formulate general conclusions about traditional Japanese martial art must therefore do so on the basis of some 700 exceptions.[19]

Analyzing and explaining the bugei in generic terms is a bit like conceptualizing world history, world literature, or world religion in similar fashion. Standing back far enough to examine the phenomenon in toto permits one to describe its outlines, but seeking deeper insights about its essence forces one to grapple with a volume of diversity and detail that quickly becomes overwhelming. In the case of the traditional bugei, this already herculean task is made even more difficult by the cult of secrecy that cloaks most ryūha and the resulting paucity of written texts explaining any ryūha's canon, because, as I will discuss further in chapter 4, such texts were intentionally designed to be opaque to outsiders.

The cabalistic manner in which classical bugei schools guard their doctrines thus forces the researcher to step out of the archives and into the field. Documentary evidence provides the most reliable base for reconstructing a ryūha's history, but to understand a school's philosophical principles one must *experience* them through hands-on involvement. That is, one must enter the ryūha and explore it as anthropologists enter and explore societies they wish to study. To do this in a thorough manner requires years, which in turn sharply restricts the range of bugei traditions a single researcher can practically explore.

For these reasons, the present study takes a different approach to the complex and variegated phenomenon of traditional Japanese martial art, attempting not to view the whole of the phenomenon directly but to grasp the substance and the spirit of the whole through one of its parts. That is, the study seeks to guide readers to an intuitive perception of what the bugei are and how they function through a detailed examination of a single ryūha.

No ryūha is truly representative of its fellows, so one cannot universalize any one school's dogma or otherwise project it directly onto a synthesized, generic image of Japanese martial art. But there *is* sufficient consubstantiality among all schools to permit one to interpolate a great deal about the nature and functioning of bugei in the abstract, from the interplay of martial, moral, and metaphysical concerns within a single ryūha. In other words, while the *anatomy* of each ryūha is unique, the *physiology* of most is similar. One can, therefore, learn something of broad value about the physiology of traditional Japanese martial art by carefully dissecting one school, in much the same way one can draw broad insights about the physiology of all species of mammals by dissecting any one.

The following pages explore the historical, philosophical, and pedagogical dynamics of one school of traditional martial art—the Kashima-Shinryū—presenting a case study that seeks to shed new light on an important but hitherto underexamined part of Japanese warrior culture. The intent is to take readers inside a traditional ryūha, to show them how initiates view what they do—and why. Through this, I hope to lay the foundations for a broader understanding of what the classical bugei are, what they were, and what they mean to those who practice them.

I have arranged the body of this study, the product of more than fifteen years of fieldwork and research, into three chapters and an epilogue.[20] Chapter 2 begins with an overview of the history of ryūha and the bugei, and proceeds to a more detailed discussion of the history of the Kashima-Shinryū itself. Because—as I argue early in the chapter—a ryūha as a corporate entity viewed across generations is really only a succession of master-disciple relationships, much of this discussion concerns the legacies and associations of major figures in the school's past. The chapter concludes with an examination of the organization, past and present, of the Kashima-Shinryū and of bugei ryūha in general.

Chapter 3 switches perspective from the ryūha as an entity defined by its membership through time to one defined by its doctrines; it looks at the philosophical structure of the Kashima-Shinryū, centering on the school's technical vocabulary and the interplay of mechanical, tactical, psychological, religious, and spiritual elements within the concepts represented by this nomenclature. Such terms and concepts offer the best handle by which to grasp the *art* of a traditional bugei, because an exposition built around them approximates—more closely than any other academic exploration—the view that adepts are led to construct of their art. Nevertheless, being an academic inquiry rather than a primer for initiates, my analysis reverses the order in which students normally discover their art, working inward from the broadest and most abstract principles of ryūha doctrine to the most specific.*

Chapter 4 continues and concludes this process in a discussion of martial art training and the transmission of ryūha doctrine. The traditional bugei approach to self-cultivation emphasizes that to train the mind and spirit one must first train the body. Accordingly, it prescribes three overlapping forms of practice and instruction: the physical acquisition of military skills through repetitive pattern practice, theoretical instruction through written texts, and meditation. The chapter introduces and examines each of these forms in turn.

These chapters are followed by an epilogue and two sets of appendixes featuring translations of historical documents relating to the Kashima-Shinryū and of documents relating to the organizational structure of the school today.

---

*While in premodern times the bugei were, with only a few exceptions, the nearly exclusive province of men, in more recent decades an ever-increasing number of women have taken them up. Certain weapons, among them the knife and the glaive (*naginata*, described in chapter 4), were traditionally taught to samurai women, but in modern times virtually all bugei forms, traditional and otherwise, attract female as well as male students. My usage, therefore, of "his," "he," and "him" in this and subsequent chapters to designate students and adepts is generic, not gendered. "He or she" is awkward in repetition and its occasional usage falsely implies that "he" alone elsewhere is strictly masculine. Extensive use of "one" quickly renders passages moribund, and the neutral plural ("they") does not work in all situations. "She" alone draws undue attention to itself, substituting a political statement for clarity and customary usage, while "he/she," "(s)he," and similar constructs are barbarisms.

2.
Heritage and Tradition

History is a distillation of rumour.
—THOMAS CARLYLE

One legend recalls another, and I hear tonight many strange
ones.
—LAFCARDIO HEARN

> Consider now the origins of the warrior arts of Japan. [The
> ancient records] convey that the Kashima-Shinryū began during the
> Age of the Gods, with a mission as champion for the Imperial court.
> . . . After Takemikazuchi-no-Mikoto had pursued and chastised all
> the baneful deities, he was enshrined at Kashima, in the province of
> Hitachi, becoming a martial deity worshipped throughout the ages.
> In later generations all whose names were made known in this world
> through feats of arms prayed to this deity.

THUS BEGINS the *Kashima-Shinryū hyōhō denki*, a record of successive headmasters of the Kashima-Shinryū. Claiming a heritage
spanning nineteen generations from its genesis in the late 1400s,
the Kashima-Shinryū today represents some five centuries of living
history. It also represents more than five centuries of legend and
folk tradition. Such intertwining of legend and fact gives the school
a rich and fascinating legacy, but it makes it difficult to establish
what really happened with complete satisfaction. Few written
records on the school's past survive. Few of these contain much
detail, and fewer still are objective. The most abundant information
is on the ryūha's founders and successive teachers, and most of this
comes from documents written and maintained by the school itself
and/or by other schools that also claim these figures within their
own traditions. Unfortunately for the would-be objective historian,
the documents of the various schools are as often as not at odds with
one another on even basic issues.

This chapter comprises an attempt to examine the history and
organizational structure of the Kashima-Shinryū, and to place them

within the context of the general development of Japanese martial art. While every effort has been made to untangle and illuminate the actual past, this has not always proved possible. When objective information could not be found or conflicting accounts resolved otherwise, the Kashima-Shinryū's traditional version of events has been followed. Thus this account remains to some extent a parochial history—a description of a tradition. It need not, however, be less enlightening an account for that.

Ryūha and the Origins of the Bugei

Martial training and the profession of arms has a long tradition in Japan, one that stretches back before the dawn of recorded history. Indeed, the foundation legends of the imperial state are replete with images of weaponry and tales of combat.[1]

Between the late seventh and early eighth centuries, the newly created state established elaborate procedures for recruiting and drilling fighting men for its armies, police forces, and palace guard units. During the ninth century the court shifted its focus to co-opting men who arranged for their own training and provided their own equipment, and by the middle of the Heian period (794–1185), literary accounts indicate that warriors had developed extensive regimens for practicing with their principal weapon: the bow and arrow. The Heian period also saw the beginnings of the Ki, Tomo, and Sakanoue schools of archery, traditionally held to have been founded by Ki no Okimichi, Tomo no Wataketamaro, and Sakanoue Tamuramaro, respectively. Most scholars, however, consider these early "ryūha" to have been a very different sort of institution from those of later ages; in any case, the form of archery they taught was ceremonial—not warlike—in design and practice.[2]

An anecdote from a Heian period tale collection entitled "How the Former Governor of Mutsu, Tachibana Norimitsu, Cut Down Some Men" suggests that the Japanese had developed some concept of identifiable styles of swordplay by the late tenth century. Norimitsu, who "although not of a warrior house, was stout of heart, discerning of judgment, and strong of body," served in military posts at court including the Office of Imperial Police (*kebiishi-chō*), the Left Gate Guards (*saemonfu*), and later as governor of Noto, Tosa, and Mutsu provinces. The incident in question took place in the mid-990s.[3]

Late one evening, on his way to visit a young woman, Norimitsu was set upon by a band of armed thugs. When one of these jumped in front of him with his sword raised, Norimitsu drew his own blade and cut in the same motion, splitting the attacker's head in two. Immediately another bandit attacked. Without pausing to return his sword to its scabbard, Norimitsu pinched it under his arm and ran—but the bandit gave chase. Suddenly Norimitsu dropped to the ground; the robber, unable to stop in time, stumbled and fell forward; Norimitsu cut him down before he could regain his feet. Now a third bandit rushed forward. "Holding his sword like a spear," Norimitsu turned to face his attacker and charged. The robber attempted to strike but misjudged the distance and, as he was too close, was unable to cut even Norimitsu's clothing. Norimitsu's sword pierced him clean through, coming out his back. As the bandit fell, Norimitsu withdrew his blade and sliced off his attacker's sword arm at the shoulder.

After making sure there were no further attackers, Norimitsu ran away. He then washed the blood from his sword and stole back to his room to sleep. He awoke the next morning to a great commotion, as news of the discovery of the bodies spread. Reluctantly, joining the crowd viewing the bodies, he overheard one investigator observe: "It was peerless swordplay. At first I thought that they had killed each other, but upon looking closer it became clear that the same sword work [killed the three of them]." While the crowd chattered and speculated as to who the mysterious swordsman might have been, a man known to have been an enemy of the three stepped forward to claim credit. Having no wish to be involved in a murder investigation, Norimitsu decided to remain silent on his part in the affair. Years later, as an old man, he finally related the story to his children.

The point of interest in this tale is the investigator's statement that examination of the bodies disclosed both the quality and the consistency of the swordwork that dispatched them. Scenes in which a swordsman's ryūha is deduced from the wounds left on the bodies of his victims are a stock feature in popular Japanese films on the samurai of later ages.[4] While it is likely that such feats of conjecture find their source in the imaginations of the public at large rather than in historical fact, it is significant that the notion that a warrior's tactics could be routinized to the extent of being readily identifiable was already current among the Japanese of the late tenth century.

Nevertheless, true bugei ryūha were a post-fifteenth-century development, a belated part of the medieval trend toward systemization of knowledge in various pursuits. During Japan's middle ages, virtuosos of poetry, the tea ceremony, flower arranging, music,

Nō drama, and the like began to think of their approaches to their arts as packages of information that could be transmitted to students in organized patterns, and to certify students' mastery of the teachings by written documents. Similarly, samurai who hoped to survive and prosper in the *jakuniku-kyōshoku* (literally, "the weak are meat; the strong eat") world of the Sengoku era sought out warriors with reputations as expert fighters and appealed to them for instruction. Such masters of combat in turn codified their knowledge and experience and methodized its study.[5]

The 250-year Pax Tokugawa that began in the early seventeenth century brought fundamental changes to the practice—as well as the teaching—of martial art. For one thing, combat itself took on new forms. With the passing of the Sengoku age, samurai were far more likely to engage in duels and street brawls wearing ordinary clothing than in pitched battles wearing full armor. This meant that the sword, which was carried about as everyday armament, was now likely to be the principal weapon, whereas during the Sengoku period it had been auxiliary to the spear, bow, and gun. Fighting without armor, samurai quickly discovered, also meant greater mobility and a greater choice of targets, calling for new postures and new tactics. Accordingly, combatants began to stand more upright and hold their weapons higher, enabling them to strike at longer distances from their opponents than before. At the same time, bugei training became increasingly formalized and businesslike, with ryūha headmasters and other adepts opening commercial training halls and instructing students for fees, turning the teaching of martial art into a full-time profession. But most significantly, the motives and goals for the study of the bugei changed. Samurai now approached martial art not simply as a means to proficiency in combat, as their ancestors had, but as a means to physical and spiritual cultivation of the self.[6]

Spiritual training in the bugei probably originated as a practical military consideration. In combat, the fear of injury or death poses a severe handicap. Fear distracts, destroying concentration, reactions and timing. Technical virtuosity with weapons is useless to a warrior who cannot control his fear—as in the familiar case of athletes who perform flawlessly in practice but are unable to function in important competitions. Ultimate proficiency in deadly combat, then, requires the ability to set aside fear—to maintain a kind of detachment from the possible consequences of the activity.

Warriors were not, in fact, the only ones in medieval Japan seeking to transcend their corporeal fears, for much medieval religious training focused on similar goals. Most interesting, albeit often overlooked in this context, were the practices of *Shugendō*, a peculiar blend of shamanistic and other pre-Buddhist Japanese folk beliefs, esoteric Buddhist rituals and cosmology, and Taoist magic that promises those who master it not only spiritual tranquility, but supranormal, even magical or supernatural mental and physical powers.

Shugendō training centers on ascetic rites performed in sacred mountain areas. Many of these involve confrontation with death as a means of spiritual purification. Trainees are, for example, obliged to traverse multiday courses along narrow mountain paths, at times jumping across perilous chasms or swinging themselves out over cliffs around protruding boulders that block their route. In premodern times, those who for reasons of fatigue or illness were unable to complete the course were deserted or even cast off precipices so as not to obstruct the progress of the other ascetics. One of the most dramatic rituals, still practiced today, is that of "abandoning the body" *(shashingyō)*, in which trainees are suspended head downward and lowered over the edge of a cliff by ropes. At the completion of this exercise, as the rope handlers haul the trainees back up, they loosen their grips for a fraction of a second, allowing the trainees a brief, terrifying moment of free fall before catching them and pulling them to safety. Such exercises are designed to clear and focus the mind, to free it of all wordly distractions and direct it toward enlightenment.[7]

Warriors appear to have begun adapting the methods of religious ascetics to their own purposes by the early sixteenth century. From the use of spiritual exercises to enhance one's fighting ability, it would have been but a short step to the insight that the process could also work the other way around—that study of the bugei could itself be a means of spiritual discipline. And indeed, the groundwork for such an insight had already been laid by the medieval proponents of other arts and activities.

The concept of *"michi,"* or "path," both defined and unified medieval Japanese art and religion. In the Heian period (794–1185), the term referred to specialization or proficiency; experts of all sorts were called "persons of the ___ path" *("___ no michi no hito")*. But during the middle ages, "michi" took on a deeper meaning, as it merged with implications drawn from a worldview common to Buddhism, Taoism, and Confucianism.

All three philosophies embrace the idea that some extraordinary level of understanding exists at which one can comprehend the phenomenal world as a whole, and that this level of understanding is attainable by virtually any human being who seeks it diligently enough. Followers of Confucianism or Taoism call this achievement *sagehood;* those of Buddhism, *enlightenment* or *satori.* While the cosmological premises underlying Confucian or Taoist sagehood and Buddhist enlightenment differ radically, the three states share a unitary or totalistic notion of human perfection. All recognize only two forms of human endeavor: those that lead to ultimate knowledge and understanding, and those that do not. Any and all variations of the former must, then, lead to the same place; there is no such thing as specialized perfection in the modern Western sense that recognizes the mastery of the piano as a distinct but coequal achievement to mastery of physics. All three doctrines express this principle in the concept of michi. All insist that there may be more than one path, but that all true michi (as opposed to erroneous ones) lead to a singular destination.

The medieval Japanese concept of michi, then, saw expertise in activities of all sorts—from games and sports to fine arts, from practical endeavors to religious practice—as possessing a universality deriving from its relationship to a common, ultimate goal. Concentrated specialization in any activity was held to be an equally valid route to ultimate attainment of universal truth; complete mastery of even the most trivial of pastimes was believed to yield the same truths as can be found through the most profound.[8]

Within this cultural and philosophical milieu, the bugei took their place alongside calligraphy, flower arranging, poetry composition, Nō drama, the tea ceremony, incense judging, and numerous other medieval michi. Later, the peaceful conditions of the Tokugawa age further enhanced this aspect of bugei training, as samurai who no longer expected to spend time on the battlefield sought and found a more relevant rationale for continued devotion to their arts.

A gnawing problem in any discussion of schools of traditional Japanese martial art is the question of just exactly what constitutes a ryūha, as viewed over the course of several generations. For unlike most schools of tea ceremony, flower arranging, or calligraphy, traditional bugei schools can really be identified as institutions only in retrospect. Master-disciple relationships can be traced backward through time to establish the continuity of lineages, but few martial art adepts prior to modern times were part of any single exclusive lineage. Few, moreover, had only a single successor. Instead, lines of descent from famous warriors tend to branch again and again, like streams endlessly dividing as they flow outward from their common source. For this reason there now exist more than 700 schools of swordsmanship *(kenjutsu)* alone.[9]

Most bugei ryūha did not develop the articulated organizational structure common in some other traditional Japanese arts. In the latter, senior disciples receive licenses to teach and to open branch schools. Those of sufficient rank are even permitted to certify their own students to open subbranches. But the authority for all instruction at all levels is derived from the ryūha's headmaster, or *iemoto*. Branch instructors *(natori)* link students to the iemoto, who retains full and exclusive control of the ryūha's doctrine and passes this on to only one successor per generation. Senior disciples not chosen as the next iemoto normally remain within the structure of the ryūha as branch instructors.

Martial art ryūha, by contrast, have historically tended to practice total transmission, in which all students certified as having mastered the school's kabala are given "possession" of it. As figure 1 demonstrates, such former students normally left their masters to open their own schools, teaching on their own authority; masters retained no residual control over former students or students of students. Each new graduate was free to modify his master's teachings as he saw fit, adding personal insights and/or techniques and ideas gleaned from other teachers. It was common practice for such graduates to change even the names of their styles, in effect founding new ryūha and independent branches of ryūha in each generation.

The principal reason bugei ryūha did not follow the iemoto/natori pattern was political. Both the daimyō and the shogunate (after 1605) sought to minimize association between samurai from different domains. The subversive potential of a network of warrior natori under the authority of a single iemoto but extending across several domains was not missed by either level of government. Thus, until modern times, the formation of articulated ryūha organizations was discouraged by various daimyō and shogunal laws.[10]

Over the course of its long history, the Kashima-Shinryū has embraced many patterns of organization and transmission. I will return to the topic of ryūha structure at the end of this chapter, after I have first examined the master-disciple lineages through which the teachings have passed.

The Kashima Grand Shrine and Takemikazuchi-no-Mikoto

At the wellspring of the Kashima-Shinryū tradition is the Kashima Grand Shrine, one of the oldest religious institutions in Japan. A nineteenth-century compendium of shrine history gives two possible dates for its establishment, noting that worship was first conducted there "in the age of Emperor Sujin," but also that the institution was built on the orders of Emperor Tenji. The problem with the first of these dates is that Sujin is of uncertain historical veracity, and the traditional dates for his reign (97 BCE to 30 CE) are not taken seriously by any modern historian. The second date, which would place the shrine's establishment sometime between AD 646 and 672, is more believable, but some scholars have argued that the shrine already existed before Tenji's reign. In any event, the earliest extant reference to the Kashima Grand Shrine is an AD 758 entry in a court history, which reports an increase of 218 servants to the shrine's inventory.[11]

Kashima, located about one hundred kilometers northeast of Tokyo in Ibaraki prefecture, enshrines Takemikazuchi-no-Mikoto, a sword spirit, deity of thunder, master of water serpents, protector of eastern Japan from earthquakes, tutelary deity of the Fujiwara imperial regents, avatar of several Buddhist divinities, and patron deity of warriors and the warrior arts.* According to court mythology, not long after heaven and earth first separated, two deities—Izanagi-no-Mikoto and Izanami-no-Mikoto—set about the task of solidifying and completing the land, which hitherto had "resembled floating oil and drifted like a jellyfish."[12] Standing on the Heavenly

---

*Takemikazuchi-no-Mikoto (also called Takemikazuchi-no-Kami in some texts) is an extraordinarily complex deity, possessing multiple identities, of which the list in the main text represents only the best known. Some authorities have even questioned whether Takemikazuchi, who is also worshipped at the Kasuga Grand Shrine in Nara, was in fact the original deity enshrined at Kashima. Early documents on the Kashima deity are both scarce and unreliable. More exasperatingly, local documents refer only to "Kashima-no-Kami" and do not specifically identify Takemikazuchi. Some suspect that an indigenous Kashima deity, perhaps one identified from early on as a diety of thunder and lightning, became associated with Takemikazuchi during the early eighth century as a result of Takemikazuchi's connections with the Fujiwara. These connections date back to pre-Taika times, when the Fujiwara—then still known as the Nakatomi—served as hereditary guardians of both the Kashima Grand Shrine and its neighboring Katori Shrine. In the early eighth century, the Fujiwara brought both the Kashima and the Katori deities to Kasuga, supplanting the original Nakatomi deities.

See Ouwehand, *Namazu-e and Their Themes*, 57–63; and Allan Grapard, *Protocol of the Gods*, 31–33, 36–38, and 82–83.

Figure 1. Principal teacher-student relationships of the Kashima-Shinryū and branch schools

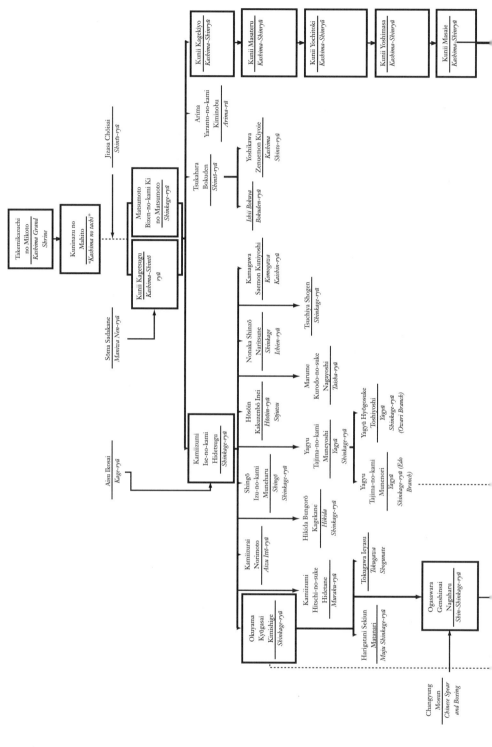

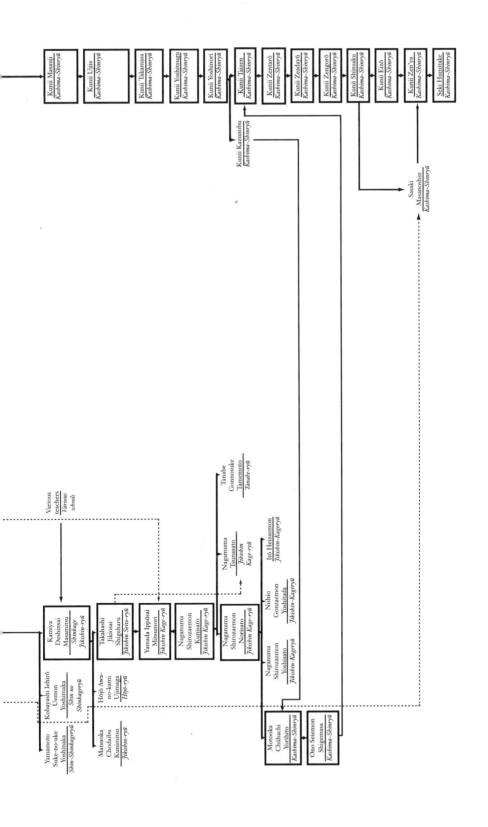

Floating Bridge, they took up a jeweled spear, dipped it into the sea, and stirred. When they withdrew the weapon, the drops that fell from the tip coagulated into the Japanese islands.

The pair then descended to this new land, where they gave birth to and otherwise begat a plethora of additional islands and deities. At length, however, Izanami bore Kagutsuchi-no-Kami, the fire deity, and in so doing burned her genitals and perished. Heartsick and enraged, Izanagi unsheathed his sword and slashed off the head of his offspring. Takemikazuchi sprang forth from the blood that dripped from Izanagi's sword guard.

The most important of Izanagi's offspring was Amaterasu Ōmikami, the sun goddess, to whom Izanagi gave rule over the High Plain of Heaven, the abode of the heavenly deities. Some time later, Amaterasu directed that her grandson, Ninigi-no-Mikoto, should descend and take charge of the earth. He reported back that the land was in an uproar and that a deity called Ōkuninushi and his descendants refused to acknowledge his (Ninigi's) authority. Takemikazuchi, accompanied by Futsunushi-no-Mikoto, the deity later celebrated at the Katori Grand Shrine, was dispatched to settle the matter.[13]

Ōkuninushi and his eldest son readily agreed to the terms Takemikazuchi presented—impressed, no doubt, by the fact that the thunder deity chose to conduct his negotiations sitting cross-legged on the point of his upturned sword. But a second son, Takeminakata-no-Kami, challenged Takemikazuchi to a test of strength. First demonstrating his own prowess by twirling a huge boulder on his fingertips, Takeminakata then attempted to take hold of Takemikazuchi's arm. The latter, however, changed the arm into a column of ice, and then changed it again into a sword blade, causing his opponent to draw away in fear. When, in his turn, Takemikazuchi took hold of Takeminakata's arm, "it was like taking hold of a young reed; he grasped it and crushed it, throwing it aside. Immediately [Takeminakata] ran away."[14] At this, Ōkuninushi and his sons pledged to obey Ninigi, who then descended once again to take up his rule of the earth. His grandson was later enthroned as Emperor Jimmu, the first human ruler of Japan. Takemikazuchi, his martial prowess having thus been demonstrated, became a patron deity of military men.

The first human to benefit from Takemikazuchi's guidance was Kuninazu-no-Mahito, a legendary attendant at the Kashima Grand Shrine during the seventh century. "The August Deity [enshrined at Kashima]," notes the compendium cited earlier, is the ancestral deity of the imperial nation's martial art; thus was this military science passed on from of old. . . . All the numerous schools of this world take their source in this teaching. . . . Kuninazu-no-Mahito, successor to Kuninazu-no-Ōkashima-no-Mikoto, grandson of Amenoko Yane-no-Mikoto, built an altar at Takamanohara and offered devotions. Receiving the guidance of the August Deity, he revealed the divinely wondrous art . . . and passed this on to later ages.[15]

The art that Kuninazu discovered became popularly known as *Kashima-no-tachi*—literally, "the sword of Kashima." He reportedly derived this from an exorcising ritual called *harai-tachi, ontachi-barai,* or *mitsugi-barai*, performed at the Kashima Grand Shrine since its inception. Harai-tachi, in turn, is said to have been based on the swordplay of Takemikazuchi when he chastised and pacified the disobedient deities of the earth. In the modern Kashima-Shinryū version of this technique, the sword is drawn horizontally from the scabbard and then swept upward in a diagonal cut from right to left *(kasumi-giri);* the blade is then turned and brought downward, again in a diagonal cut, from left to right *(kesagiri);* finally, the sword is raised slowly along the same right-to-left diagonal as the first cut and then drawn horizontally at about shoulder level, from left to right, before being returned to the scabbard. The diagonal cuts stand for Takemikazuchi's castigation of the offending deities; the horizontal drawing motion, his pacification and forgiveness of the chastised gods. The exorcism ritual employed at the Kashima Grand Shrine today is very similar to this, albeit performed with a wand wrapped in paper rather than a sword. Sword dances *(kenbu)* remain an essential element of other important shrine rituals as well.

Tradition has it that Kuninazu developed from harai-tachi a series of techniques that he called *shinmyō-ken* ("sword of divine mystery"). Also known as *nukiuchi* ("extricating strike"), these techniques aim at what is termed "silent victory" *(otonashi-no-kachi),* whereby one defeats an opponent without blocking or striking his weapon with one's own. Most commonly, this involves making an opening attack—a cut or thrust—that the opponent will attempt to turn aside. The instant before the defending weapon contacts the attacking one, the direction of attack is changed; the weapon spins around the block and strikes down the opponent in the same motion.

By the medieval period, the Kashima Grand Shrine had become an important center for the study of the military arts. It had also become a major landholder, with an income exceeding 25,000 *koku* of rice annually.* In the late twelfth century, Kashima Rokurō Munemoto, a ranking attendant *(gūji)* to the shrine, established what later became known as Kashima Castle or Yoshioka Castle.[16] For the next four centuries his heirs functioned as both castellans and head priests to the shrine, while their principal vassals also served as subordinate attendants *(negi* or *hafuri)*. In 1590, Kashima Harutoki, a thirteenth-generation descendant of Munemoto, was killed and his stronghold reduced by Satake Yoshishige. Yoshishige (1547–1612) was a major power in eastern Japan during the late sixteenth century, controlling most of Hitachi, Kazusa, and Shimōsa provinces. His son Yoshinobu (1570–1633) inherited his father's lands in 1590 and ruled the area until about 1600, when, as punishment for his attempt to remain neutral in the struggle that brought Tokugawa Ieyasu to national hegemony, he was moved to Dewa province and replaced in Hitachi by the Mito branch of the Tokugawa house. His progeny remained in Dewa until the Meiji (1868–1911) period.[17]

The Three Founders

Kashima-Shinryū martial art took birth through the combined insights and discoveries of three sixteenth-century warriors: Matsumoto Bizen-no-kami Ki no Masamoto (or Masanobu), Kunii Genpachirō Kagetsugu, and Kamiizumi Ise-no-kami Fujiwara no Hidetsuna (or Nobutsuna).†

The pivotal figure here was Matsumoto, the scion of one of the four principal vassal families to the house of Kashima (the other three being the Yoshikawa, Ogano, and Gakuga) and a hereditary attendant of the Kashima Grand Shrine. Matsumoto was a warrior of consummate skill—one source credits him with participation in at least twenty battles, in three of which he took more than seventy enemy heads. In spite of this, he did not achieve the fame of his protégés Kamiizumi Hidetsuna and Tsukahara Bokuden (see below). This is probably because unlike the latter two, who traveled exten-

---

*A *koku* is a unit for measuring income in terms of rice or rice-equivalents. Defined as the amount of rice needed to support one person for one year, it was standardized during the early modern period at about 180 liters.

†Documents belonging to the Jikishin-kageryū identify the school's founder as "Sugimoto Bizen-no-kami Ki no Masamoto." Most authorities believe this to be the result of a copyist's error, substituting the character "sugi" (杉) for "matsu" (松), but Ishigaki Yasuzō is emphatic that this is not the case. He compares outsiders

sively and engaged in duels and matches throughout Japan, Matsumoto never left the Kashima area and never—at least insofar as the written record attests—participated in a duel; his reputation was based entirely on his battlefield achievements.[18]

As is the case with many Sengoku era samurai, the dates of Matsumoto's birth and death are uncertain. A medieval war tale and two nineteenth-century historical compendiums state that he was killed in 1524, at the age of 57, in a spear exchange with one Tsuga Daizen during the battle of Takamagahara.* The Matsumoto family death register, however, places his demise in 1534, while the records of the Kunii family say he was killed by a stray arrow during a battle in 1543, at the age of 67. There is, however, reason to doubt all three of these dates.

The aforementioned medieval war tale is the only extant record of Matsumoto's participation in the 1524 battle it details, and was the source for both of the nineteenth-century compendiums, while the 1543 campaign described in the Kunii family records is similarly suspect: No other documents corroborate either the campaign itself or Matsumoto's actions in it. The 1534 date suggested by the Matsumoto family death register, on the other hand, is probably a misinterpretation, resulting from a typographical error. The register survives as a single volume, with the first entry dated 1680, and it is therefore clearly at least the second of what was originally a set of volumes. The entry dated "Tenbun 3 (1534) fifth month, second day" on page 9 of this register is preceded by an entry dated 1725 and followed by one

---

presuming to dispute what a ryūha's documents say about its own founder to thieves breaking into a man's house and rearranging his most intimate possessions. Proprietary emotion notwithstanding, Ishigaki's conclusion is contraindicated by all outside evidence: Corroborating references to "Matsumoto Bizen-no-kami Ki no Masamoto" can be found in various public and private documents, but no sources other than the Jikishin-kageryū records confirm that "Sugimoto Bizen-no-kami" ever lived (although a schematic of the Jikishin-kageryū lineage in the *Shinsen bujutsu ryūso roku* [p. 167], completed around 1843, also gives the name of the founder as "Sugimoto Bizen-no-kami"). Ishigaki's argument appears in *Kashima Shinden Jikishin Kageryū gokui tenkai*, 54–57.

"Kamiizumi" is the most common reading for Hidetsuna's surname, but some scholars believe that he actually pronounced it "Kōizumi."

*Takamagahara, the spot where Kuninazu-no-Mahito is said to have received his oracle concerning martial art from Takemikazuchi-no-Mikoto, was also the site of a brutal battle in 1524, climaxing a struggle for power within the house of Kashima. The events of this feud are chronicled in the *Kashima jiranki*, 49–54. An extensive discussion of Takamagahara and its history appears in Tō Minoru, *Kashima jingū*, 92–106.

for 1743. "Tenbun (天文) 3," then, is most likely a miswriting of "Genbun (元文) 3" (1738), which would fall logically between the dates of the entries that flank it. The "Matsumoto Heiueimon Masamoto" referenced in this entry must therefore have been an eighteenth-century descendant of the Kashima-Shinryū founder.[19]

At any rate, in the fifteenth and sixteenth centuries Kashima was a gathering place for samurai seeking instruction in the military disciplines; Matsumoto thus spent his adolescence and early years of training surrounded by some of the best warriors in Japan. Among others, he probably studied with Iizasa Yamashiro-no-kami Chōisai, the founder of the Katori-Shintōryū and the most illustrious bugei exponent in the region during Matsumoto's youth.[20]

The hagiographic traditions concerning Matsumoto, like those surrounding most founders of shrines, temples, artistic lineages, and other important institutions in medieval Japan, cite divine intervention as the source of his creative genius. After reaching adulthood, he reportedly found himself unfulfilled by what he had been taught. Seeking to go beyond it, he undertook a protracted regimen of meditation, purification ritual, and other devotions at the shrine. At length the inspiration he sought came to him in the form of a dream in which Takemikazuchi-no-Mikoto visited him and presented him with a scroll revealing secret principles of martial art. At about this same time, the tale continues, Matsumoto entered into collaboration with Kunii Kagetsugu, a warrior from Shirakawa, in the southern part of Mutsu province.

Kunii reportedly had studied an early form of the Nenryū—a style that claims roots dating back to the early 1400s—but was unsatisfied by it. He cloistured himself in the Kashima (branch) Shrine in Shirakawa and, like Matsumoto, performed devotions to Takemikazuchi-no-Mikoto until he received a revelatory oracle concerning martial art. He developed this inspiration on his own for a while, calling his new style the Kashima-Shintōryū. Later he traveled to the Kashima Grand Shrine in Hitachi, where he pooled his insights with those of Matsumoto. According to one account, this synergy began with the arrival at Kashima of one Hayakawa Tōzaemon. Hayakawa, who was traveling about the country sharpening his martial skills under various teachers (a practice known as *musha shugyo*—see chapter 4), had recently spent some time with Kunii in Shirakawa. After telling Matsumoto about Kunii's Kashima-Shintōryū, he engaged one of Matsumoto's students, Arima Yamato-no-kami Kiminobu (who later founded the Arima-ryū), in a match.

In any case, the meeting of minds between Matsumoto and Kunii marked the birth of the Kashima-Shinryū. The ryūha's official historiography recognizes Matsumoto, who was apparently senior in years to Kunii, as the founder of the resulting school, and ascribes to Kunii the status of counselor to the founder.[21] The *Kashima-Shinryū hyōhō denki* relates that Matsumoto called his new style the Shinkage-ryū (the "Divine Shade," or "Abetted by the Gods" style) to acknowledge its source—his revelation.*

The centerpiece of Matsumoto's swordsmanship was the concept of *ichi-no-tachi*. "*Ichi*" ("one") refers here to "number one"— that is, the best, the foremost; it is also a homophone for "position," and thus means the most advantageous position; and it carries the additional meaning of "one dimension." "*Tachi*" means "sword" or "sword stroke."† The technique is at once simple and brilliant in conception. Similarly, it is not physically demanding, but is nonetheless very difficult to master. To perform ichi-no-tachi the swordsman enters his opponent's striking range, drawing an attack, which he makes no attempt to block or otherwise divert. Instead, he steps inside—through, not around—and past the blow, to deliver a decisive strike of his own. Ichi-no-tachi is an extraordinarily subtle technique hinging on the swordsman's timing, the position to which he steps, and the angle at which he strikes. Properly performed, it is virtually impossible to counter.[22]

Matsumoto's most important students were Arima Yamato-no-kami Kiminobu, Tsukahara Bokuden, and, according to Kashima-Shinryū and Jikishin-Kageryū lore, the third of the Kashima-Shinryū founders, Kamiizumi Ise-no-kami Fujiwara no Hidetsuna.‡ Although

---

*"*Kage*," which literally means "shade" or "beholden to," was also commonly used in sixteenth- and seventeenth-century texts on martial art in the meaning of "heart" or "mind." Okada, *Kengō*, 35.

†Some authors render the characters for "*ichi-no-tachi*" as "*hitotsu-no-tachi*," but Kashima-Shinryū adherents prefer the former reading. "*Hitotsu*" is a cardinal number, while "*ichi*" is an ordinal one. Thus "hitotsu," meaning "single," misses most of the nuances of "ichi," particularly those that derive from its homophones. The reading "hitotsu-no-tachi," which translates relatively well as "single stroke," is a logical mistake, insofar as ichi-no-tachi in application always involves dropping the opponent with a single blow, but it does not capture the real essence of the concept.

‡Bokuden (1490?–1571) was a swordsman of legendary stature. The founder of the Kashima-Shintōryū (not to be confused with Kunii Kagetsugu's school), he is also believed to have instructed the thirteenth and fifteenth Ashikaga shōguns,

there are no reliable records of either his birth or his death, Kamiizumi appears to have been born sometime between 1505 and 1510 in Kamiizumi village in Kōzuke province (present-day Maebashi City in Gumma prefecture). He began his career in service to the keeper of Minowa Castle in Kōzuke. Both the castle and the loyalties of Kamiizumi's master changed hands three times between 1552 and 1563, after which Hidetsuna briefly took service with Takeda Shingen, who gave him the character "shin" (also read "nobu") to use in his name—hence his alternative appellation, Nobutsuna.* Later that same year, however, he left Shingen's employ to further his study of the bugei. He spent the next eight years wandering, teaching, and training before returning to Kōzuke in 1571, where he died around 1577.[23]

Like most warriors of his age, Kamiizumi apparently studied under a variety of teachers. The *Hyōhō denki*, a document common to the Kashima-Shinryū and the Jikishin Kageryū, states that he acceded to Matsumoto Bizen-no-kami's Shinkage-ryū but that, intimidated by the power of the character "shin" (meaning "divine" or "deity") in Matsumoto's orthography, he substituted another character also pronounced "shin," but meaning "new." Kamiizumi's style was thus the "New Shade," or the "New Abetment" school of martial art. This version of things is not, however, without problems.

Yoshiteru and Yoshiaki, as well as Takeda Shingen and his general Yamamoto Kansuke. In his travels about Japan, leading an entourage at times numbering more than 800, he is said to have fought at least nineteen duels with live blades and participated in some thirty-seven battles, during all of which he bested more than 212 opponents. He was never defeated, receiving only six arrow wounds in the course of his career. (*Kashima shi*, 490–491.)

Not all scholars and traditions accept the idea of Bokuden as Matsumoto's student. The Kashima-Shintōryū, for example, traces its lineage from Iizasa Chōisai to Bokuden's father, Yoshikawa Kakuyoshi, to Bokuden. This is also the version related in the late eighteenth century bugei history, *Nihon chūkō bujutsu keifu ryaku* (p. 122), while the earlier (published 1716) *Honchō bugei shōden* (p. 57) describes Bokuden as a direct student of Iizasa. Iizasa, however, is also claimed as the founder of the Katori-Shintōryū, which does not practice ichi-no-tachi. Bokuden, on the other hand, is famous for his mastery of this technique. Iizasa then, could not have invented ichi-no-tachi and passed it on to both Matsumoto and Bokuden. Bokuden must therefore have either acquired the technique from Matsumoto or discovered it independently—but at virtually the same time. The *Honchō bugei shōden* (p. 58) credits Matsumoto with inventing the technique and implies—but does not state directly—that he taught it to Bokuden.

*Shingen was offering Kamiizumi the use of a character from his own name. This was one of the highest honors that a samurai lord could bestow on one of his retainers.

To begin with, it is by no means clear that Matsumoto ever actually used the name "Shinkage-ryū" for his style. The appellation appears in no records other than the *Hyōhō denki* and, aside from Kamiizumi, none of Matsumoto's other students used this name. Arima Kiminobu called his style the Arima-ryū, Kunii Kagetsugu originally called his the Kashima-Shintōryū (while his descendents at some point shortened this to the Kashima-Shinryū), and Tsukahara Bokuden dubbed his methods the Shintō-ryū, or the Kashima-Shintōryū. Iizasa Chōisai, Matsumoto's teacher, moreover, also called his style the Shintō-ryū.

A second puzzle is Kamiizumi's choice of the character "shin/new" to replace "shin/deity." Presumably he must have had some reason for selecting this character instead of any of a dozen or more other homophones for "shin/deity." Yet "shin/new" is an exceedingly odd choice if Kamiizumi saw himself as principally following in Matsumoto's footsteps. The most logical possibility is that he believed he had added substantially to what Matsumoto had taught him.

Of course, arguments based on nomenclature are anything but decisive. This is particularly true in the case of Kamiizumi, who was not entirely uniform in his own orthography, although he did consistently use one set of characters or another that formed homophones for "Shinkage-ryū." A document he gave to Marume Kurando-no-suke Nagayoshi and dated "second month, 1567," for example, writes the name of the style with an entirely different character for "kage" (one meaning "reflections," "silhouette," or "shadow"), while another dated three months later (and also given to Marume) employs that same character for "kage" but renders "shin" with a graph meaning "true" or "sincere."[24]

An alternative origin for Kamiizumi's "Shinkage-ryū" is suggested by the diploma he gave to Yagyū Muneyoshi on "an auspicious day in the fifth month of 1566." Here Kamiizumi relates that

> there is the Jōko-ryū, there is the Chūko-nenryū; there is also the Kage-ryū; and there are uncountable others. In my studies I penetrated into the deepest foundations of the various styles, but in particular I drew out the mysteries of the Kage-ryū and [therefore] call [my own school] the Shin ["New"] Kage-ryū.[25]

Most authorities identify the Kage-ryū referred to in this document with Aisu Ikōsai Hisatada (1452?–1538?), one of the premier swordsmen of the late fifteenth century.[26] The text quoted implies that Kamiizumi studied under Hisatada or one of his pupils and

added to this what he learned from Matsumoto and other teachers
to produce his own "New Kage" style of martial art.

But some scholars have questioned whether Kamiizumi ever studied under Matsumoto at all. In point of fact, the available evidence
makes a convincing argument—one way or the other—elusive at
best. For while it is true that there are no written records other than
the *Hyōhō denki* to connect the pair, it is equally true that this absence
of documentation does not prove the negative. Attempts at analysis
of circumstantial evidence seem similarly inconclusive.

Okada Kazuo argues, on the basis of birth and death dates for the
two warriors, that the window of opportunity in which Kamiizumi
could have met Matsumoto was too short for meaningful contact
between them. Kamiizumi, he contends, was born in 1508, and
would have been only 16 years old at the time of Matsumoto's death
in 1524. If, then, he trained under Matsumoto, he must have done
so for a very brief time and at the age of 15 or younger.[27] Okada's
argument, however, rests on at least two erroneous assumptions.

First, it postulates an unwarranted precision in dating the lives of
both swordsmen. As discussed above, the dates of neither
Kamiizumi's birth nor Matsumoto's death can be established with
certainty, whereas a margin of error as small as one or two years in
one or both dates makes an enormous difference to Okada's conclusions. Adjusting both dates by two years places Kamiizumi at
anywhere from 11 to 19 years of age at Matsumoto's death; assum-
ing Kamiizumi to have been born in 1505 and Matsumoto to have
died in 1543 would make Kamiizumi 38 at the time!

Second, Okada overestimates the length of the training period
common in the sixteenth century. With the professionalization of
bugei teaching during the early modern period, students came to
serve long-term apprenticeships prior to being graduated—a situation that continues today. But this was not the case in Kamiizumi's
time, as certificates of mastery from the period readily demonstrate.
A diploma Kamiizumi awarded to Hōzōin In'ei on "an auspicious
day, eighth month, 1567," for instance, states that Hōzōin had "diligently applied himself to the study of the Shinkage-ryū *since spring,*
and the style . . . had been transmitted to him in its entirety"
(emphasis added). If Kamiizumi could pass on his knowledge in toto
in six months or so, surely he could have absorbed a great deal from
Matsumoto in as much—or even a bit less—time.[28]

Nakabayashi Shinji also questions Kamiizumi's relationship to
Matsumoto, observing that the nomenclatures for principles and

techniques used by the two warriors, as recorded in documents they left behind, bear little resemblance to one another.[29] But while there is some merit to this argument, a case *for* Matsumoto as Kamiizumi's teacher can also be made on very similar grounds.

Kamiizumi's swordsmanship centered on *katsujin-ken*—one of a pair of key concepts in martial art theory—and rejected its antipode, *setsunin-tō*. The two terms derive from Buddhist allegory and literally mean "life-giving sword" and "killing sword," respectively. In classical bugei parlance, however, their connotations are more concrete: The "sword," in both cases refers not to the weapon itself but to its usage; and it is not the opponent himself who is killed or given life, but his responses and fighting spirit. When a combatant uses force of will to overpower, immobilize, and strike down an opponent before he can react, this is called "setsunin-tō" (i.e. "sword[smanship] that transfixes," or "swordsmanship that kills response"). "Katsujin-ken" ("Sword[smanship] that animates"), on the other hand, involves drawing out the opponent, inducing him to strike, and then going inside his technique, countering it either at the moment of its origination or at the point of its most complete extension. Setsunin-tō is an egoistic and risky approach to combat—the slightest miscalculation will result in the swordsman walking straight into his opponent's counterattack. Katsujin-ken, by contrast, involves a sophisticated manipulation of the opponent and his actions by means of utter selflessness; properly conducted, it is virtually undefeatable.[30]

Matsumoto Bizen-no-kami's ichi-no-tachi is the essence of katsujin-ken, and its most sublime expression. This, then, strongly suggests the influence of Kashima martial art on Kamiizumi. That being the case, Matsumoto, as the senior exponent of the Kashima style during Kamiizumi's early life, was a likely source.*

In any event, a connection between Matsumoto and Kamiizumi is certainly plausible, if not provable. Perhaps, however, the most important words on Kamiizumi's teachers were his own:

---

*It is, of course, conceivable that Kamiizumi's introduction to Kashima bugei could have come from Matsumoto's student Tsukahara Bokuden, rather than Matsumoto himself. At least two chronicles of the late medieval period—the *Hōjō godaiki* and the *Kanhasshū kosenroku*—describe Bokuden as Kamiizumi's teacher. On the other hand, at least three early modern texts—the *Gekken sōdan*, the *Honchō bugei shōden*, and the *Meiryō kōhan*—say that Kamiizumi instructed Bokuden. (*Gekken sōdan*, p. 193; *Honchō bugei shōden*, pp. 57, 75; Ishioka et al., *Nihon no kobu-*

In my studies I penetrated into the deepest foundations of the various schools but . . . [while] I did not abandon the various styles, neither do I recognize them. In truth I am like one who, having caught a fish, forgets his lure.[31]

Clearly Kamiizumi did not think of himself as the heir to any particular tradition, but as the pioneer of his own.

The foregoing questions notwithstanding, Kashima-Shinryū tradition posits Matsumoto as its founder and traces his legacy through two lineages. The first, the *sōke*, or "Founder's House," derives from Matsumoto's student Kunii Kagekiyo, a son of Kagetsugu. This lineage has continued within the Kunii family to the present-day (twenty-first-generation) sōke, Kunii Michiyuki. The second line, the *shihanke*, or "Instructor's House," separated from the sōke lineage with Kamiizumi and continued for nine generations, until the eighteenth century, when Kunii Taizen received certificates of mastery from both his father, Yoshinori, and Ono Shigemasa, the eleventh-generation shihanke, and merged the two lines. Both lines then remained within the Kunii family until the eighteenth-generation sōke/shihanke, Kunii Zen'ya, split them again in the late 1960s. The two lineages are outlined in figure 2.

The Students of Kamiizumi Ise-no-kami and the Shihanke Line

Kamiizumi had a dozen or more students later acknowledged as masters in their own right (see figure 1, pp. 20–21), including Hikida Bungorō Kanekage, the founder of the Hikida Shinkage-ryū; Marume Kurodō-no-suke Nagayoshi, who established the Taisha-ryū; Hōsōin

---

jutsu, 36–37; Okada, *Kengō shidan*, 29–30.) Moroda (*Kensei*, 156–162) gives a spirited defense of the latter relationship, but it is most unlikely. Not only did Bokuden establish his reputation several decades earlier than Kamiizumi, but he called his style the Shintō-ryū, as did Iizasa and Kunii Kagetsugu—Matsumoto's teacher and collaborator, respectively—while Kamiizumi called his the Shinkage-ryū.

The fact that the various texts contradict one another on this indicates, more than anything else, the level of confusion that prevailed about the relationship in the decades after the two swordsmen became famous. The most likely explanation for all this is that neither studied under the other, but both were students of the same teacher: Matsumoto. On the other hand, this would not preclude the possibility that Kamiizumi also studied under Bokuden. Bokuden was, after all, fifteen or more years Kamiizumi's senior and also outlived Matsumoto by some thirty to fifty years. If Kamiizumi was, in fact, Matsumoto's student, it is not difficult to suppose that he might have also received advice and instruction from his senior fellow pupil.

Kakuzenbō In'ei, the progenitor of the Hōsōin-ryū of spearmanship (sōjutsu); Komagawa Saemon Kuniyoshi, the founder of the Komagawa Kaishin-ryū; Kamiizumi Norimoto, the founder of the Aizu Ittō-ryū; Kamiizumi Hitachi-no-suke Hidetane, who originated the Muraku-ryū; and Yagyū Tajima-no-kami Muneyoshi, who founded the Yagyū Shinkage-ryū. His successor within the Kashima-Shinryū tradition, however, was Okuyama (Kyūgasai) Magojirō Taira no Kimishige.

Okuyama, who is best known by his Buddhist appellation, Kyūgasai, was originally named Okudaira Sadakuni. Born in 1526 in Mikawa province, he traveled to Kōzuke as a young man to study with Kamiizumi. Upon his return to Mikawa, he settled in the village of Okuyama, whence his acquired surname. He later caught the eye of the young Tokugawa Ieyasu, who invited him to serve as his fencing instructor. Ieyasu also gave him the character "kimi" to use in his name, and he was thereafter known as Kimishige. He died in 1602—at the age of 77—in the home of his old master, Okudaira Sadataka.[32]

Sometime after his return from Kōzuke, Kyūgasai is supposed to have spent a hundred days in prayer and meditation at a branch of the Kashima Shrine in Okuyama in pursuit of his own divine oracle concerning the mysteries of martial art. The orthography he chose for his school's name, which differed from Kamiizumi Ise-no-kami's, reportedly acknowledges this new revelation. According to the *Kashima-Shinryū hyōhō denki*, the character read as *"kage"* in Matsumoto Bizen-no-kami's original orthography was intended to convey that the school was a direct transmission from Takemikazuchi-no-Mikoto. In its Japanese reading (kage), it carries the meaning of indebtedness for favors granted, of invisible backing and support. But in its Chinese reading (*yin* in Mandarin; *in* or *on* in Sino-Japanese), it has connotations of negativity and darkness. Kamiizumi, says the document, retained this character but changed the graph for "shin" from Matsumoto's shin/deity to shin/new, and Okuyama then restored the original shin/deity, but changed the character for "kage" to one without the negative connotations of the original. The new character (kage/silhouette—pronounced *ei* in its Sino-Japanese reading) means "reflection," "figure," "light," "shadow," or "tracings," in addition to the meanings of indebtedness and assistance carried by kage/shade. Okuyama's Shinkage-ryū, therefore, translates as the "Silhouette of the Gods," or "Divine Shadows" style.

Figure 2. Kashima-Shinryū *sōke* and *shibanke* lineages

Masumoto Bizen-no kami Ki no Masamoto → Kunii Genpachirō Kagetsugu

Shihanke

Sōke

Sōke	Shibanke
Kunii Gengorō Minomoto no Kagekiyo	Kamiizumi Ise-no-kami Fujiwara no Hidetsuna
Kunii Yatarō Minamoto no Maseteru	Okuyama Kyūgasai Taira no Kimishige
Kunii Yagorō Minamoto no Yoshitoki	Ogasawara Genshinsai Minamoto no Nagaharu
Kunii Yashirō Minamoto no Yoshimasa	Kamiya Denshinsai Taira no Masamitsu
Kunii Yahachirō Minamoto no Masaie	Takahashi Jikiōsai Minamoto no Shigeharu
Kunii Kogorō Minamoto no Masauji	Yamada Ippūsai Fujiwara no Mitsunori
Kunii Shingorō Minamoto no Ujiie	Naganuma Shirozaemon Fujiwara no Kunisato
Kunii Zenpachirō Minamoto no Takamasa	Naganuma Shirozaemon Fujiwara no Norisato
Kunii Shinpachirō Minamoto no Yoshitsugu	Motooka Chūhachi Fujiwara no Yorihito
Kunii Gentarō Minamoto no Yoshinori	Ono Seiemon Taira no Shigemasa
Kunii Taizen Minamoto no Ritsuzan	
Kunii Zentarō Minamoto no Ritsuzan	

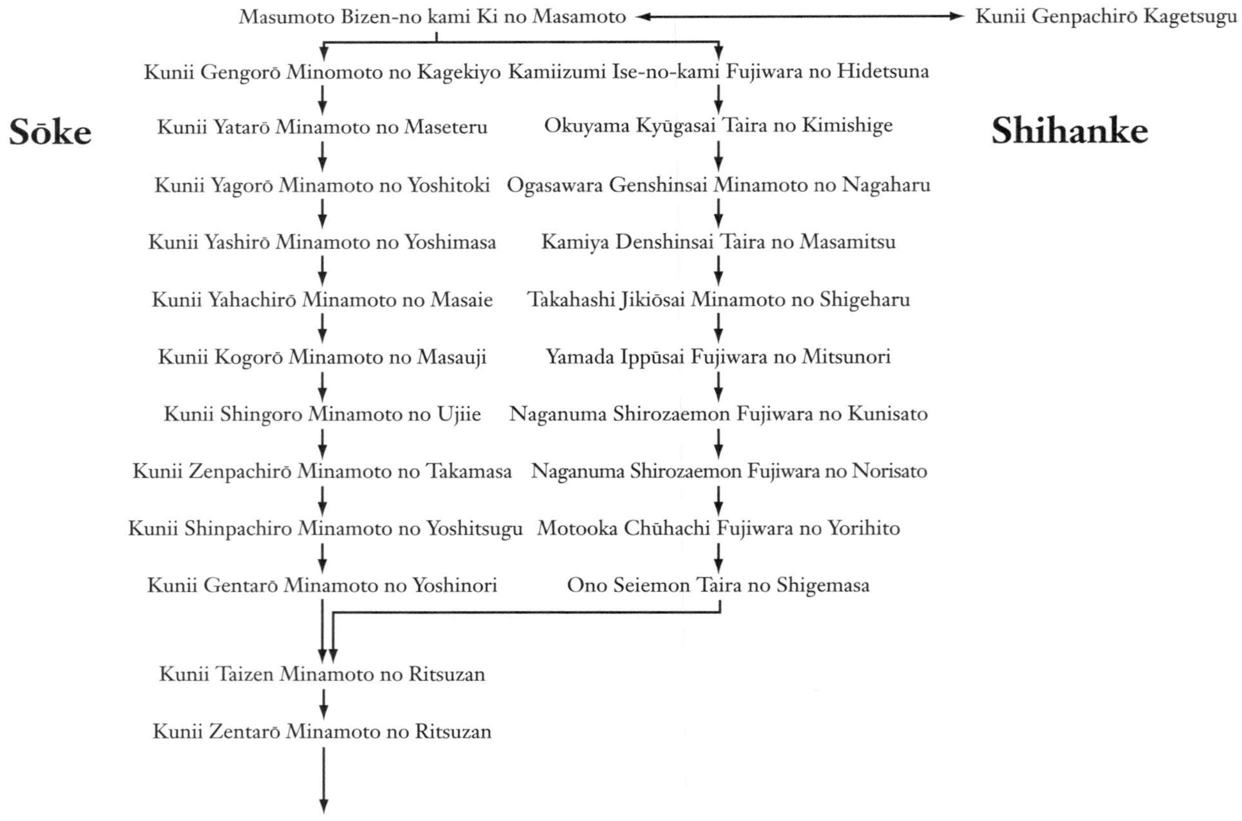

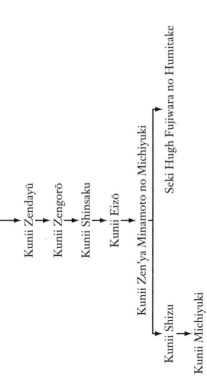

Kunii Zendayū → Kunii Zengorō → Kunii Shinsaku → Kunii Eizō → Kunii Zen'ya Minamoto no Michiyuki → Seki Hugh Fujiwara no Humitake

Kunii Shizu → Kunii Michiyuki

Okuyama was followed by Ogasawara (Genshinsai) Kinzaemon Minamoto no Nagaharu of Tōtōmi province (present-day Shizuoka prefecture). Ogasawara began his career in service to Imagawa Yoshimoto, joining Tokugawa Ieyasu after Yoshimoto's death in 1560.* He later left Ieyasu for Takeda Shingen's heir, Katsuyori, and then jumped to Hōjō Ujimasa when Katsuyori was killed in 1582, only to find himself masterless yet again in 1590 when Toyotomi Hideyoshi destroyed Ujimasa.†

By this time Ogasawara had changed sides at least once too often, and in so doing earned the wrath of Ieyasu—to the point that Ieyasu, upon coming to power, ordered the family head, Harunori, to commit suicide. Wishing to avoid a similar fate, Genshinsai fled to China. After wandering about for a short time, he opened a martial art school in Beijing, where he taught Japanese bugei and studied Chinese boxing and spear methods. Following Ieyasu's death, Ogasawara returned to Japan and settled in the Kosami district of Edo, near present-day Nihonbashi. He called his style the Shin-Shinkage-ryū, adding the character "shin," meaning "true," to Kamiizumi's original shin/new and kage/shade to produce the "True Shinkage-ryū," possibly to distinguish his style from the Yagyū Shinkage-ryū.[33]

Kamiya (Denshinsai) Bunzaemon Taira no Masamitsu (1582?–16??), the fifth successor in the shihanke lineage, became a student of Ogasawara Genshinsai at the age of 42, after losing a match to

*Imagawa Yoshimoto (1519–1560) was a major power in central Japan, controlling the provinces of Mikawa, Tōtōmi, and Suruga until his death at the hands of Oda Nobunaga in the battle of Okehazama. Tokugawa Ieyasu, the founder of the Tokugawa shogunate, was born to a minor daimyō house in Mikawa province. His family served as vassals of Imagawa Yoshimoto until Okehazama, after which Ieyasu broke with the Imagawa to join the victorious Nobunaga.

†Takeda Katsuyori (1546–1582), Shingen's third son, succeeded his father in 1573. In 1575 his power was broken by Nobunaga at the battle of Nagashino; in 1582 Nobunaga and Ieyasu routed him again at Temmokuzan, and Katsuyori committed suicide together with his son Nobukatsu. Hōjō Ujimasa (1538–1590) controlled most of the Kantō region until he made the error of refusing to accept vassalage under Toyotomi Hideyoshi, who destroyed him in 1590 and gave his lands to Ieyasu.

Hideyoshi, the son of a farmer, began his career as a peasant foot soldier (ashigaru) and worked his way up through the ranks to become one of Oda Nobunaga's top commanders. Following Nobunaga's death, Hideyoshi declared himself to be his (Nobunaga's) successor; by 1585 he had secured the obedience of all the daimyō in Nobunaga's coalition. By 1590 he was supreme in Japan. He died of natural causes in 1598, setting off a new struggle for power.

Genshinsai's younger brother. Prior to this, he had trained in several styles of martial art under a variety of teachers. When he left Ogasawara's tutelage, Kamiya, like Ogasawara, Okuyama, and Kamiizumi before him, retitled the style he had received, dropping the shin/true character used by his mentor and appending the Buddhist phrase "*jikishin,*" to produce the Shinkage-Jikishin-ryū. "Jikishin" (literally, "upright heart" or "direct will") indicates a state of untroubled, uncomplicated purity of thought and action. The *Kashima-Shinryū hyōhō denki* ascribes Shintō and neo-Confucian overtones to the term as well, opining that Kamiya used it to emphasize that a warrior must allow his will to be directly shaped by the (always correct) mind of the deities.[34]

Kamiya had some thirty-three students to whom he awarded certificates of mastery. Of these, the one most important to this study was Takahashi (Jikiōsai) Danjōzaemon Minamoto no Shigeharu of Kii province. Takahashi's association with the Kashima-Shinryū began when he was serving as a page *(koshō)* to Abe Shirōgorō, a direct retainer *(hatamoto)* of the shōgun. Abe was at the time receiving instruction from Kamiya Denshinsai and arranged for his young page to train with him, too. Takahashi's own teaching career extended from the Kan'ei (1624–1644) through the Genroku (1688–1704) eras, and included posts as fencing instructor to two daimyō before he opened a private school *(dōjō)* in what is now the Kuroda ward of Tokyo.

The mid-seventeenth century was the heyday for the formation of new martial art ryūha, a phenomenon that inevitably led to substantial confusion regarding the pedigrees of bugei teachers. This development—particularly the appearance of a plethora of schools unrelated to the Matsumoto Bizen-no-kami/Kamiizumi Ise-no-kami tradition but calling themselves by some variation of "Shinkage-ryū"—purportedly disturbed Takahashi, who henceforth referred to his own ryūha as the Jikishin-Seitō-ryū ("True Lineage of the Jikishin-ryū") to distinguish it from the others.[35]

Among Takahashi's students during his tenure at Takatsuki was a retainer of Nagai Naotaka, Yamada (Ippūsai) Heizaemon-no-jō Fujiwara no Mitsunori. Already middle aged when he first met Takahashi, Yamada had previously trained in the Edo branch of the Yagyū Shinkage-ryū. At first he was an enthusiastic convert to Takahashi's methods, but midway through his training, Yamada had a falling out with his new teacher and left his tutelage for further study with the Yagyū. At length, however, the two swordsmen were

able to settle their disagreement; Yamada returned to Takahashi, at
least long enough to acquire a certificate attesting to his mastery of
the Jikishin-Seitō-ryū. Perhaps owing to his close connection with
the Yagyū branch of the Shinkage-ryū tradition, Yamada seems to
have been distressed by Takahashi's dropping of the "shinkage"
from the school's name. Accordingly, he restored it, calling his style
the Jikishin Kageryū ("Reflections of the Upright Heart Style").[36]

Yamada's third son, Naganuma Shirōzaemon-no-jō Fujiwara no
Kunisato (1688–1767), was one of the most important figures of the
middle Edo period in martial art history.* He followed his father as
fencing instructor to the daimyō of Takatsuki domain, but resigned
this post at the age of 26 to open a private school in Edo. He is
believed to have taught more than ten thousand students in the
course of his long career. Among other achievements, Naganuma
was a pioneer in the development of protective gear for the chest
and wrists and associated training techniques, such as free-sparring,
that eventually led to modern kendō, the sportive adaptation of
Japanese fencing.[37]

Having inherited the Kashima-Shinryū tradition from his father,
Naganuma passed it on to at least two of his own sons, one natural
and one adopted. His initial heir was his third (natural) son,
Norisato, but when Norisato died in 1777, at the age of only 36,
Kunisato adopted his great-nephew Tadasato to continue his house.
(Tadasato, however, died of illness while still a child; the continua-
tion of the line was therefore maintained by arranging for Tadasato
to adopt the son of his guardian, Itō Masamitsu, as his own son,
Sukesato.) Very late in his life, Kunisato also adopted one of his
senior students, Saitō Shōbe, and sent him to serve as instructor to
Tsuchisaki Yamashiro-no-kami, the daimyō of Numada domain, in
what is now Gumma prefecture. Shōbe, who henceforth called himself Naganuma Tsunasato, later opened his own school in Edo.
Naganuma Kunisato's lines of descent, genealogical and institutional, are outlined in figure 3.[38]

From this point the lineages of what are today called the
Kashima-Shinryū and the Jikishin-kageryū diverged, the latter continuing under Shōbe/Tsunasato and his successors and the former
under another of Norisato's students, Motooka Chūhachi Fujiwara
no Yorihito. Motooka had once been a student of Kunii Kazunobu,

---

*Ippūsai's original surname was Naganuma; he acquired the name Yamada
through his adoption by a maternal uncle.

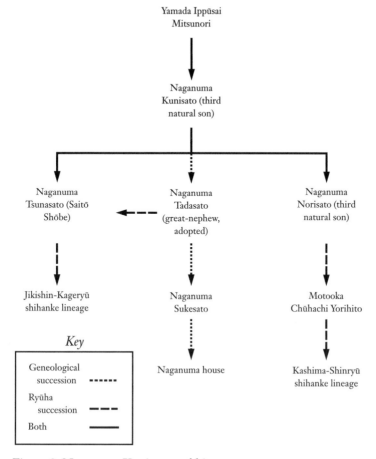

Figure 3. Naganuma Kunisato and his successors

a son of Yoshinori, the eleventh-generation successor to the sōke line. His student Ono Seiemon Taira no Shigemasa in turn trained Kunii Taizen Minamoto no Ritsuzan, who, having acquired a certificate of mastery from his father, Yoshinori, as well as from Ono, merged the shihanke and sōke lineages. For the next two and a half centuries, the Kashima-Shinryū continued as a family ryūha, passed down within the Kunii house.

The Kunii House and the Sōke Line

The Kunii are a branch of the Seiwa Genji, the Minamoto line descended from Emperor Seiwa (r. 858–876), as a result of the imperial family's practice of disposing of extraneous princes by granting them a surname (usually Minamoto or Taira) and demoting them from princely to commoner status. (The term Genji derives from the Sino-Japanese reading of the surname Minamoto.) Emperor Seiwa had nineteen sons, the descendants of nine of whom bore the Minamoto name. The lines of most interest to military historians claim descent from Seiwa's sixth son, Sadazumi, through his son Tsunemoto, who fathered nine sons, at least three of whom became warriors of some reputation. The most important of these was his eldest son, Mitsunaka. It is of Mitsunaka and his progeny that historians generally speak when they refer to the Seiwa Genji. The Kunii trace their ancestry to Mitsunaka's third son, Yorinobu, through his fifth son, Yoshimasa (see figure 4).[39]

Yoshimasa, who had garnered a respectable reputation as a warrior fighting under his elder brother Yoriyoshi in the Former Nine Years' War of 1051–1062, settled in Hitachi province after a stint in the provincial government office there.[*] He and his descendants adopted the surname Kunii, and by the 1160s had established themselves as the hereditary stewards of a block of lands held by the Yoshida Shrine (located in what is now the city of Mito) called Kunii-hō.[40] Sometime in the late thirteenth or early fourteenth century they left Hitachi and moved north to Shirakawa (in present-day Fukushima prefecture), where they became local magnates of some importance.[41]

As we have seen, the Kunii house's relationship with the Kashima-Shinryū began in the early sixteenth century, with Kunii Genpachirō Kagetsugu, Matsumoto Bizen-no-kami's coadjutor in the creation of the ryūha. Kagetsugu had a distinguished career on the battlefield, as well as in the training hall, fighting under the banner of Takeda Shingen. In his retirement, he moved a few dozen kilometers east of Shirakawa, to the village of Funao, near present-day Iwaki City in Fukushima prefecture, where he died of natural causes in the spring of 1591.[42]

---

[*]The Former Nine Years' War, waged against Abe Yoritoki and his son Sadatō, did much to enhance the prestige of the Minamoto as leaders of the emerging warrior order. The Abe were powerful local figures in northeastern Japan who found themselves involved in a rebellion against the authority of the provincial governor (Yoriyoshi) who was commissioned to suppress them. Yoritoki was killed in 1057, but Sadatō was able to hold out for five years longer before he too, met his end. The name "Former Nine Years' War" is something of a misnomer for a conflict that lasted twelve years. It probably results from confusion between this campaign and one dubbed the "Latter Three Years' War," fought in this same region from 1086 to 1089 by Yoriyoshi's son, Yoshiie.

Kagetsugu's son Kagekiyo trained under both his father and Matsumoto, becoming the second sōke after Matsumoto. His son Masuteru fought alongside his father and grandfather under Takeda Shingen. Following Shingen's death (in 1573) and the final destruction of the Takeda under Shingen's heir Katsuyori in 1582, he briefly became a vassal of Oda Nobunaga. He left Nobunaga after less than a year, however, owing to disagreements with the latter's policies and approach to governance.

The fourth-generation sōke, Yoshitoki, served in the army of Katō Kiyomasa during Toyotomi Hideyoshi's ill-advised attempts to subjugate China and Korea in the 1590s.* During the winter of 1598, Kiyomasa's army was trapped for more than two months in the Japanese fortress at Ulsan, about 80 kilometers up the coast from Pusan, by a besieging Chinese army under Yang Ho. Supplies gave out quickly, forcing the Japanese to eat their horses and to depend on melted snow for water. As both the strength and the morale of the defenders began to falter, Yoshitoki, together with a comrade, Iida Kakubei, managed to break through the enemy encirclement and return carrying sacks of rice for their troops. Yoshitoki's actions helped stave off enervation until a relief force was able to rescue the garrison a few weeks later.[43]

Hideyoshi's death brought an end to the Korean campaign later that same year, but it also created new troubles at home, both to Japan as a whole and to the Kunii house. His formidable political acumen notwithstanding, Hideyoshi left behind only the shakiest of arrangements for succession within his regime: a five-year-old heir, Hideyori, and a council of five regents pledged to look after his (Hideyori's) welfare. Predictably, the most powerful among the regents came into conflict almost immediately. Within two years of Hideyoshi's death, Japan was divided into two major camps: an Eastern alliance led by Tokugawa Ieyasu and a Western alliance under Ishida Mitsunari. In the ninth month of 1600, the two sides came to blows on a plain called Sekigahara, in what is now Gifu prefecture. Ieyasu's forces carried the day, leaving him without effective opposition in Japan. In 1603 Ieyasu took the title of shōgun and set about creating an enduring regime through which to rule. He secured his final victory in two campaigns fought during the winter of 1614–1615 and the following summer, by eliminating Hideyori and his remaining supporters.

*Kiyomasa (1562–1611) was the daimyō of Kumamoto domain in Kyushu. He headed one of Hideyoshi's two main armies in the first Korean campaign, the other being led by Konishi Yukinaga.

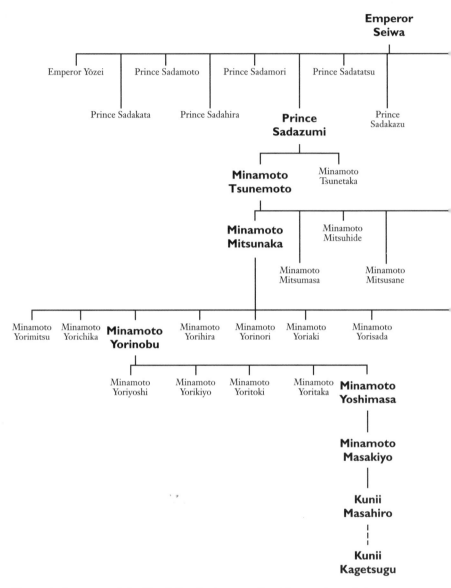

Figure 4. Ancestry of the Kunii family (source: *Sonpi bunmyaku* vol. 3; *Kunii-ke keizu*)

The advent of Tokugawa power marked the beginning of a whole new political, social, and economic order for the samurai. What had been an order of landed, feudal warriors was transformed in the space of a few decades into a caste of urbanized, stipended retainers. No longer fighting men serving independent barons, the early

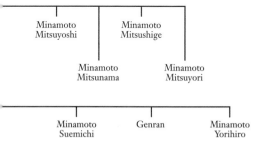

modern samurai became primarily bureaucrats, gathered in castle towns or in the shogunal capital of Edo and performing administrative duties for their daimyō.

For the Kunii house, this brave new world was particularly inhospitable. Yoshitoki and his son, the fifth-generation sōke Yoshimasa, fought with the Western forces at Sekigahara, attached to the forces of Ukita Hideie.* Yoshitoki was killed in the struggle; Yoshimasa, though wounded, was able to escape alive. He spent the winter hiding and convalescing on Mt. Ibuki, in Ōmi province. From there he made his way to Toyama, in Etchū, disguised as an itinerant medicine peddler to avoid detection by Tokugawa forces engaged in mop-up operations. At length he was able to return to his home in Funao, taking care the entire way to evade the watchful eyes of Tokugawa spies and informers.

In the post-Sekigahara order, Funao became shogunal house land (*tenryō*), administered directly by appointees of the Edo government. Yoshimasa and his descendants assumed a somewhat nebulous status as *gōshi*—or country samurai—retaining the formal privileges of the warrior class but residing on the land, in a lifestyle more akin to that of the peasantry than to the samurai of the castle towns and cities. At the same time, their devotion to the bugei continued undiminished; Yoshimasa's son, Masaie, made Kashima-Shinryū a compulsory part of the education of each successive heir. Henceforth the Kunii eked out their living through farming, while continuing to teach and study martial art.

Masaie's great-great-grandson, Yoshitsugu, was placed in charge of a storehouse for tax rice belonging to the shogunate, a post that became hereditary within the Kunii house for the next three generations. Between 1783 and 1787, when Yoshitsugu's great-grandson, Taizen, was serving in this capacity, Japan was struck by a series of bad harvests and natural disasters known to historians as the Temmei Famine after the calendar era (1781–1788) in which it occurred. Seeking to relieve at least a part of the suffering of the peasants in his district, Taizen petitioned the shōgun's regional representative (*daikan*) to open the emergency rice stores, but the government refused his request. After repeated pleas with similar results, he took matters into his own hands, opening the storehouses and distributing a part of the grain. He then reported what he had done to the shogunate, fully expecting to be ordered to commit ritual suicide (*seppuku*), the normal form of capital punishment for

*The Ukita comprised a powerful daimyō house in western Japan. Hideie, who was only a child when his father Naoie died in 1582, was raised by Hideyoshi and became one of his top commanders. At the time of Hideyoshi's death, he controlled most of Bitchu, Bizen, and Mimasaka provinces. After the defeat at Sekigahara, he fled to Kyushu, but was later discovered and exiled to the island of Hajijōjima, off the coast of Izu.

samurai. In the event, however, the government judged his actions
to have been unselfish and well intended, if inappropriate, and simply allowed him to resign his position and his samurai status.
Afterward, he opened an inn and devoted the remainder of his
energy to farming.

Taizen earned certificates of mastery from both his grandfather,
Yoshinori, and Ono Shigemasa, thus merging the shihanke into the
sōke line. He also originated the concept of *musōken*—literally, "the
unbeheld sword." In essence, musōken is an extension of
Matsumoto Bizen-no-kami's ichi-no-tachi, whereby the swordsman stops an opponent's technique by positioning himself so as to
distort the opponent's perception in a manner that prevents him
from completing the attack. The archetypical example of this is the
sword drawing *(battō-jutsu)* technique called musōken. Here the
opponent attacks from the front, the side, or even from behind, with
a straight vertical cut to the head. The swordsman performing the
technique steps into the blow, at the same time drawing his own
sword and flipping it with his wrist so that it points at the opponent's eyes. At the finish of this movement, his sword is held flat
before him, with the blade facing to his left, and in precisely the
opponent's line of vision. This angle makes the blade invisible, pre-
venting the opponent from discerning its length or the position of
its tip, and forcing him to break off his attack or risk stepping right
into the point.

For the next six generations the Kunii maintained a quiet existence as country squires in northern Japan, at the same time continuing to practice Kashima-Shinryū. In this respect, Kashima-
Shinryū development during the eighteenth and nineteenth
centuries departed considerably from the pattern followed by bet-
ter-known ryūha, such as the Yagyū Shinkage-ryū, the Jikishin
Kageryū, or the Ono-ha Ittō-ryū. For while these latter traditions
were perpetuated by professional teachers operating commercial
schools in cities or holding posts as personal instructors to daimyō
or shōguns, the Kashima-Shinryū was carried on in relative obscu-
rity, as a family tradition within the Kunii house. In the twentieth
century, however, the art reached a new peak of development and
fame under Kunii Zen'ya, the eighteenth-generation sōke.

Zen'ya, who, as we observed in chapter 1, became known by such
sobriquets as "the modern [Miyamoto] Musashi" and "the last
sword-saint," was one of the true greats of Japanese martial art history. A master in every sense of the term, he was undefeated during

a career that spanned six decades and included scores of formal and informal matches and duels. More importantly, he combined the insights gleaned from a lifetime of severe physical and spiritual training to reexamine, revise, and refine almost every aspect of Kashima-Shinryū technique and philosophy. He was born on January 20, 1894. He began training in martial art at the age of 8. At 16 he had his first taste of real combat.

In 1910, northern Japan was a poor, mainly agricultural region, an economic backwater that had not yet caught the wave of industrialization pushing outward from Tokyo. Recurrent famines in the area around the Kunii home in Fukushima had given rise to night-time raiders stealing farm produce; in a few instances, farmers attempting to protect their possessions had been severely injured by the thieves. Late one night, Zen'ya was sitting guard alone in his house when he heard a suspicious noise and went to investigate, taking his sword with him as a precaution. He discovered a band of men loading watermelons and other goods from his family's storehouse onto a wagon. Kunii ran toward them shouting, "Stop, thief!" as most of the group beat a hasty retreat, pulling the wagon after them. Two of the thieves, however, remained behind.

As he drew closer, Kunii saw something flicker—something that reflected the bright moonlight—at the sides of the two. Surmising that they had drawn swords, he stopped his approach. At this, however, the two thieves began to advance toward him. Kunii drew his own weapon as the first of the thieves raised his blade over his head and charged, only to be cut down by Zen'ya's ichi-no-tachi stroke. The second thief froze momentarily and then carefully resumed his advance, also holding his sword over his head. Hoping to avoid a second duel, the 16-year-old swordsman turned to escape, but the thief ran after him. As soon as he realized this, Kunii turned once more to face his attacker. When the thief had closed to just outside of striking range, Kunii stepped forward and attacked with a diagonal strike to the side of the head (a *kurai tachi*—see chapter 4). The thief tried to bat this down, whereupon Zen'ya slipped neatly around the countertechnique and sliced across his opponent's chest, killing him instantly.

Shaken by the encounter, Kunii ran back to his house and closeted himself in his room until morning. Later he reported the incident to the authorities, who did not at first believe him. The police, as it turned out, had already researched the identities of the slain thieves and determined them to have once been fencing instructors of some status and reputation. It was, the police opined, simply not possible that such men could both have been bested by a 16-year-old boy. Further investigation, however, confirmed Zen'ya's version of events, while a court inquiry determined that he had acted legally and in self-defense.[44]

When he was 19, Kunii spent several months training under Sasaki Masanoshin of Ibaraki prefecture, a master of the Shinkage-ryū and a former student of Zen'ya's grandfather. Before this he had also studied the Maniwa Nenryū under Suhara Kuniyasu. At 20, he succeeded his father as the eighteenth sōke of the Kashima-Shinryū. That same year he graduated from Fukushima Agricultural High School and enrolled for further study at the Kōdō Gakuin. Subsequently he saw action with the Japanese army in China during World War I and, following his discharge, continued his studies of the Japanese classics *(kokugaku)* under Imaizumi Teisuke at Kokugakuin University.*

Politically, he was fiercely conservative and patriotic to the point of chauvinism, becoming active with such prewar ultrana-tionalist organizations as the Imperial Rule Association (Nippon Kōseikai), the Blood Pledge Corp League for Asian Development (Ketsumeidan Kōa Dōmei), and the Japan Youth League (Nippon Seinen Renmei). He also served as an instructor at the Toyama Military Academy, Kinshū Girls' High School, Ritsumeikan University, and the Kashima Grand Shrine. In addition, he helped found the Japan Society for the Promotion of Classical Martial Art (Nihon Kobudō Shinkyokai).†

Kunii saw his political posture as the continuation of a long fam-ily tradition of imperial loyalism, a tradition that began in the four-teenth century with activities on behalf of the Southern Court.‡ This spirit of antishogunal allegiance to the throne reemerged, in

---

*Kokugakuin University was founded in 1890 in what is now Iidabashi, in Chiyōda-ku, as a center for the study of *kokugaku.* "Kokugaku," literally "national studies," was a school of indigenous historical and literary scholarship based on the Japanese classics. It began in the eighteenth century as an effort to recover a liter-ary and historical heritage for Japan and rapidly developed into an intellectual movement for a return to Japan's spiritual roots.

†Toyama Military Academy was founded in 1876 in Toyama-chō of Ushikumi-ku, in Tokyo, as an institution for training officers for the Japanese army. Ritsumeikan University is a private university in Kyoto, founded in 1869.

‡The events that gave birth to Japan's second shogunate trace back to 1259, when a succession dispute split the imperial house into rival Senior (Jimyōin) and Junior (Daikakuji) branches. By 1290 the Kamakura shogunate had managed to

Zen'ya's view, when Kunii Taizen was forced to resign his post as steward of the shōgun's tax-rice storehouse. Both Taizen and his son, Zentarō, he maintained, used their inn as a base for covert involvement with anti-Tokugawa activists. Zentarō's son, Kyūuemon, even moved to Mito in order to train restorationist guerrillas in Kashima-Shinryū.[45]

In his later years Kunii Zen'ya trained dozens of notable students, including the actor Nakadai Tatsuya, who came to him on various occasions for help with the skills he needed for parts. Down to his death in August of 1966, at the age of 72, Kunii was widely believed to be Japan's most skilled practitioner of martial art. The epitaph on his tombstone in the family burial plot in Iwaki City, Fukushima prefecture, reads in part:

> The master prayed regularly to the Deity of Kashima, never laying aside his diligence. Awake or asleep he kept to his sword, unifying deity and man and repeatedly receiving divine guidance. At length he attained consummate skill. He opened a school in Tokyo's Takinokawa district.
>
> He was pure and sincere of temperament, loyal to his friends and associates, and disinterested in money. He would delight in becoming gloriously drunk and singing. Always in his martial art he was as severe as the autumn frost. Disciples flocked to him with students from other styles at their heels, begging for instruction.
>
> Into his seventy-second year he practiced martial art morning and evening. At length he came to death, stricken with a sudden illness of the heart. It was autumn, the seventeenth day of August, in the

---

bring the problem under control by instituting a somewhat shaky compromise whereby the two branches would alternate with one another in providing succeeding emperors. The system held together reasonably well until 1331. In that year Emperor Go-Daigo, of the Junior line, began an ill-advised rebellion aimed at eliminating both his rival Senior line and the shogunate. He was rapidly defeated, captured and exiled, but managed to escape in 1332, only to find that his cause had become a rallying point for a number of anti-shogunate warrior leaders. In Go-Daigo's name, an army under Ashikaga Takauji captured Kyoto and a second under Niita Yoshisada destroyed Kamakura and the shogunate.

Takauji was not long, however, in deciding that his new sovereign had outgrown his usefulness. In 1335 he turned against Go-Daigo, drove him out of Kyoto, and set Kōmyō of the Senior line on the throne in his place. The Niita and numerous other major samurai houses supported Go-Daigo against Takauji, but after some intitial setbacks, the Ashikaga were victorious. Go-Daigo and his followers fled to Yoshino, in the mountains south of Kyoto, where they set up a rival (Southern) court that continued to contest with the Kyoto court for legitimacy until 1392. Takauji, in the meantime, arranged to be given the title of shōgun, and established a new warrior regime in the capital city.

forty-first year of Shōwa [1966]. On the day of his funeral, the thunder roared incessantly, mourning the passing of the sword-saint.[46]

Kunii Zen'ya's passing marked the end of an era in more ways than one. Not only was "the Modern Musashi" the last of a breed—a swordmaster who held even his own life in lower regard than his pursuit of mastery of the bugei, and a true samurai, utterly unaffected by Westernization—but he broke with a centuries-old family tradition to name Seki Humitake as the nineteenth-generation shihanke of the Kashima-Shinryū and the principal heir to his teachings. Under this arrangement, the sōke title became essentially honorific and ceremonial, with day-to-day responsibility for teaching and propagating Kashima-Shinryū bugei resting mainly with the shihanke. Zen'ya's succession decision marked the first time in nearly two hundred years that the shihanke line had passed out of the Kunii family, and the first time since the early sixteenth century that the head of the Kunii house was not actively practicing and teaching Kashima-Shinryū. Zen'ya himself, however, saw this less as a break with the past than as a revival of an older tradition: the existence of separate shihanke and sōke lines of succession. Accordingly, his widow Shizu became the nineteenth-generation sōke after Zen'ya's death. When Shizu died in December of 1992, Zen'ya's son Michiyuki succeeded her in this capacity.

Zen'ya's successor as shihanke, Seki Humitake, was born on December 14, 1937, and raised in central western Japan. An individual of remarkably diverse talents, he holds a Ph.D. in marine biology from the University of Tokyo, is a past winner of the Okada Prize, awarded by the Oceanographical Society of Japan, and has served on the faculties of the University of Tokyo, Waseda University, and since 1976, the University of Tsukuba in Ibaraki prefecture.

Seki's association with Kunii Zen'ya and the Kashima-Shinryū began in March of 1960, during his senior year in college, when he presented himself at Kunii's school in Tokyo's Takinokawa district and asked for instruction. Within four years he had distinguished himself as Kunii's ablest student. In February of 1964 Kunii arranged a no-rules match (taryū-jiai) for him with a fifth *dan* proponent of Shōtōkan karate (at the time, fifth dan was the highest rank awarded by the Shōtōkan organization). Seki's victory in this bout earned him promotion to the Kashima-Shinryū's highest level of initiation: *menkyo-kaiden*.* Nine months later,

---

*Kashima-Shinryū initiation levels are explained in the following section.

Kunii named him his designated heir as shihanke after Seki further distinguished himself in a similar match against an eighth dan aikidō expert. He formally took over as shihanke following Kunii's death in August 1966.

Although considerably less aggressive than his predecessor about challenging or seeking out challenges from other martial artists, Seki has more than equaled Kunii's passion for promoting the welfare and reputation of the Kashima-Shinryū. He has authored three books and dozens of magazine and journal articles about Kashima-Shinryū history and theory, and has further organized and systematized both the school's curriculum and its administrative structure, in the process establishing a network of branch clubs and schools—mostly at colleges and universities—around Japan and in foreign countries. A skillful and charismatic teacher whose students now number in the hundreds, he has acquired a reputation for formidability that rivals Kunii Zen'ya's. Between 1967 and 1969, for example, while conducting research near Nanaimo, British Columbia, Canada, Seki taught Kashima-Shinryū tactics to the Royal Canadian Mounted Police. On one occasion, one of his pupils reported having halted a beer hall brawl without laying a hand on any of the participants, simply by announcing himself to be "one of Dr. Seki's jūjutsu students."[47]

Seki's proudest bugei achievement, however, occurred on November 2, 1981, when he was invited to lecture for the late Shōwa emperor, Hirohito. The lecture itself was on marine biology, but in the course of the discussion period that followed it, the emperor raised questions about Seki's book on Kashima-Shinryū and praised it to the then-crown-prince, Akihito, who was also present. Bugei exponents have traditionally regarded being invited to perform a match before *(tenran-jiai)* or present writings concerning their schools to *(tenran o aogu)* an emperor to be the highest possible honor. Seki is, in fact, only the second figure in the Kashima-Shinryū shihanke lineage to have received this accolade, the first being Kamiizumi Ise-no-kami Hidetsuna in 1570.[48]

The Kashima-Shinryū as an Organization

The Kashima-Shinryū sōke and shihanke lineages date back nearly five hundred years, but the school as a structured organization is a phenomenon of far more recent origin. During its early years the ryūha appears to have had no institutional structure at all, which is one of the reasons that it is so difficult to establish even teacher-student relationships for the first few generations. Sengoku-period swordsmen like Kamiizumi Hidetsuna and Okuyama Kyūgasai traveled about, instructing students as and where they found them; some students followed the teachers from place to place, and others trained under them for short periods while the teacher was in the area. In either case, during this era a ryūha had little practical existence beyond the man who taught it.

In point of fact, it is probably inaccurate to speak of the Kashima-Shinryū as one ryūha until almost two centuries after Okuyama's death. For—notwithstanding the Kunii family's traditional historiography positing a single entity transmitted in parallel lineages—there is no documentary evidence indicating any direct contact between the sōke and shihanke lines until the late eighteenth century. Nor would the political circumstances of the Tokugawa period have been favorable to an ongoing relationship between the Kunii in Funao and samurai serving as instructors to daimyō in other domains or operating commercial schools in Edo. From Matsumoto Bizen-no-kami Masanobu's time until Kunii Taizen's, then, the Kashima-Shinryū was, for all intents and purposes, two ryūha—one maintained by the Kunii as a family art, and the other transmitted through Kamiizumi Hidetsuna and his students in the shihanke line.

One of the first steps toward institutionalization of bugei ryūha was the issuing of diplomas and licenses to students, beginning in the late sixteenth century with graduation certificates given to those the teacher believed to have mastered what he had to offer. Kamiizumi Hidetsuna was among the earliest instructors to adopt this practice.[49] Sengoku bugei masters seldom formally differentiated students by level prior to graduation; there was little need for such distinctions inasmuch as the period of tutelage was, as we have already observed, usually brief—sometimes only a few months. But during the Tokugawa period, as instruction became more professionalized and more commercialized, apprenticeships became longer; and along with this, more elaborate systems of intermediate ranks began to appear, allowing students a more tangible measure of their progress.

Today the governing bodies of virtually all the modern cognate martial arts (including karate, kendō, jūdō, aikidō, *iaidō*, *kyūdō*, and *naginata-dō*), as well as those of many other arts and sports (including calligraphy, abacus, and even yo-yo and skiing), have adopted a standardized system of ranks and grades (*dan-kyū*—often symbolized by

colored belts worn over practice uniforms) based on the one introduced by jūdō pioneer Kanō Jigorō in the late nineteenth century.*
Prior to Kanō's innovation, however, each bugei ryūha maintained its
own system of ranks and often its own terminology for them. Even
names used in common, such as *"mokuroku"* (literally, "catalog" or
"list"), sometimes represented completely different levels of achievement from school to school.

Under the current headmaster, the Kashima-Shinryū marks a
student's progress from beginner to expert with a series of seven
diplomas and licenses. Unlike those of the modern dan-kyū system,
however, Kashima-Shinryū ranks do not represent certification of
skills mastered so much as initiation into new and deeper levels of
training. Promotion in "rank," in other words, signifies the granting of permission for students to move on to the next level of their
training. The principal criteria for promotion are aptitude (mental
as well as physical) and moral fitness to be allowed to share in the
teachings of the school at a higher and deeper level, and to be
trusted with more of its secrets.

A student's first diploma is called *kirigami*, or "pledge." Literally
"cut paper," this is an abbreviation of the phrase *kirigami no menkyō*,
which referred originally to the slips of paper on which the certificates were brushed. Kirigami is a commonly used rank in the bugei
and in other traditional Japanese arts; its receipt indicates formal
initiation into the master's tutelage. From there, students progress
through the levels of *shōmokuroku* ("little catalog," or "apprentice"),
shoden ("first step into the tradition," or "novice initiate"), *chūden*
("midway into the tradition," or "intermediate initiate"), *okuden*
("the heart of the tradition," or "deep initiate"), and *kaiden* ("the
tradition accomplished," or "complete initiate"). The final student
rank, *menkyo-kaiden* ("licensed kaiden," or "licensed initiate"), is
also widely used in much the same meaning by other ryūha in and
out of the bugei. "Menkyo" means "license" or "permission" and
originally signified permission to use the name of the master's ryūha
in dealings with persons outside the school—such as in duels and
competitions—and to certify students of one's own. It therefore
represented a student's graduation from the master's tutelage and
was awarded only to those who were considered to have exhausted

---

*Kanō's system of colored belts represented one of the first attempts to associ-
ate student ranks with visible badges worn in practice sessions. He introduced this
innovation as a means of identifying the skill levels of students he did not know,
when he visited high school and other jūdō clubs throughout the country.

all that the school had to offer. The Kashima-Shinryū today uses it in somewhat devalued form to denote a status analogous to the doctorate in the American educational system. That is, it now marks a student's completed initiation into the ryūha and his privilege of complete possession of its secrets, rather than his graduation from it.

Under Kunii Zen'ya and his forebears, promotion in rank normally involved a combination of demonstrated ability in formal practice exercises, aptitude for further advance, and successful participation in duels and matches with adepts from other schools (taryū-jiai). In general, Kunii demanded that his students defeat opponents with at least one and a half times their experience. But because these matches, conducted without rules and without referees, often resulted in the serious injury or even death of one of the participants, the Japanese government took steps to eliminate them in the late 1960s. Seki Humitake thereby replaced taryū-jiai with more extensive formal-exercise testing and with written exams. The latter cannot, of course, predict a student's ability in actual combat, but Seki believes that they at least ensure that the student thoroughly understands ryūha principles. If, in other words, the new testing system does not guarantee that new generations of students can actually fight, it does—he maintains—vouchsafe their ability to *train* students who can, should taryū-jiai ever again become a regular practice in Japan.

As they codified the process and stages of their students' training, early Tokugawa-period bugei masters also fixed and formalized the sites where they offered instruction. Most martial training during the medieval period was conducted outdoors, usually in unspecialized venues temporarily appropriated for the purpose, such as open fields or the grounds of shrines or temples. This stemmed partly from a wish to have students practice in environments similar to the battlefields on which they would apply what they learned, and partly from simple logistics, inasmuch as few teachers of the era remained in one locale for very long. Some daimyō set aside areas in the courtyards of their castles or homes for military training, but even here instructors tended to come and go frequently.

Private bugei academies began to appear in the seventeenth century, when unemployed samurai *(rōnin)* flocked to Edo, the shōgun's new capital, in search of work and, finding none, hung out shingles and sought to make a living teaching martial skills. By the time of the fourth shōgun, Ietsuna (r. 1651–1680), practice sites had become considerably more developed. Picture scrolls and other art-work show elaborate halls or gardens specifically designed for bugei practice, with training floors, racks for storing practice weapons, areas for students and spectators to rest or observe training, and raised platforms on which the teacher could sit to supervise prac-tices. The shift to indoor halls or enclosed courtyards was probably an effect of the commercialization of bugei instruction, as teachers sought to prevent prying eyes from stealing their secrets and thereby disrupting their livelihoods. Ogasawara Genshinsai was the first fig-ure associated with the Kashima-Shinryū tradition known to have operated a private academy—in Edo, near what is now Nihonbashi.

Training halls ranged in size from tiny rooms 3 or 4 meters square, such as the Kashima-Shintōryū school in Kashima-machi, Ibaraki prefecture, to somewhat larger buildings such as the Yagyū family's Edo facility, which has since been moved to the Kashima Grand Shrine, and is about 14 by 10 meters (both halls are still used for training today). By the late nineteenth century, some also included dormitory facilities for students.

Such training sites were known by a variety of names during the early modern period. The most popular of these was "*keikoba*", which translates simply as "practice place," or more literally as "place for reflecting on the past," "the past" being the teachings of the ryūha master and his antecedents. The term "dōjō," which has now come into virtually universal use among martial art practition-ers in and out of Japan, did not become especially popular until the Meiji period. Literally "place of the way," "dōjō" is a Chinese term that originally designated a site in the imperial palace set aside for Buddhist ceremonies. By extension it came to signify temples in general, and in this latter capacity it was carried to Japan in the Heian period. Its application as a name for a place of bugei instruc-tion seems to date from mid-to-late Tokugawa times.[50]

Traditionally, bugei teachers were usually very careful about selecting students and controlling them during their periods of apprenticeship, an attitude which served a number of purposes. For one thing, the school's secrets represented the teacher's most valu-able financial asset; students who freely passed on what they learned to outsiders could rapidly undermine the teacher's livelihood. Moreover, students who involved themselves in duels or brawls in which they made poor showings could easily cast public doubt on the efficacy of the style they had learned—a particularly acute dan-ger in the case of students in early stages of their training, when they might have mislearned or misapplied the ryūha's techniques. But most importantly, instruction to the wrong sort of person could pose severe moral problems, insofar as a bugei ryūha's focus was instruction in methods of deadly combat. As G. Cameron Hurst has observed, the behavior of students of low moral character could easily become a source of embarrassment to teachers of the tea ceremony or flower arranging, but a misbehaving bugei student, who might very well cripple or kill someone, was a serious threat to society and a disaster for the reputation of his teacher.[51]

For these reasons, most bugei ryūha developed elaborate procedures for screening new students. Letters of recommendation were usually required, and the backgrounds of all applicants were investigated. Only after passing such screenings were prospective students admitted for study. The Kashima-Shinryū followed similar practices until the present generation; under Kunii Zen'ya, applicants could not be considered unless they obtained the sponsorship of at least two persons having close ties to the school.

By early modern times, successful applicants for bugei instruction were initiated into their ryūha as though into a brotherhood or secret society. Some schools staged entrance ceremonies ranging from the simple to the very ornate. Most collected initiation gifts and fees. And all ryūha required students to sign written pledges, or *kishōmon*, in which they promised to abide by the school's rules and to keep its secrets.[52]

The practice of kishōmon dates back to the Kamakura period (1185–1333), when the shogunate made them a regular part of the documentation for lawsuits.[53] By late medieval times, bugei masters became increasingly concerned with the exclusivity of their teachings and they began forbidding students to pass on any ryūha confidences without explicit permission, and obliging students to swear to this in written oaths that invoked divine wrath upon those who broke their word. Early modern instructors commonly demanded kishōmon from students not only at their entrance to study, but at each new promotion and advance into new levels of training, when they received licenses to teach, and at many other points in their careers. Pledges of this sort were required of all students, no matter how high their social rank; not even shōguns and daimyō were exempt from the custom.[54]

Kishōmon varied in format, but most featured two main parts: one listing the rules the student was expected to follow, and the other detailing the punishments he could expect to incur—at the hands of various Buddhist and Shintō deities—should he fail to live up to his promise.[55] The pledges were often but not universally sealed with the student's own blood, pressed onto the paper next to the student's signature or cypher *(kaō)*. Some ryūha prescribed fascinatingly detailed rituals for accomplishing this. One, for example, directed initiates to "draw blood from the nail root of the left ring finger and, after receiving that blood onto the forefinger of your right hand, press below your name." Another read:

> To imprint a blood seal, first turn the back of your left hand downward and the palm upward. Pinching a thick needle between your thumb and forefinger, such that only the tip protrudes, curl the left ring finger into a loop and pierce it below the nail to draw a small amount of blood. Thereupon press the blood seal below your name, using your ring finger.[56]

The oath of initiation still demanded of Kashima-Shinryū students today dates back to at least the early eighteenth century, and is virtually identical to one used by the Jikishin-Kageryū:[57]

> Oath for instruction in the warrior arts:
>
> Item: Being most grateful for permission to become a student of the Kashima-Shinryū, also known as the Shinkage-ryū or the Shin-Kageryū, I will never reveal even a little of the traditions I learn to outsiders.[58] I will return all scrolls and other texts I may receive as soon as I have finished studying them, and I will always handle them with the utmost care.
>
> Item: Needless to say I will devote myself to practice morning and evening, concentrate on the intuitive principles *(ri)* [of the Kashima-Shinryū], and refrain from doing wrong. Moreover, I will not test myself against other styles without obtaining permission in advance.
>
> Item: I will not cause the senseless destruction of life, nor will I criticize others.
>
> Item: From the time I take up my discipline I will never engage in any shady or deceitful acts. Even when I cannot avoid expressing my own views, I will always comprehend and observe instructions.
>
> Should I ever turn my back on the above promises,[59] I should suffer unto death the divine punishment not only of the August Divinity of Kashima, but of all the myriad gods and spirits. Under these terms I hereby affirm this request for instruction.
>
> Addressed to his lordship, the headmaster of the Kashima-Shinryū
>
> Date   Name

The Kunii family administered the Kashima-Shinryū with a minimum of formal structure beyond the rules set forth in this kishōmon, even after Kunii Zen'ya opened his training hall in Tokyo. After World War II, however, American Occupation-imposed agrarian reforms deprived the Kunii of rental income from their farmlands in Fukushima, necessitating a more elaborate set of rules and a fee structure in order to provide for the cooperative upkeep of the school by its students. Kunii Zen'ya thereby adopted a fifteen-article code spelling out the curriculum, a monthly tuition ranging from one to three hundred yen per month (depending on the age of the student), practice times, procedures and fees for entrance and withdrawal from study, and proper conduct in and out of the training hall.[60]

After Zen'ya passed away in 1966, his successor Seki Humitake continued instruction under this format for several years. A number of problems soon developed, however, necessitating another reorganization and further institutionalizing of the ryūha. The result was the inauguration of the Kashima-Shinryū Federation of Martial Sciences (Kashima-Shinryū budō renmei) on April 1, 1973. The constitution for this organization appears in English translation in appendix II.[61]

In the 1980s, a number of foreign students returning from Japan were authorized to establish branch schools in the United States. The growing need for an association to oversee instruction and to coordinate communications among these schools and between the American schools and the parent organization in Japan led to the establishment in 1990 of a subfederation, the Kashima-Shinryū Federation of North America. The constitution for this body, formally adopted in 1993, is reproduced in appendix II.

At the time of this writing, training continues under the format prescribed by these organizations. There are at present fifteen branch training schools in Japan, five in the United States, and one in Germany.

3.

The Philosophy and Science of Combat

"The question is," said Alice, "whether you *can* make words mean so many different things." "The question is," said Humpty Dumpty, "which is to be master—that's all."
—LEWIS CARROLL,
Through the Looking Glass

The important thing about any word is how you understand it.
—PUBLILIUS SYRUS

THE TERM "ryūha," prosaically translated as "school," can be more literally and more evocatively rendered as "branch of the current." The current here represents the onward flow of a stream of thought—an approach to an art—through time; the branches betoken the partitioning of that thought, the splitting off and the new growth that occurs as insights are passed from master to students, generation after generation. In their essence, ryūha are timeless, defined not by their membership but by their doctrine, or *ryūgi*—the kabala through which they formulate their art. They exist not to foster physical skills but to hand on knowledge. For skill cannot be taught or learned—it can only be acquired through long training and practice. Skill is for the most part self-discovered, imposed on students from within by their own aptitude and discipline. But knowledge can be bequeathed. The perceptions, inspirations, experiences and wisdom collected over a lifetime can be imparted to students so that each generation can build on the privity of those that came before, and each new student will not have to begin the process of discovery afresh.

The kabala of the Kashima-Shinryū centers on the arts of war and has been built by accretion over the course of more than a millennium. According to its own traditions, it began with Izanagi and Izanami's creation of the Japanese islands and with Takemikazuchi-no-Mikoto's tests of strength against the rebellious deities, only to be rediscovered by Kuninazu no Mahito in the seventh century. Historically, it traces back to Matsumoto Bizen-no-Kami's fifteenth-century reformulation of Mahito's shinmyō-ken as ichi-no-tachi, and has been further developed by nineteen generations of Matsumoto's students in the sōke and the shihanke lineages.

Over this long span of time, the art has acquired a rich lexicon of ideas and concepts, often expressed in colorful but seemingly opaque terms and phrases. This opacity was largely intentional; techniques and principles were given names designed to be evocative to the initiated, but to reveal little to outsiders: *enbi-ken* ("flying swallow sword"), a counterstrike that dips and slides around an opponent's blow, like a swallow in flight; *chūkoroshi* ("intermediate killing"), to modify one's techniques so as to destroy—kill—an opponent's capacity to fight, rather than taking his life; or *inazuma* ("thunderbolt"), extremely quick counterstrikes applied against major nerve centers at the precise instant the opponent reaches the focal point of his strike.

Buddhist, Confucian, neo-Confucian, Taoist, and Shintō terms feature prominently in this vocabulary, but it would be a mistake to conceptualize the Kashima-Shinryū as a particularized expression of any religious tradition. The bugei are fundamentally secular arts in which pietistic-sounding locutions often mask entirely down-to-earth pieces of information. While spiritual conditioning—moral cultivation and concentration—is an essential aspect of bugei training, in most ryūha the religious context of this spiritual conditioning is a personal matter, to be decided upon by each individual practitioner. In purely practical terms, Kashima-Shinryū martial art is—and always has been—compatible with almost any religious affiliation or lack thereof, accommodating Matsumoto Bizen-no-Kami's attendance on the Kashima Grand Shrine and the deity Takemikazuchi-no-Mikoto, Kamiizumi Ise-no-Kami's interest in Zen Buddhism (expanded upon considerably by his student Yagyū Muneyoshi and *his* successors), the Pure Land Buddhist leanings of others in the shihanke lineage, Kunii Zen'ya's State Shintō and kokugaku activism, and the agnosticism of many contemporary students—all with equal comfort.

At the same time, it would also be an error to minimize the significance of the traditional vocabulary, for both the art itself and the locutions used to explain it are products of the times in which they developed. Prior to the late nineteenth century and the introduction of Western worldviews, liturgical and ritual systems centered on shrines and temples were the vehicles through which the Japanese conceptualized their universe, and they provided the only available terminology for questions of physical science or philosophy. For this reason, any effort to completely secularize bugei principles and concepts would do violence to the cultural context in which they originated.

Kashima-Shinryū bugei, as might be expected from an art claiming birth in a series of divine revelations from Takemikazuchi-no-Mikoto, ostensibly draws its cosmological framework from Shintō. In the sixteenth century, Kunii Genpachiro Kagetsugu, through what he perceived as a divine oracle, determined that the same cosmological principles underlay both the rites for spiritual purification *(chinkonhō)* practiced at the Kashima Grand Shrine and the shinmyō-ken of Kuninazu no Mahito's martial art, but that their application in these two spheres of activity had become arbitrarily and unnaturally distinguished. He therefore remerged the religious and martial applications of the principles in his rediscovered version of Kashima-no-tachi.[1]

But "Shintō cosmology" is, as every beginning student of Japanese history or religion learns, an extraordinarily elusive construct. While the origins of the diverse local spirit cults that today are collectively labeled "Shintō" reach back to the dawn of Japanese civilization, none of these cults produced scriptures or other explanatory writings until centuries after their contact and fusion with Buddhist, Taoist, and Confucian ideas. Indeed, even the term "Shintō," literally "way of the [native] divinities," was a neologism, adopted in reaction to the imported religious constructs and practices; it scarcely existed prior to medieval times and did not come to denote an independent religion or theology until after 1868, when the modern Japanese government ordered a systematic, albeit new and artificial, dissociation of doctrines and rituals directed at "native" deities from those invoking Buddhist divinities. Premodern Japanese religious traditions were, to borrow Allan Grapard's term, "combinative": mixtures of elements derived from shamanistic cults, Buddhism, Confucianism, and Taoism.[2] "Shintō," the worldview underlying the art of Kashima-Shinryū, then, must be conceived broadly, "as the *ensemble* of contradictory and yet peculiarly Japanese types of religious beliefs, sentiments, and approaches, which have been shaped and conditioned by the historical experience of the Japanese people from the prehistoric period to the present."[3]

One feature of this premodern Japanese worldview key to under-standing Kashima-Shinryū conceptualization is what Joseph Kitagawa terms its "monistic" or "unitary world of meaning." The ancient Japanese, he observes, sought no higher orders of meaning behind the phenomenal realm, affirming instead that the natural or manifest world is also the real world. The relationship between sentient and nonsentient beings, between humans and nature, is to be understood in terms of direct, interactive participation—nature's participation in human lives, as well as human participation in the life of nature. That is, this worldview posits "an intimate correlation between the rhythm of nature and that of human life" in which "the meaning of each being [is] not sought in itself but in its mutual participation, continuity, and correspondance to and with others within the total framework of the monastic world of meaning." This unitary cosmos is permeated throughout by sacred, or *kami* nature, according to an "aesthetic, magico-religious apprehension of the primeval totality as well as everything within it not as representations of *kami* but as *kami*." (Kami is, of course, another concept that defies succinct translation or even explanation, refering to both the numinous, the impersonal quality that Kitagawa calls "kami nature," and to the numina, the specific beings—human, superhuman, animate or inanimate—endowed with the kami nature.) Thus in the traditional Japanese religious universe, all things and all beings, including animals, celestial bodies, and even physical elements such as wood, stone, fire, and water, partake of the kami nature, and all forms of human activity—including the bugei—can be considered religious acts.[4]

At the same time, each phenomenon of the universe has an inner, unrevealed mien as well as its outer, obvious visage. The Japanese call the former the *ri* or *ura* and the latter the *hyō* or *omote*. In the natural order of things, these two aspects function in complete harmony, inseparable even in conception. The inner and outer surfaces of a drop of water, or the front and back sides of a piece of paper, for example, cannot be disjoined; each is but a facet of the other. Also, neither ura nor omote is more real than the other; both simply *are*, at once and always. Kashima-Shinryū cosmology expresses this notion in the phrase *"hyōri ittai,"* or "Outside (omote) and Inside (ura) as One." Only in the realm of human affairs can the relationship between ura and omote become confused, omote severed from its proper ura, as when kind words (omote) are used to mask evil intentions (ura). But as humans and human affairs, too, are as much phenomena of the universe as are drops of water, actions that sunder ura from omote must be violations of the rightful order of nature and should be shunned.*

Outside and Inside as One has important applications in the field of martial art. Kashima-Shinryū bugei as practiced today consists of twelve particularized military disciplines (bujutsu), divided into two broad groups: the omote arts, consisting of kenjutsu (swordsmanship), battō-jutsu (sword drawing), *naginata-jutsu* (use of the *naginata*, a kind of glaive or voulges), sōjutsu (spearmanship), *kenjutsu-tachiai* (use of the sword against other weapons), and *shuriken-jutsu* (use of throwing darts); and the ura arts, consisting of jūjutsu (grappling), *kenpō* (striking and kicking), *bōjutsu* (use of the long staff), *jōjutsu* (use of the short staff), *kaiken-jutsu* or *tantō-jutsu* (use of knives and short swords), and *tasuki-dori* or *hōbaku-jutsu* (tying or binding an opponent).[5] But all these disciplines intertwine and coexist as components—facets—of a single whole. Each contains all the others and is in turn contained by all of the others. Each draws on the same principles of thought and movement, differentiated only by the interaction of these principles with the distinctive characteristics of the weapon around which it revolves. None is complete in and of itself. Kashima-Shinryū bugei, as an entity beyond a simple collection of tricks and strategies for fighting, materializes when taken in total, when all twelve bujutsu disciplines that comprise it are melded into a single budō.

Each concept and every technique of Kashima-Shinryū bugei, moreover, is meant to be understood on multiple levels. At the very least, each has a military (omote) and a moral (ura) usage, a physical (omote) and a psychological or spiritual (ura) component, standard (omote) and variant (ura) applications, a mechanical (omote) and a philosophical (ura) explanation, and so forth, and each of these applications and components has an ura and an omote facet as well, as does each of *those* facets. No one of the multiple levels stands alone; each contains and is contained by all of the others. To fully analyze—even to fully understand—the entirety of any bugei concept in linear, compartmentalized fashion is a futile undertaking,

---

*The construct of ura and omote bears some semblance to the more familiar Sino-Japanese doctrine of yin and yang (discussed further below), but the two are not the same. Yin and yang represent primeval forces or essences that mix and interact with one another to produce the myriad things of the universe; they are distinguished by their nature. Ura and omote merely describe differing facets of these things; they are distinguished by perspective, not essence.

comparable to attempting to describe precisely what one sees in two mirrors positioned so as to reflect one another. Ordinarily, bugei practitioners make no such efforts. Instead they deal rationally with one or perhaps a few of the multiple layers at any one time, and allow their intuition or subconscious to perceive the rest along with the connections between them.

Budō, the martial path, begins with bujutsu—the practical arts of war. These arts are, as might be expected, largely collections of particulars. In the traditional training process (discussed in chapter 4), bugei masters teach mainly through example and hands-on practice, guiding their students from physical mastery of specific moves applied in specific circumstances to a gradually broadening intuition of the abstract principles underlying all such actions. Along the way, initiates assimilate hundreds of individual techniques, strategies, terms and concepts.

These terms and concepts offer the best handle by which to grasp the art—the kabala—of the Kashima-Shinryū, the best tool by which to forge an understanding of the conceptual structure of a traditional bugei. By building my exposition around the school's vocabulary, I can, better than by any other means, approximate for academic audiences the view of the Kashima-Shinryū that adepts are led to construct. And this sort of view is, in turn, crucial if one is to appreciate just what the bugei themselves really are.

Nevertheless, intellectual understanding of the bugei as cultural phenomena need not be the same as mastery of any of them as arts. Therefore, while the samurai who studied it (and those who practice it today) learned and viewed the kabala of their ryūha not from the outlines inward, but from the contents outward, grasping the essence of the art through its details, the following analysis will reverse the path of discovery traveled by ryūha initiates. I will begin with the broadest and most abstract tenets of the art and work inward in concentric circles toward the more specific. This process, which I will conclude in the next chapter in my discussion of the school's methodology of training and transmission, necessarily involves some repetition and backtracking, for the terms, like the Shintō universe in which they originated, are all interpenetrated and interrelated.

Shinbu and the Martial Way

The term "budō" teams the ideograph *dō/michi* 道, meaning "path" or "way," with *bu* 武 ("military affairs, arms, bravery, martial power").

Chinese Taoist-inspired etymology traces the origin of this latter character to the combination of ideographs for "spear" 矛 and "stop" 止 ; "bu" is thus said to have originally meant "to stop a spear" or "to end conflict." The Japanese martial art tradition, however, associates "bu" phonetically with the native term "musu*bu*"—"to give birth," "to bring together," "to create," or "to give life." In the Japanese conceptualization then, "bu" is a proactive, constructive idea, meaning "to bring forth peace."* Peace cannot be created through military affairs alone. In its broadest sense, therefore, "bu" also refers to agriculture, manufacture, and all other forms of production. Japanese budō posits the <u>sword as a symbol</u> for all the tools of these peace-creating trades, in the same way that Kashima-Shinryū bugei takes the sword as its nucleus, representative of all the other weapons of the various disciplines.[6]

Both the goal and the essence of Kashima-Shinryū budō are expressed in the word "shinbu." The most common orthography for this term modifies the character "bu" with *shin/kami* 神 ("divine, spirit, deity"), but alternative renderings use *shin/ma* 真 ("truth, reality") or *shin/makoto* 誠 ("sincerity, fidelity, honesty, genuine"). "Shinbu" thus translates inexactly as "divine valor," "true martial art," "spiritual martial power," or "sacred martialism."

In its narrowest sense, "shinbu" means "sublime martial moral power, like that of the deities; or to rectify turmoil as would the deities." This is the notion hinted at in the famous phrase *"shinbu ni shite fusetsu"* ("to attain shinbu and kill not"), which appears in a number of Tokugawa period treatises on the bugei, the best known of which is the early eighteenth century *Neko no myōjutsu*.[7]

But the concept of shinbu embraces physical and metaphysical as well as ethical ideas. In its fullest sense, it describes the condition that holds when all the essential principles of martial art are put into application simultaneously and in proper balance. Shinbu is, in other words, the summation of idealized budō, that which at once epitomizes and transcends physical combat.†

---

*An archetypical example of the use of a destructive weapon for procreative purposes can be seen in the mythological account (discussed in chapter 2) of Izanami no Mikoto and Izanagi no Mikoto creating the Japanese islands with a jeweled spear.

†Use of the term *"shinbu"* in this context has a venerable history in Japan, one that predates ryūha bugei by many centuries. The eleventh-century wartale *Mutsuwaki*, for example, describes the illustrious Minamoto Yoshiie (1041–1108) as a man of "surpassing courage who shot arrows from horseback like a god. . . .

While epitomizing and transcending physical combat may seem incompatible goals, traditional bugei thinking asserts that neither is in fact possible without the other. Thus, for the Kashima-Shinryū, the highest expression of shinbu is *tatazu-no-kachi* ("victory without a stand"): to defuse a confrontation or subdue the opponent without recourse to clash of arms. Moreover, the essence of tatazu-no-kachi—or any other form of shinbu—lies in the physical, mental, and spiritual skill of *hōyō-dōka* (roughly: "acceptance and resorption"). This construct provides an excellent illustration of the multiple levels of omote and ura at which bugei terms and principles must be understood (diagrammed in figure 5). Kunii Zen'ya described hōyō-dōka as follows:

Ken ni ken nashi; tai o motte ken to nasu.	In the sword there is no sword; make a sword of the body.
Tai ni tai nashi; shin o motte tai to nasu.	In the body there is no body; make a body of the spirit.
Keizen motte, maruku; kizen motte, akiraka nari.	Like a firefly, round; by its radiance, apparent.
Matazu, hakarazu, omowazu, tomarazu,	Waiting not, scheming not, thinking not, pausing not,
Banjō ni maru o mawasu ga gotoku,	As if turning circles on a stage,
Suichū no hisago o assuru ga gotoshi.	As if pressing a gourd in water.[8]

Hōyō-dōka and related expressions employed by other ryūha provide the derivation for the phrase, "become one with the opponent," popularized by writers of films and novels dealing with the martial arts. The narrow (omote) sense of this construct is evoked by the "Axiom of the Moon on the Water" (*suigetsu no gokui*), which instructs that a warrior must respond *with* his opponent, in the same way that the moon, reflected on a body of water, responds with the movements of the waves and current, neither swimming against them nor being carried away by them. He must, in other words, embrace his opponent, flow and adapt flexibly with the opponent's mental and physical movements while neither resisting them nor allowing himself to be dominated by them. The Kashima-Shinryū lexicon expresses the omote and ura of this aspect of hōyō-dōka with the terms "*gontaiyū*" and "*aiki.*"

With his great arrowheads he shot down enemy leaders again and again, never loosing an arrow in vain, always hitting his mark. Like the thunder he rushed; like the wind he flew. He was shinbu, incarnate in this world." (*Mutsuwaki*, 25.)

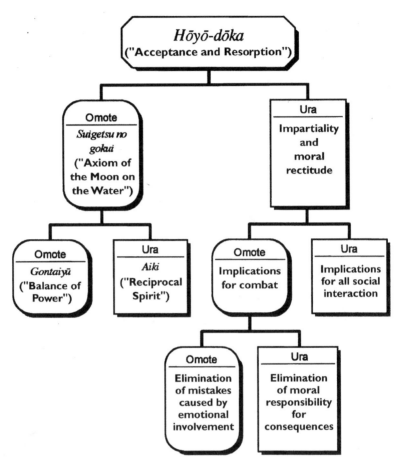

Figure 5. The *omote* and *ura* of *hōyō-dōka*

"*Gon*" refers to the weights of a beam scale, "*tai*" to one's body, and "*yū*" to fortitude and prowess. Gontaiyū, then, is the mettle that maintains a warrior's physical equilibrium. In combat a warrior must neither stubbornly resist nor surrender to the force exerted by his opponent. Rather he must neutralize it, offset it exactly so that the net application of strength between himself and the opponent is zero. From this state of equilibrium, which resembles the poise of the two sides of a scale, the warrior can easily move the opponent about and defeat him by applying only a tiny additional force—in the same way that one can easily raise, lower, or swing even the heaviest objects resting in the buckets of a balanced scale. "Aiki," or "reciprocal spirit," represents the spiritual and psychological aspects of this same skill, the ability to neither intimidate nor be intimidated by the opponent.[9]

But hōyō-dōka also has a broader (ura) meaning: that the warrior must always approach combat from a position of absolute impartiality and moral rectitude, must "delight naught in the unavailing joy of felling an enemy, of destroying evil," as one Kashima-Shinryū text puts it, because, the same text warns, "if the heart is not pure, he who willfully attacks will only be destroyed."[10] Specifically, this requires the warrior to exorcise the attitudes known as the *jūaku,* or "ten evils": insolence, overconfidence, greed, anger, fear, doubt, distrust, hesitation, contempt, and conceit.[11]

Even at the (omote) level of combat, purity of heart is seen to serve both an omote and an ura purpose. First, emotions, even relatively virtuous ones like pleasure or satisfaction derived from victory in the interests of justice, can blind a warrior, cause him to make mistakes, or otherwise interfere with his ability to function at his best. Second, by maintaining utter objectivity and detachment at every stage of a confrontation, the warrior separates himself from any moral responsibility for its outcome; he becomes essentially an instrument facilitating events, just as his weapon is. In the ethics of the traditional bugei, he can no more be blamed for injuries brought about by actions with which he has no volitional or emotional involvement than can a rock be blamed for rolling off a hill and striking someone.

Polishing one's character to this degree obviously carries benefits and applications far beyond the rather limited realm of physical combat. In its widest (ura) sense, then, hōyō-dōka represents an approach to life and to social interaction of all forms. It is the essence of shinbu, which is in turn the essence of Kashima-Shinryū budō. It is also a good illustration of the process by which pursuit of the very narrow goal of success in battle both leads to and demands a broader and more life-affirming development of the self. This process constitutes the crux of budō, the Martial Way.

The Framework of the Art: The Fivefold Laws and the Eight Divine Coordinates

Physicists assert that all natural phenomena are composed of varying combinations of matter and energy. These combinations continuously come into existence and disintegrate into their constituent parts, whereupon the parts recombine to produce new phenomena. Matter can be converted to energy and energy to matter, but neither can be destroyed outright; the sum of all energy and matter has remained constant since the universe itself came into being. Thus matter and energy, the primal stuff of the cosmos, are eternal—without beginning or end—and in this sense the myriad phenomena that result from their combination are also without beginning or end. Kashima-Shinryū cosmology expresses this ongoing integration, disintegration, and reintegration of the underlying substance of reality in the phrase "Arise, return to source, go forth" (hakken, kangen, suishin). This then, is the law or rhythm through which all natural phenomena manifest themselves.

Combat and the bugei, being themselves natural phenomena, are governed by natural law. And while no human actions can be in actual defiance of natural law—an arrow, for example, cannot be shot around a corner—certain actions are better attuned to nature than others, just as an arrow launched with the wind will carry farther than one launched against it. Similarly, Kashima-Shinryū theory insists that for optimal performance in combat, a warrior's movements and tactics must harmonize with the rhythm "Arise, return to source, go forth."[12]

Ryūha canon further identifies five essential laws that collectively describe this rhythm as it operates in martial art. Called the Fivefold Laws (goko-no-hōjō) or the Laws Governing the Ultimate Principles of the Divine School (Shinryū gokui hōjō), these laws are: Motion and Stillness as One (dōsei ittai), Origination and Manifestation as One (kihatsu ittai), Offense and Defense as One (kōbō ittai), Emptiness and Reality as One (kyojitsu ittai), and Yin and Yang as One (inyō ittai). As figure 6 illustrates, shinbu is to be found at the nexus of these five laws.

Each of the Fivefold Laws calls for the union of apparently contradictory states or qualities. This underscores the monistic nature of the worldview shaping the Kashima-Shinryū kabala by asserting that the five continua in question—action and inactivity, beginning and fruition, aggression and protection, being and nonbeing, and positive and negative—are not linear, but circular.

Analyzing the ongoing monism described by "Arise, return to source, go forth" in terms of the confluence of opposites recalls the Sino-Japanese doctrine of yin and yang, which presents metaphysical reality in terms of a pair of antipodal powers or principles. In this conception, all things and all events arise from the interplay of two elements or forces: yin (in or on in Japanese), which represents negativity, darkness, weakness, passivity, destruction, and things hidden or female; and yang (Japanese: yō), which stands for positivity, light,

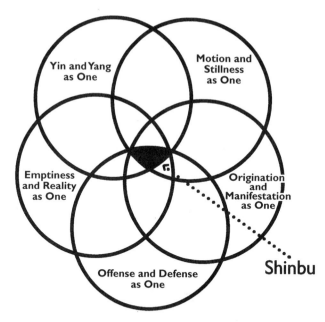

Figure 6. *Shinbu* and the Fivefold Laws (source: Seki, *Nihon budō no engen*, 19)

strength, activity, creation, and things visible or male. Written with characters depicting the shady and sunny sides of a hill, yin and yang are conceived of as complimentary, not opposing forces. Other than as abstract concepts, neither exists in its pure form anywhere or at any time; all things in the real universe contain elements of both—indeed neither exists alone even as a concept, inasmuch as neither has meaning except in reference to the other. Yin and yang are ceaselessly interactive, such that each moment in time and each phenomenon are the products of an ever-shifting balance between the two. Yin and yang cosmology, then, describes not a dualistic universe, but what historian of philosophy Wing-tsit Chan calls "a dynamic monism through the dialectic."[13]

The first of the Fivefold Laws, the principle of Yin and Yang as One, recognizes the ways in which this interplay of yin and yang permeates combat and the bugei. The mind or will (yin) fuses with the sword (yang) through the medium of the body (this aspect of Yin and Yang as One is also described as *ken-shin-tai sanmi ittai*, or "Sword, Mind, and Body as a Trinity").* More broadly, the yielding

Mind in this context translates the Japanese term *"kokoro,"* which is alternatively rendered "heart," "heart-mind," "will," or "self." In *Kurozumikyō and the New Religions of Japan* (Princeton, NJ: Princeton University Press, 1986, 18–19), Helen

passivity of yin tempers the violent aggressiveness of yang to achieve the detachment and objectivism essential to plenary (shinbu) technique. And in a more concrete sense, Yin and Yang as One forms the basis for proper application of power, as the actions of the left (yin) hand harmonize with those of the right (yang), and as energy moves from the hands (yin) to the tip of the weapon (yang) at the moment a blow is struck and then returns to the hands.[14]

The second law, the principle of Motion and Stillness as One, requires that motion always be present within stillness, and that stillness always be present within motion. On the spiritual and philosophical levels this means that a warrior must not allow his mind or spirit to stop or become fixated on any single aspect of his own or his opponent's actions, lest this cause him to neglect some other equally important aspect of the whole encounter. Nor can he allow his spirit to become agitated or disturbed; even when his body and weapon are in full motion his mind must remain quiet, so that he can respond smoothly and instantly with his opponent's every move.

As is the case in all facets of Kashima-Shinryū budō, however, the spiritual and philosophical levels of Motion and Stillness as One are to be approached and assimilated through more mundane considerations pertinent to combat (bujutsu). At this level, the concept is a rather straightforward matter of physics. Motion, a change in an object's position in space, is usually described in terms of velocity, which is simply the distance and direction the object travels in a given amount of time. An object in motion has velocity; an object with no velocity is still.* To execute a successful strike or blow, a warrior must generate sufficient power to perform the technique and must complete the blow before his opponent can block or otherwise counter it. Both factors are a function of velocity: The greater the velocity of the warrior's weapon, the greater the power with which it strikes and the less time it takes to complete the strike.† In combat,

---

Hardacre explains the kokoro as including the facilities of mind, will, and emotion. The *kokoro* is not, however, the sum of these facilities in the abstract but differs in each person according to personality traits, dispositions, and aesthetic sensibilities. When Japanese makes a distinction between "spirit" (*seishin*) and flesh (*nikutai*), the *kokoro* is associated with the spirit. The *kokoro* includes the soul (*tamashii*) but is not identical to it. After death the *tamashii* continues to exist, but the *kokoro* does not.

*In scientific notation this is expressed as $v = \frac{dr}{dt}$, where v is the velocity, d the vector of travel, r the distance traveled, and t the time.

†The power or linear momentum (p) with which an object in motion strikes another object is the product of the velocity of the object and its mass ($p = mv$).

however, both speed and power are relative considerations; the absolute power and speed of which a warrior is capable are of less importance than his speed and power relative to those of his opponent, and even this is relative. For what matters most is not which opponent is faster or more powerful, but which is faster or more powerful *at the critical moment in which a blow is delivered.* Figure 7, which compares the application of power by an expert with that of a beginner, illustrates this point succinctly. Even though the beginner portrayed in the graphs can ultimately generate greater speed and power than the expert, the expert is able to reach his peak in a much shorter interval. Until time t_1, therefore, the expert's speed and power are greater than those of the beginner, enabling him to defeat his less skilled (but stronger and faster) opponent before the latter can apply his full power.[15]

The most efficient means for the warrior to reduce the time he needs to reach the critical level of speed and power is to lessen the difference between this critical velocity and his velocity at the start of the technique. Kashima-Shinryū masters therefore insist that a warrior in combat never reach a state of absolute immobility, as this would maximize the time it takes to accelerate to the speed (and therefore the power) needed to best his opponent.* At the same

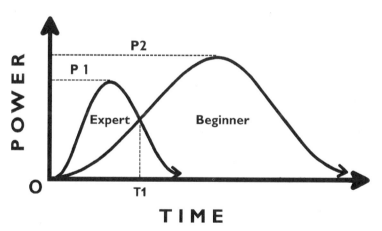

Figure 7. Comparison of the rates of application of power of a beginner and an expert (source: Seki, *Nihon budō no engen,* 20)

Generating sufficient power to perform a given task, then, is a matter of accelerating the tool with which the task is to be performed to a sufficient velocity.

*Acceleration (*a*) is a change in velocity over time ($a = \frac{v_2 - v_1}{t}$). At a given rate of acceleration, the greater the initial velocity (v_1), the greater the velocity (v_2) that

time, he cannot constantly move at full velocity, for, among other things, this would quickly exhaust him; there must be moments within techniques or between techniques when his body and/or weapon hold their positions. But such moments of "stillness" must be apparent or relative, not absolute stillness; the warrior must move constantly, if imperceptibly, even when seeming to be completely at rest.

To be able to pass rapidly from stillness into motion, a warrior must begin from a suitable fighting posture, or *kamae*. Unlike the rigid stances of karate and some other martial arts, Kashima-Shinryū kamae are conceived of as transitory positions that exist only in the fleeting moments between successive techniques—stillness within motion. Kamae for the sword (depicted in figures 8–13) include: *mugamae* ("non-kamae"), also called *otonashi-no-kamae* ("silent posture"); *kami-hassō* ("issuing from above"); *shimo-hassō* ("issuing from below"); *kurai-tachi* ("occupying sword"); *tsukikage* ("moonlight," or "moon shadow"); and *kasumi* ("mist").* In all of these, the swordsman stands with his front knee bent and his rear leg straight, keeping about 70 percent of his weight over his front leg. This position, which exemplifies motion within stillness, makes him seem always on the verge of stepping forward. The toes of both feet point outward to allow for easy movement to either side, in keeping with the principles of Offense and Defense as One and Emptiness and Reality as One, discussed below.

Motion and Stillness must also be One throughout each of the swordsman's strikes and other actions, which means he must be able to accelerate or decelerate his weapon at any stage of the strike. The pattern of movement best suited to this goal is the spiral: A weapon moved in straight lines must go from motion to absolute stillness and back to motion in order to change its direction of travel. Circles provide continuing motion (motion within stillness), but they are two-dimensional and do not permit continual acceleration (stillness within motion). Spirals, on the other hand, are three dimensional,

---

can be reached in a given amount of time $(v_2 = at + v_1)$. Thus the time required to generate the power necessary to perform any combative technique, as well as the time required to perform it, diminishes in direct proportion to the speed at which the warrior's body or weapon is moving at the start of the technique ($t = \frac{v_2 - v_1}{a}$), because $v_2 - v_1$ is greatest when $v_1 = 0$.

*The orthography for the "hassō" of kami-hassō and shimo-hassō is borrowed from a Buddhist phrase referring to the eight phases of the Buddha's life. This is probably a stand-in for a homophone meaning "start out," or "send forth".

Figure 8.
Mugamae or
otonashi-no-kamae

Figure 9.
Kami-hassō

Figure 10.
Shimo-hassō

Figure 11.
Kurai-tachi

Figure 12.
Tsukikage

Figure 13.
Kasumi

allowing continual motion *and* continual acceleration. Spirals are also the most natural form of movement, conforming closely to the laws of Conservation of Motion and Conservation of Energy in modern scientific conceptualization, and the precept "Arise, return to source, go forth" of traditional Japanese cosmology.[16] In all Kashima-Shinryū techniques, therefore, the adept's hands or weapon move in spirals, even when their positions at the decisive points of the technique form a triangle or square (see figure 14).

One Kunii family document emphasizes this point with the phrase "the square is a spiral, the triangle too, is a spiral" *(shikaku sunawachi en nari, sankaku mata en nari).* Another phrase common in traditional bugei documents and expressing the same idea is *sankakuen-no-tachi* ("the sword of the three-cornered circle").[17]

By manipulating their weapons in spirals, Kashima-Shinryū experts can strike in one seamless movement from the initial kamae to the target, without loss of energy or momentum. This, they say, enables them to change techniques at will, to flow smoothly from one movement to another, and to check attacks that do not conform to this principle at their outset. Thus the fourth of the Fivefold Laws, the principle of Origination and Manifestation as One, dictates that there be no separation between the initiation of a technique and its climax.

Strikes executed in two parts, as for example when a swordsman first raises his weapon above his head and then brings it down on the target, dissever Origination from Manifestation. The first movement—raising the weapon—is preparatory to the actual strike. This sort of one-two or cock-and-fire delivery detaches each attack or defensive action from preceding and subsequent techniques by interposing preliminary movements between them. Not only does

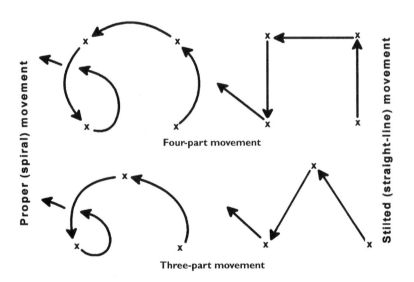

Figure 14. Three-cornered and four-cornered movement (source: Seki, *Nihon budō no engen,* 22)

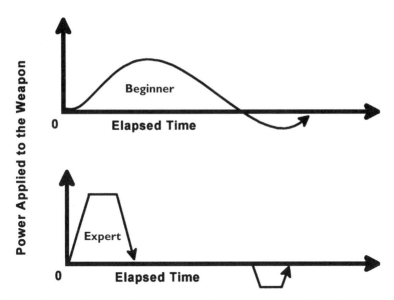

Figure 15. Application of power from the perspective of Origination and Manifestation as One (source: Seki, *Nihon budō no engen*, 20)

this make it difficult to shift smoothly from one technique to another, it renders the swordsman vulnerable to counterattack during the interval between the Origination and the Manifestation of each strike—a skillful opponent can, for example, strike just as the swordsman raises his weapon in preparation for his own blow.

Figure 15 contrasts the exertion of force by an expert who has mastered Origination and Manifestation as One with that of a beginner. Beginners require a long, running start to generate the momentum they need to reach maximum power and a long follow-through to wind it down before executing a second technique. Experts, however, can exert peak force and then return to a state of complete relaxation almost instantly.* They do this by maximizing the acceleration of their weapons, keeping their body movements small and quick and the movements of the weapons large but flickering.

The fighting movements and techniques to which beginners and experts alike apply power and speed intuitively divide into offensive and defensive actions. But Kashima-Shinryū doctrine insists that such a distinction is both unnatural and dangerous, and calls for all

---

*In terms of physics, this means that the expert is able to accelerate and decelerate to and from maximum speed much more rapidly than the beginner (because striking power, or linear momentum, is equal to the mass of the weapon times its speed at impact).

tactics to conform to the principle of Offense and Defense as One, the third of the Fivefold Laws.

Traditional Japanese bugei theory analyzes attacks in terms of initiative (*sen* or *sente*) and response (*go*), commonly distinguishing three types of initiative: *sen-no-sen*, in which one seizes the initiative and defeats the opponent with one's first strike; *go-no-sen*, in which one first blocks or dodges an opponent's strike and then delivers a counterstrike of one's own; and *tai-no-sen*, in which one attacks at the same time as one's opponent.* When one executes sen and go simultaneously, in a single technique, Offense and Defense become One, and the opponent is deprived of any opportunity to counterattack.

Offense and Defense as One follows logically from hōyō-dōka and is, in fact, impossible without it. First of all, hōyō-dōka is a principal reason why Kashima-Shinryū bujutsu rejects the go-no-sen strategy, which involves reacting *to* rather than responding *with* an opponent's actions. Moreover, to approach an encounter without the total impartiality and utter lack of concern for the outcome dictated by hōyō-dōka, to become caught up in the righteousness of one's cause and/or begin to take pleasure in defeating one's opponents—or, conversely, to fear or shrink from them—engenders a preoccupation with results that divorces Offense from Defense by focusing one's attention unduly on one or the other.

Kashima-Shinryū canon further delimits the character of attacks and counterstrikes with the principle of Emptiness and Reality as One, recognizing that the cosmological law "Arise, return to source, go forth," describes being and nonbeing as simply alternating states of the same underlying reality. Mugamae (see figure 8), the optimal prefatory stance of Kashima-Shinryū bujutsu, exemplifies Emptiness and Reality as One, the last of the Fivefold Laws, at its most basic. As its name ("the non-kamae") suggests, this posture betrays no outward signs of any readiness for action, offensive or defensive. The swordsman stands exposed, his sword lowered

---

*In his famous *Gorin no sho*, Miyamoto Musashi gives different names to the three types of initiative:

Of the "three forms of initiative," the first is when one attacks the enemy first. This is called *ken-no-sen* (forcing the initiative). Another is when the enemy attacks first. This is called *tai-no-sen* (waiting for the initiative). The other is when one attacks and the enemy also attacks. This is called *tai-tai-no-sen* (body against body initiative, when two men attack at once). These are the three forms of initiative. Any fight must begin with one of these three forms of initiative; there are no others.

(Miyamoto Mushashi, *Gorin no sho*, in *Nihon budō taikei*, 2:74.)

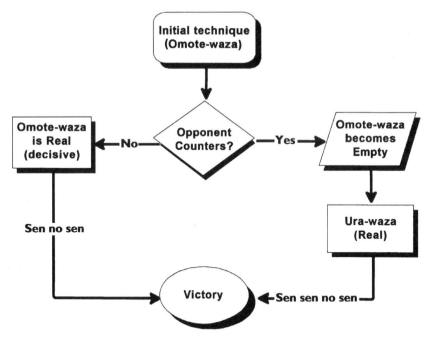

Figure 16. Interplay of attack and counterattack in the context of Emptiness and Reality as One

before him and his body square to his opponent. Its very emptiness, however, makes mugamae a position of pure, unlimited potential from which all manner of techniques (reality) can freely originate.

From mugamae, then, the swordsman launches an attack. If the opponent offers no countertechnique, this initial action becomes decisive (sen-no-sen). If, on the other hand, the opponent attempts to block or otherwise counter his first action, the swordsman simply shifts in mid-course to a new technique, which becomes decisive—a situation termed *sen-sen-no-sen.* In the first instance the initial attack was Real—decisive in and of itself. In the second, it became Empty, but then gave rise to a subsequent attack that was Real (see figure 16).*

*Practioners of modern kendō use the terms "sen-no-sen" and "sen-sen-no-sen" somewhat differently from Kashima-Shinryū masters. In kendō, "sen-sen-no-sen" describes an attack launched before the opponent begins a strike, while "sen-no-sen" indicates an attack initiated in the same instant in which an opponent's strike has begun. See Jeffrey Dann, "Kendō in Japanese Martial Culture" (Ph.D. dissertation, University of Washington, 1978) 159–161.

When the swordsman's execution embraces Emptiness and Reality as One, sen-no-sen and sen-sen-no-sen become alternative manifestations of a single action—the swordsman's initial attack—and the Emptiness of the first attack coexists with the decisive Reality of the second as a single technique, not a combination or series of techniques. The second attack exists *within* the first, imminent even when unrevealed. For this reason, bugei theorists refer to it as an *ura-waza*, an "inner technique" or "obverse technique" enshrouded in the lining of the "outside" or "manifest technique," the *omote-waza*. The ura-waza and the omote-waza each contain the other and each is at once both Empty and Real. When an encounter ends in sen-no-sen, the omote-waza is Real, while the ura-waza remains unmanifested and Empty. When the combat proceeds to sen-sen-no-sen, the ura-waza becomes Real and the omote-waza becomes Empty. In either event, the interconnection of the omote-waza and the ura-waza deprives the opponent of any opportunity to counter successfully.[18]

While the Fivefold Laws outline the conceptual structure (omote) of Kashima-Shinryū budō, the physical structure (ura) of Kashima-Shinryū bujutsu is framed by the Eight Divine Coordinates *(hasshin-den)* designating the positions of eight guardian deities believed to surround the emperor (and by extension, every individual acting in accord with the principles of imperial justice, impartiality, and mercy). Kashima-Shinryū fighting techniques arise when an adept moves his body or weapon from one of these coordinates to another.[19]

As figure 17 illustrates, the Eight Divine Coordinates define five basic vectors of spatial motion. The diagram is two-dimensional, but the coordinates are more properly conceived of as surrounding the individual like a sphere, so that in combative applications the five vectors are named relative to the vertical plane connecting the centerline of one's body with that of one's opponent: perpendicular *(hō)*, spiraling *(en)*, diagonal *(kyoku)*, direct *(choku)*, and the acute angle or wedge *(ei)*.*

In their purest form, perpendicular, diagonal, and direct movements can be seen in horizontal, oblique, and vertical cutting motions. Spirals, as we have already observed, underlie all Kashima-Shinryū techniques and connect the other vectors to one another

---

*In bugei jargon, both this plane and the centerlines are termed "shin," written with a character designating the wick of a candle.

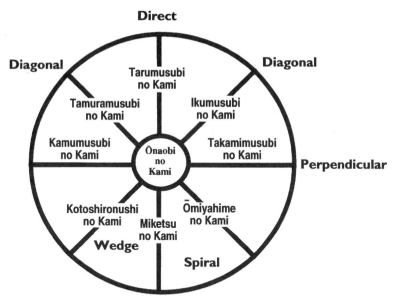

Figure 17. The Eight Divine Coordinates and the five vectors of Kashima-Shinryū martial art (source: *Kunii-ke sōden Kashima-Shinryū jūjutsu menkyo kaiden mokuroku*)

when they are applied in combination. Blows delivered at an acute angle utilize the mechanical principles of the wedge and the lever to simultaneously deflect and counter an opponent's attack.

Kashima-Shinryū doctrine further identifies five fundamental patterns through which the five vectors combine in Kashima-Shinryū fighting techniques. (Figures 18–22 depict unarmed applications of each of the five patterns.) In the first of these, *kyoku henjite hō to naru* ("a diagonal becomes perpendicular"), one avoids the opponent's attack by stepping diagonally past it and counters with a horizontal strike or throwing action. In the second, *ei henjite en to naru* ("a wedge becomes a spiral"), one deflects the opponent's strike with an angular blow of one's arm or weapon, and then throws or pins the opponent with a tight spiraling motion (of the arm or weapon). The third pattern, *ei henjite kyoku to naru* ("a wedge becomes a diagonal"), involves redirecting the opponent's attack with a wedging blow or thrust of one's own and then cutting or toppling him with a diagonal slash or throwing action. *Ei henjite choku to naru* ("a wedge becomes direct"), the fourth pattern, transforms an angular parry into a straight thrust or vertical blow. And in the fifth pattern, *ei choku kyoku choku* ("wedge is direct; diagonal is

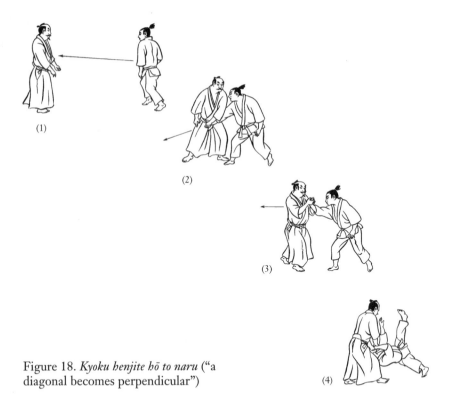

(1)

(2)

(3)

(4)

Figure 18. *Kyoku henjite hō to naru* ("a diagonal becomes perpendicular")

(1)

(2)

(3)

(4)

Figure 19. *Ei henjite en to naru* ("a wedge becomes a spiral")

Figure 20. *Ei henjite kyoku to naru*
("a wedge becomes a diagonal")

Figure 21. *Ei henjite choku to naru* ("a wedge becomes direct")

direct"), an angular blow or diagonal movement simultaneously deflects an attack and defeats the opponent. All Kashima-Shinryū bujutsu tactics, then, are variations of one of these five patterns.[20]

Figure 22. *Ei choku kyoku choku* ("a wedge is direct; a diagonal is direct")

Applied Constructs

Collectively, the Fivefold Laws and the Eight Divine Coordinates delimit the conceptual universe of discourse within which successive generations of Kashima-Shinryū masters have formulated their art. But to understand Kashima-Shinryū bugei as a historical phenomenon, to appreciate it and its sister martial art ryūha as functioning components of samurai lives and culture, we must focus more closely on how these principles function in practical application.

The Certificate of Mastery issued to successful students by recent generations of headmasters summarizes Kashima-Shinryū canon by listing the Fivefold Laws, followed by twenty applied constructs, or *ōyō-shinri*. Fifteen of these also appear in a copy of a Jikishin Kageryū Certificate of Mastery dated "an auspicious day in the second month of the ninth year of the Genroku era [1696]." Both the Kashima-Shinryū and the Jikishin Kageryū documents simply inventory the concepts by name, without commentary, making it impossible to determine the extent to which contemporary interpretations of them conform to earlier ones. Nevertheless, it is clear that the constructs themselves date back at least as far as the seventeenth century.[21]

As their name implies, the applied constructs denote particularized applications of the broad principles expressed in the Fivefold Laws and the Eight Divine Coordinates. Examining them, therefore, will help to flesh out our sketch of the philosophy and science of Kashima-Shinryū bugei, and provide further illustrations of the way in which the terminology adopted by bugei ryūha serves to at once illuminate and conceal. Four of the twenty applied constructs (nukitachi-no-koto, tatazu-no-kachi, gontaiyū, and aiki) have already been introduced. For analytical purposes, we can divide the rest into two broad catagories: those that pertain to the application or development of physical and/or psycho-spiritual skills, and those pointing to issues of strategy and tactics.

The most fundamental of all physical considerations in the bugei is the issue of stance. A warrior's manner of standing or walking while in combat forms the base or platform upon which he builds all his techniques. Kashima-Shinryū thinking holds that three conditions, called the "three aversions" *(mittsu no kirai)*, should be shunned at all costs: "fixed feet" *(sue-ashi)*, "floating feet" *(uki-ashi)*, and "jumping feet" *(tobi-ashi)*.

The first means to distribute one's weight equally over both legs, while the second refers to planting all one's weight on one foot, to shifting one's weight continually from one leg to the other, or to constantly shifting the position of one's feet. All these tactics, Kashima-Shinryū masters caution, will restrict a fighter's freedom of movement; no longer able to step smoothly and instantly in all directions, he must hop or leap about in sharp, choppy, sparrowlike steps in order to overcome the inertia or the instability of his stance. Either error often leads to the third "aversion," tobi-ashi, in which the warrior springs forward, backward or to the side causing both feet to leave the ground at the same time. This is considered precarious in the extreme, as he cannot halt or change his direction of travel while in midair, and, while off the ground, he has no platform from which to draw power for his techniques.[22]

Properly executed Kashima-Shinryū technique calls for the sword, the mind, and the body to operate as three integrated phases of a single phenomenon (Sword, Mind, and Body as a Trinity; see page 69). To know and control the actions of an opponent's sword, then, a warrior must know how to observe the movements of both his body and his mind. The traditional term for this is *metsuke* ("eye placement"). The eyes—the proverbial windows to the soul—are the key to reading the actions of the mind; the light or gleam in an adversary's eyes is as revealing as the movements of the rest of his body. Kashima-Shinryū initiates are therefore told to observe an opponent's eyes, his body as a whole, and his weapon with equal attention, focusing on all three at the same time and fixing their gaze on no one of them.[23]

Observing three things at once must, of course, incorporate something more than visual perception in the ordinary sense. In fact, bugei adepts often claim the ability to feel or sense an opponent's actions and to manage them even as they occur, rather than seeing them in a normal manner and then reacting. This enhances not only their power to control an attacker, but their power to do so without inflicting unnecessary harm, another fundamental implication of hōyō-dōka. Kashima-Shinryū instruction explains this ability as a specific application of the notion of aiki, or "reciprocal spirit." Aiki, as we noted earlier, broadly denotes an ura aspect of hōyō-dōka and the Axiom of the Moon on the Water, the skill of remaining in emotional and spiritual balance with the opponent. The specific mechanism at work here involves manipulation of the *ki* or *reiki*, the universal and fundamental energy that, according to traditional Sino-Japanese physiology, circulates within all living things.[24] Adepts learn to harmonize their ki with that of their opponents, so that the aura of the opponents' ki touches on their own. Changes in the flow of an opponent's ki—as when he contemplates attacks or other actions—are said to oscillate against the adept's aura, enabling him to read the opponent's movements before they become physically perceptible by other means.

Bugei jargon refers to the manner by which a warrior grips his weapon, and by extension to skill or technique, especially the skill of applying power and energy through one's weapon, as *te-no-uchi*, or "palm of the hand." One of the most important forms of Kashima-Shinryū te-no-uchi is *kiriotoshi* ("cutting down"), another of the ōyō-shinri appearing in both Kashima-Shinryū and Jikishin Kageryū documents. In this maneuver, also called *sokui-tachi*, or "sticky rice sword," a swordsman cuts downward through the middle of an attacking weapon, just before it reaches the focal point of its swing. The swordsman handles his own weapon as though it were made of something soft and tacky, so that it adheres to the attacking weapon and forces it toward the ground. Performed correctly, kiriotoshi is supposed to absorb the energy of the opponent's attack, momentarily rendering his weapon dead, and forestalling any countertechnique. It therefore exemplifies hōyō-dōka ("acceptance and resorption") in its most literal sense. Other sorts of percussive blocks, by contrast, are held to be dangerous because they actually add momentum to the attacking blade, momentum a skilled opponent can easily redirect to continue the attack.

To maximize his power for kiriotoshi and other applications, a Kashima-Shinryū adept seeks to concentrate the resources of his entire body in a single direction or at a single point, completely eliminating any extraneous muscle tension or nervous energy—any force not essential to the execution of task at hand. He acquires this ability, called *sōtai-no-shime* ("concentering the body," or more literally, "to draw in the body as a whole"), by focusing and disciplining his body through exercises like the kesagiri of Kashima-Shinryū kenjutsu or the *Reiki-no-hō* of Kashima-Shinryu jūjutsu (both described in chapter 4), in the same way that one focuses and disciplines the mind and spirit through meditation.[25] For advanced bugei practitioners, "concentering the body" involves integrating muscular or biomechanical strength with biospiritual energy, or ki. With proper training an expert can even use the ki itself as a weapon.

Kiate ("striking with the ki") forms the foundation of *kiai-jutsu*, the art of *kiai*—that is, the art of controlling one's own and one's adversary's psychospiritual and physical energy by manipulating the breath. "Kiai," literally "confluences of ki," represent a tool and a construct applied by virtually all traditional bugei ryūha. They are usually conceived of as a concentration and projection of the spirit, or as one author has described, a marshalling of

> the potential power which governs the course of human life, and the source of energy inherent in the human race. . . . Psychologically [kiai-jutsu] is the art of concentrating the whole of one's mental energy upon a single object with the determination to achieve or subdue that object. Physically it is the art of deep and prolonged breathing.[26]

Written with the same ideographs as "aiki," but in reverse order, "kiai" represents the omote of aiki. Both terms refer to the marshalling of one's ki and the harmonizing of one's energies with those of the opponent, but while aiki accents embracing the opponent's ki onto oneself, kiai emphasizes projecting one's ki onto the opponent.

Novices and nonpractitioners of the bugei commonly associate kiai with the "karate shout" emitted by adepts at the focal point of a blow, but this sort of vocalization—closely related to those of weight lifters, shot-putters, and other athletes as well as to the "rebel yells" of troops on the battlefield and the grunts of laborers at moments of intense physical exertion—can be both more and less than a true kiai. To begin with, while their projection often takes the form of a shout, kiai can be silent as well as voiced. More importantly, true kiai must involve the *opponent's* energy as well as one's own.

Kiai-jutsu theory holds that the physical and spiritual strength of all living things ebbs and flows with the intake and outflow of the breath, in a process sometimes likened to pushing a stone up and down a mountain: As one inhales, one's potential power builds, like the latent energy stored in a stone as one moves it uphill. As one exhales, the power is released, like the energy of the stone as it rolls down the mountain. Gravity, in this analogy, enhances the momentum given the stone by the pusher; in like manner the release of the breath enhances any application of strength.

But just as the stone will have exhausted all of its energy upon reaching the bottom of the mountain, living things experience an instant of physical and spiritual weakness in the interval after the breath has been expelled completely and before the next inhalation begins. The most basic application of kiate exploits this phenomenon with a short, powerful kiai delivered at the precise instant an adversary finishes exhaling, shattering his composure and destroying his capacity to attack or respond. Kashima-Shinryū kiai-jutsu warns, however, that a warrior using this technique must be careful to use only about three-fifths of his lung capacity for the kiate. Exhaling completely at the end of a kiai forces a break between this and any subsequent actions. The warrior's techniques, therefore, become disjointed, allowing his opponent to attack the interval between them, a situation known as "having the tail of one's kiai caught." Properly applied, kiate would seem to be a formidable weapon. Stories abound of experts felling birds from the sky and repelling attackers with the power of their kiai alone.[27]

In fact Seki Humitake, the current Kashima-Shinryū shihanke, relates an interesting experience of this sort that happened to him during a research trip to Canada in 1969. Late one afternoon, Seki, accompanied by an assistant, was returning to his laboratory after collecting samples from a salmon stream in the nearby woods. All at once he was struck by sense of danger *(sakki)* seemingly emanating from someone nearby. Because the only person he could see was his assistant, who he was sure bore him no harm, he ignored the feeling and continued on his way. A few steps later he saw a dark shape move in the bushes next to the path and, before he could react, a large black bear reared up on its hind legs before him, less than 2 meters away. The bear, clearly as startled and confused as the men, advanced slightly; Seki, realizing that the animal was now close enough to rake him with its claws before he would be able to scramble out of range, stood his ground and watched carefully. As the bear grew more agitated, its breathing became rougher and more exaggerated, suggesting to Seki a possible way out of his dilemma. Just as the bear finished one exhalation and before it could begin its next inhalation, he applied a sharp kiate attack. The bear stopped all movement for an instant, looked confused, and then, dropping back to all fours, turned and lumbered off into the woods, leaving the two scientists to continue cautiously homeward.[28]

As we observed earlier in our discussion of hōyō-dōka, however, skill—even of this esoteric sort—is of little value to a warrior emotionally unprepared for battle. Apprehension and nervousness can sabotage the execution of any task. Anxiety renders a warrior's performance awkward and ineffectual, rapidly dissolving skills acquired over years of careful training and practice along with his composure. Optimum performance demands mental and spiritual calm. If this consideration is important to athletes, entertainers, and students taking examinations, it is even more so to warriors in combat. Battles or duels leave little room for error; a single mistake can cost one's life. This reality makes retaining one's composure in combat both essential and elusive, for the higher the price of failure caused by being flustered, the greater the provocation to be flustered. For a warrior about to enter battle, then, assaying his mental and spiritual readiness is as essential as checking over his weapons or determining his physical condition.

Kashima-Shinryū teachings include methods, called *gimmi*, for testing one's composure—and, if necessary, for regaining it—before engaging an opponent. The simplest of these calls for checking the pulse simultaneously at the left wrist and at both carotid arteries. When one is properly calm, the pulse at all three points should beat in unison; dissipation among the three pulse beats indicates spiritual agitation, which can be corrected through breathing exercises or self-applied acupressure techniques.[29]

In addition to calming their own spirits, the samurai also worried about staying the spirits or souls of slain enemies to prevent their return to this world. The need for such an action, called *todome* (literally, "to stop"), comes from a Chinese-derived folk belief that divides the human soul into two parts. One, the *kon* (called the *hun* or *ming* in Mandarin), is associated with yang, and one, the *haku* (in Mandarin, *kwei* or *p'o*), is associated with yin. After death, the kon normally resides in the body for a short time and then ascends to the heavens, while the haku returns to the earth from which it originally came. Care must be taken, however, that the kon is properly stilled lest it remain on earth to do mischief. Unless properly attended, the soul of one whose life has been ended violently or prematurely in particular may become trapped in this world or may return to seek vengeance.*

Broadly speaking, a samurai might have struck down an enemy for any of three principal reasons. For each of these, Kashima-Shinryū lore offered an appropriate means of accomplishing the killing and/or treating the corpse afterward so as to stay the newly dispatched soul from returning. Collectively called *todome-sandan* ("three-fold todome"), all involved stabbing the victim somewhere on his left side.

When a warrior killed on the order of his superior, a situation known as *gyoi-uchi* ("striking for the honorable will"), he would normally have presented the victim's head to the lord who ordered the execution, making it desirable for him to minimize any damage to the corpse. The ideal means to accomplish both this and the appropriate todome was to stab the enemy in the sole of his left foot. Transpiercing this spot, a major nerve center and a vital point known as the "spring of life" *(inochi-no-izumi)* in acupuncture theory, will produce almost instant death. This target was, moreover, readily accessible on an enemy kneeling in the formal posture *(seiza)* customarily adopted by Tokugawa period samurai in the presence of their equals or superiors.

A samurai might also dispatch an enemy of his parents on grounds of filial piety. In this instance, called *teki-uchi* ("striking for vengeance"), the proper todome was to stab the victim below his left ear so as to sever the carotid artery. This is, in fact, the only spot on the head or neck that is both a vital point and soft enough to be

---

*Fear of the trouble a restless soul might visit on the living also formed one of the motives behind the custom of burying bodies sitting up *(kussō)* rather than prostrate. Folding the body and burying it upright so that its knees pressed against its chest prevented the kon from escaping before it was ready to make its heavenward journey. The Japanese buried their dead in this manner from the Yayoi period (ca. 300 BC–AD 300) or earlier through the Edo era (1600–1868).

easily pierced by a knife or sword. Because of the manner in which the blood drains from a wound of this sort, the victim's face would not become distorted, and his head would therefore remain presentable for exhibition to the samurai's parent or for offering to the parent's grave.

The third reason for killing, *ishu-uchi* ("striking of one's own accord") demanded special caution. For unlike gyoi-uchi or teki-uchi, in which the warrior's role in the killing was simply that of an instrument carrying out the orders of his superior or the demands of justice, in ishu-uchi the decision to kill originated with the warrior himself. The enemy was the warrior's own enemy, killed because of the warrior's enmity toward him; responsibility for the death therefore rested with the warrior himself, whereas in the other cases, his ethical responsibility was considered to have been minimal. Regardless, therefore, of how the enemy was struck down, his soul needed to be arrested by stabbing the victim just below the left nipple and twisting the blade from edge up to edge downward as it was withdrawn.[30]

Kashima-Shinryū initiates were further advised to take care that slain foes fell forward as they died so as not to bring undue dishonor to the victim. Samurai mores saw facing upward in death as a proper posture for women, but not for men; thus a warrior found dead on his back would be scorned as having died in a "womanly" fashion. This is the same reason that samurai performing seppuku, or ritual self-immolation, carefully tucked the sleeves of their kimono under their knees to ensure they would fall forward as they died.[31]

In a less esoteric application, the characters for todome-sandan can also be read as *"tome-sandan,"* a reading unique to the Kashima-Shinryū. Tome-sandan means to arrest or halt an opponent's strikes at three (the head, the torso, or the legs) physical levels.[32] One cannot simply block the opponent's blows, as blocking is defensive, receptive—and, ultimately, passive—and thus lies outside the boundaries of Offense and Defense as One. Blocking a strike may thwart the strike itself, but it cannot stop the *attack*, of which the strike formed a part; when blocked, an opponent can simply redirect either the original or a follow-up blow and continue the attack; blocking leaves the opponent in control, forcing one to perform block after block in response to what the opponent does. Instead, one must truncate the attack in mid-course, literally cut it off with a strike of one's own. The *Kihon-tachi* series of techniques for the sword, described in detail in chapter 4, illustrate this principle, also called *kiridome* ("to stop by cutting").

Constructs like mittsu-no-kirai, metsuke, sōtai-no-shime, te-no-uchi, kiriotoshi-no-koto, kiate, gimmi, and todome-sandan concern fundamental physical and/or psychospiritual skills, and as such, they represent principles applicable to any number of traditional and non-traditional bugei. Tome-sandan and the remaining eight applied constructs focus more narrowly on the strategy and tactics that underlie specific fighting techniques. Kashima-Shinryū interpretations of these terms, then, are exclusive—or nearly so—to the ryūha.

The cornerstone to Kashima-Shinryū strategy rests in applying *shikake*, or initiating techniques, as the Emptiness of Emptiness and Reality as One; in other words, to attack first, as a means for drawing out an opponent's response in accord with Kamiizumi Ise-no-kami's broader principle of katsujin-ken (see chapter 2). A warrior in combat has but two options: to attack or to wait for his opponent's attack. Many ryūha, especially those of modern cognate arts such as aikidō or karate, stress the latter tactic, underscoring the self-defensive objectives and attenuating aggressive applications of the fighting skills they propagate. Perhaps the best-known expression of this sentiment is Funakoshi Gichin's "karate ni sente nashi" ("In karate there is no first strike"), which appears even on his tombstone.* The Kashima-Shinryū approach to combat might, by contrast, be summarized as "shinbu ni sente nomi" ("In shinbu, there is *only* the first strike").

Kashima-Shinryū strategy aims at controlling the entire encounter, at containing both the opponent's aggression and one's own. It teaches that a swordsman who waits for his opponent to make the first move surrenders the initiative (sen), and thereby control of the fight, to him: He then moves according to the opponent's timing with actions dictated by those of the opponent. If, on the other hand, he seizes the initiative for himself, he forces his *opponent* to respond within a range of choices limited by his opening move and at a moment of his own choosing. If, moreover, the swordsman's shikake is wholly in accord with the principles of Emptiness and Reality as One and with Origination and Manifestation as One, this opening action must become decisive, whether as sen-no-sen or sen-sen-no-sen (see page 77); he needs no second strike.

Initiating techniques can be as overtly threatening as a cut or strike, or they can be as subtle as placing one's self within the opponent's

---

*Funakoshi Gichin (18??–1957) was the pivotal figure in the introduction of karate to Japan from Okinawa.

striking range. In either case, even though shikake are used to force a response from the opponent, they must be *opening techniques*, not pure feints. To perform them inattentively or without content is to flirt with defeat, as a skillful opponent will simply ignore a feint and seize the initiative (sen) for himself. One must fully commit to the shikake and yet, at the same time, not be so firmly locked into it as to be unable to readily adapt it to the opponent's response.

This consideration has a special significance when the swordsman's shikake consists of simply offering his opponent an easy target. A wary adversary will not take an opening he suspects might be part of a ruse. To be sure of drawing out the opponent, therefore, the swordsman must convince him that he is not only willing to risk death, but that he *expects* to die. And he cannot do this by pretense; to convince the opponent he must first convince himself. He must, in other words, surrender himself wholly to the shikake by actively seeking death, and then snatching himself back from its edge only when the opponent has fully committed himself. The mental gymnastics involved in this sort of embrace of death are a little like those of a person playing Russian roulette. The difference between the swordsman and the Russian roulette player, however, turns on preparation and control. The latter entrusts his fate to probability and chance alone, the former to his training and his acquired reflexes. And yet the reality of death and its acceptance are similar in both cases. A part, therefore, of budō as the martial path to self-development lies in the heightened realization of living that accompanies the practitioner's regular forays toward death.

To become fully ensnared by an opponent's technique and yet turn the opponent's own moves against him and seize victory from defeat is called *yabure-gachi* ("breaking up the victory"). Kashima-Shinryū canon maintains that so long as both combatants use only techniques consistent with all of the Fivefold Laws, yabure-gachi is impossible. Should the actions of either, however, be deficient in even one of these principles, yabure-gachi becomes not only feasible, but probable. The Kashima-Shinryū sword technique *naori-taichūken* (literally, "the sword rectified to the body's center"), used to reverse the Ono-ha Ittō-ryū's famous *uke-nagashi* ("to receive and let flow away") technique, provides an excellent illustration of this concept in application.[33]

Uke-nagashi is a flowing block that parries the force of an opponent's attack and uses it to generate momentum for a counterstrike. To perform it, a swordsman responds to a straight vertical attack to his forehead by rolling his hands upward to his left, raising his blade with the cutting edge up and the tip angled slightly downward to his right so that it protects his forehead. In the instant in which the attacking sword collides with his, he steps forward and slightly to the left with his right foot, allowing the power of his opponent's strike to push the tip of his blade downward as he slips out from under it. In this way, the attack slides harmlessly off his sword, much like water off a roof, while at the same time imparting momentum to the defending weapon, which the swordsman uses to spin his blade around and deliver a counterblow of his own.

Skillfully applied, uke-nagashi is a devastating technique, but its weakness lies in the fact that the swordsman's counterattack cannot begin until after his opponent's sword has made contact with his own; it thus separates Offense from Defense and Origination from Manifestation. A swordsman whose opening strike fully embraces all of the Fivefold Laws can use the interval between these elements—no matter how brief—to recover and defeat the technique. Kashima-Shinryū adepts accomplish this by means of naori-taichūken: When an opponent attempts to use uke-nagashi to counter his opening attack, the Kashima-Shinryū swordsman, at the instant in which his weapon makes contact with the opponent's, immediately relaxes all power behind his strike, making his blade cling to his opponent's. As he does this, he pivots to his right to follow the opponent (who is attempting to step out from under the strike), always keeping his sword poised directly over the opponent's head and perpendicular to his own shoulders, thereby checkmating the opponent, who, unable to get out from under the attacking sword, cannot complete his counterblow.

Combat reconciled to shinbu—actions fully incorporating the Fivefold Laws—should leave an opponent no openings through which to stage a successful attack. But tactics falling short of this ideal create brief periods of vulnerability. Kashima-Shinryū strategy recognizes three errors in particular as especially dangerous. Collectively called the "three unpermissible moments" (*mittsu no yurusanu tokoro*), these represent the most opportune instants in which to attack. They are:

1) A shift in kamae or a change in technique; unlike the flow of omote-waza to ura-waza consistent with Emptiness and Reality as One, true changes of kamae or tactics involve a transition from one state of mind to another. Thus, until the change is completed and the

warrior has fully revised his mental (and physical) posture, his spirit is unfocused and he cannot respond properly to an attack (or any other action) directed at him.

2) The gap between the Origination and the Manifestation of a technique; two-part or "cock-and-fire" actions create an interval during which the fighter has fully committed himself to the preparatory movement but has not yet begun the actual strike. If attacked during this interval, the fighter will be mentally unready to respond—as his thoughts are focused on his own strike rather than on defense—and physically unable to do so, as he must first halt his current action and then initiate a new action to block or counter the attack. A warrior can, therefore, easily prevent the completion of an opponent's technique by checking it at its moment of origin.

3) The end of a kiai; as we have noted, a fleeting instant of physical and spiritual weakness follows the end of a kiai. To avoid this problem, Kashima-Shinryū students are taught to exhale no more than three-fifths of the air in their lungs while performing a kiai.[34]

Each of the hundreds of bugei ryūha in Japan embraces a repertoire of kamae or prefatory stances, some common, others unique—or nearly so—to a particular school. The Kashima-Shinryū for example, utilizes six main postures (see page 73) plus a handful of special kamae for particular weapons or situations. Modern kendō uses five kamae, while the Katori-Shintōryū employs ten, the Jikishin Kageryū seven, and the Shinkage-ryū seventeen. If, then, ryūha average around nine basic ready postures, a hypothetical match between two swordsmen from different schools involves some eighty-one possible combinations of kamae. Even when both schools' repertoires of postures overlap perfectly (that is, both use the same nine kamae), the probability of both swordsmen choosing the same ready posture should be only one in nine; if, as is more likely, the overlap is less than perfect (the two ryūha sharing some but not all of their respective kamae), the probability is even lower. In spite of this, opposing combatants very commonly square off in identical postures, a situation known as *aigamae*, or "reciprocal postures." While this may seem odd from a purely mathematical perspective, it is far less puzzling when one considers the specific dynamics of a sword fight.

Most kamae impose limitations on the variety of attacks or defensive actions a swordsman can initiate: A given kamae is a viable beginning position for only a finite number of blows or techniques, and an *ideal* beginning for a smaller number still. The relative effectiveness of specific strikes and counterstrikes further limits a swordsman's range of choices, for he will wish to avoid attacks easily defended against from the posture assumed by his opponent, and will not wish to be caught in a position unsuitable for defense against the techniques most easily or most probably launched from his opponent's kamae. Instead, he will seek to adopt a ready posture ideally suited for both attacking and countering the best moves that readily flow from his opponent's posture, and will, in so doing, effectively neutralize some—perhaps even most—of his opponent's best options. For this reason, when two combatants begin from differing kamae, only a few combinations of techniques become likely.

This can be better understood by analyzing a specific example: Two swordsmen face one another from about a pace outside of striking distance. The first adopts a *seigan-kamae*, holding his weapon straight in front of himself, the tip pointing at his opponent's eyes (this is perhaps the most common ready posture in Japanese swordplay); the second also holds his blade straight before himself, but points the tip downward, in a *gedan-kamae*. (Seigan-kamae and gedan-kamae are both postures used in modern kendō. Neither is employed in Kashima-Shinryū swordplay.) Gedan-kamae is a relatively weak defensive position, but it is ideally suited to quick, upward thrusting attacks. Seigan-kamae, on the other hand, is a good posture for blocking almost any attack, but requires a swordsman to first raise or otherwise withdraw his weapon before launching an offensive strike of his own. The two combatants in this example, then, are very nearly stalemated (unless one is much faster or stronger than the other). The second swordsman cannot deliver his low thrust without stepping straight into the tip of his adversary's blade; the first swordsman, however, cannot raise his weapon to strike without opening himself to the second swordsman's thrust.

When, by contrast, both swordsmen utilize the *same* kamae, the number of plausible combinations of techniques increases considerably, as both combatants are positioned for the same set of strikes and counters. This, then, explains why contending opponents are so often drawn to aigamae; the most common example of this is probably the seigan-kamae versus seigan-kamae encounters favored by kendō players.

Aigamae is thought to be less compelling in Kashima-Shinryū bugei than in other forms of martial art because both kamae and techniques are structured so as to embody the principles of Motion and Stillness as One and Origination and Manifestation as One. Thus *any* Kashima-Shinryū technique can be initiated effortlessly from *any* Kashima-Shinryū kamae. All Kashima-Shinryū techniques follow spiraling paths to their targets, beginning from postures in which, although apparently static, the weapons actually move in imperceptible loops. Spirals being effectively without beginnings or ends, strikes executed from any of the postures depicted in figures 8–13 differ only in the position on the spiral from which they begin, and can be performed identically in all other respects. Unless, therefore, he deviates from the principles set forth by the Fivefold Laws, a warrior's freedom of action should be utterly unrestricted by either his own or his opponent's kamae.

In encounters between experts of similar ability, aigamae often leads to *aishin* ("reciprocal wills"), wherein the two opponents—each seeking to begin with the most effective strike possible from the kamae he has adopted—launch identical attacks.[35] Aishin *can* result in both opponents killing one another *(aiuchi)*, but if the techniques employed are properly grounded in Offense and Defense as One, the outcome will be a momentary deadlock in which the attacks cancel each other out, the weapons meeting harmlessly in mid-air *(kirimusubi)*

The five techniques that make up the Kashima-Shinryū's *aishin-kumitachi* series epitomize this concept in practical operation and also illustrate the means by which a swordsman can recover from this sort of stalemate. In the first and perhaps most interesting of these, *kumi-tachi-kiridome*, for example, both swordsmen attack simultaneously, stepping forward with their right feet, their weapons meeting in the kurai-tachi position (see figure 11). They each attempt to break this deadlock by striking around the other's blade, in great counterclockwise arcs aimed at the left side of the other's forehead. Once again, however, their swords clash harmlessly in the air. At this juncture, one swings his sword around at about eye level, in a flat clockwise arc, attempting to sweep his opponent's blade aside and then deliver a follow-up strike. But when the first swordsman's weapon has traveled around to within about 45 degrees of striking his own, the second brings the tip of his sword around in a small circle, and cuts downward and through his opponent's attack, using kiriotoshi. He then brings the tip of his blade to the first swordsman's wrist, thereby taking control of his subsequent movements.

Two adversaries about the same size contending with weapons of the same length have exactly the same reach—they can strike each other in the same places from the same distance. This condition represents the construct *aijaku* ("reciprocal reach" or "matching length") in its simplest and most literal sense. But while situations of this sort are common in training where students use standardized practice weapons and in sportive competition where rules often govern the pairing of opponents and the dimensions of the weapons, they are much less likely to occur in actual combat where warriors must face antagonists much larger or smaller than themselves bearing all manner of ordnance.

The wider sense of aijaku, then, is also known as *chōtan ichimi* ("long and short in congruence") and refers to the concept of compensating for the apparent advantage of an opponent armed with a weapon of greater reach than one's own. One can, for example, strike the opponent on the parts of his body closest to oneself, such as the wrists, while taking care to offer him no such extended targets. One can also step inside the normal striking range of an adversary's weapon, jamming his movements but retaining complete freedom in one's own.

Aijaku is the principle underlying Kashima-Shinryū techniques for using swords against naginata, spears, long and short staffs, and various other weapons, or for using short swords or knives against long swords. But its highest expression can be seen in *shirahatori*—the use of unarmed (jūjutsu) techniques against a sword-wielding opponent. Shirahatori requires a warrior to mesh perfectly with an opponent's attack, to make his own technique flow from inside the opponent's. It is, therefore, also an expression of the principle of Outside and Inside as One.[36]

Aijaku and related constructs demonstrate that the omote arts of Kashima-Shinryū bugei, such as kenjutsu, are differentiated from the ura arts, such as jūjutsu, not as distinct realms on opposing sides of a clearly defined border, but as positions on a continuum. At the poles one finds sword techniques that are purely omote and unarmed techniques that are purely ura, but between these points lies a hazy frontier zone of techniques that partake of both jūjutsu and kenjutsu. This is one of the most important implications of the principle of Outside and Inside as One.

Swords, glaives, spears, and staves are designed for cutting, stabbing, or bludgeoning adversaries, but these are not their only uses. Blow and counterblow with any of these arms often cancel each other out, leaving the weapons locked together (kirimusubi) and producing a stalemate, unless one or both combatants either find a way to disengage and attempt another strike, or use jūjutsu techniques to flow around the deadlock and topple or otherwise arrest their opponent. Moreover, on the battlefield, where armor protects combatants from all but the best-timed and -directed slices, stabs, and hits; in contests where training weapons (such as wooden or bamboo swords), protective gear, or rules make it difficult to deliver an unambiguously decisive strike; or in any encounter in which one opponent wishes to avoid killing or maiming the other, using a weapon in a jūjutsu-like manner to immobilize or throw the opponent can offer the most efficient means to victory.*

Whether a result of deadlock or sought voluntarily, the transition from kenjutsu to jūjutsu begins when the opponents close to jūjutsu fighting range *(maai)*, usually with their weapons meeting hand guard *(tsuba)* to hand guard, in what bugei jargon terms the *gasshō* ("praying hands") or *tsubazeri* ("vying tsuba to tsuba") position. There are two means of arriving at this position, depending on the initial distance between the combatants.

When swordsmen begin only a pace or two apart, the encounter is classified as a *tachiai*, or "standing meeting." To reach the gasshō position from a tachiai, the swordsmen hold their weapons before them and slide or step forward, bringing their blades directly together just above the hand guards. As they close, they point their swords perpendicular to the line of combat and at an acute angle to the vertical. This action is called *tai-atari*, "to meet with the body." An engagement in which the swordsmen approach one another from several paces apart is termed a *yukiai* ("advancing meeting") and requires the swordsmen to first make contact with each other's blades near the tips, and then slide along the length of the blades until the hand guards meet. This action is called *tachi-atari*, "to meet with the sword."

---

*The movie *Seven Samurai* (Tōhō Productions, 1954) gives an excellent example of the problems involved in resolving contests governed by rules. In one scene, a master swordsman engages a challenger with wooden swords. The challenger and his friends declare the match a draw, claiming that both contestants struck each other at the same instant; the master swordsman, however, calmly states that his blow was a fraction of a second faster. The angry challenger insists on a rematch, this time with live blades, which, predictably, results in his death. Such I-got-you-no-you-didn't arguing occurs only when the contesting warriors have agreed to pull their blows a fraction of an instant before actual contact. It is neither necessary nor possible when one combatant throws or pins his opponent instead. On the battlefield, warriors followed up such locks, throws, or pins with cuts or thrusts to the openings in their fallen opponents' armor.

Kashima-Shinryū techniques executed from the gasshō/tsubazeri position all apply the "Axiom of the Moon on the Water," particularly the gontaiyū aspect of this construct. This means that a swordsman must neither push nor withdraw, but maintain a perfect balance of zero against the power applied by the opponent. This zero figure indicates the relative application of power by both opponents, not the absolute power applied by either. The Axiom of the Moon on the Water must be maintained throughout when executing tai-atari, tachi-atari, and any subsequent technique.

*   *   *

In the foregoing pages I have attempted to take readers inside Kashima-Shinryū bugei, to offer a glimpse of one traditional ryūha's martial philosophy and science as initiates view them. Readers finding themselves overwhelmed by the number and variety of terms introduced need not despair, for it was never my intention to teach the terms themselves. My analysis has, by design, been evocative rather than exhaustive, seeking in the main to illuminate the texture and dynamics of a kabala never meant to be learned or understood in purely linear, academic terms.

The traditional bugei are extraordinarily complex arts, especially at their most fundamental levels as methodologies of combat and war. On this plane they are largely collections of particulars, expressed in hundreds of individual techniques and strategies, described in a profoundly unsystemized, sometimes opaque, and often overlapping argot of names and terms. Much of this apparent chaos is intentional, for—at least in traditional times—the ryūha, as competitive organizations training warriors for deadly combat, deliberately strove to keep outsiders from grasping the essence of what they taught.

And yet each ryūha's kabala *does* have an essence, a conceptual core around which the details of the school's art revolve. This core becomes increasingly perceptible to initiates as they advance in their studies, particularly as they turn their attentions beyond the initiatory functions of the bugei as arts of war (bujutsu) to their deeper purpose as arts of peace and self-realization (budō). To adepts who have entered this realm, each one of their ryūha's terms and concepts reveals multiple levels of meaning—mechanical, psychological, moral, and so forth—conceptualized as indicating not sequential steps, but interpenetrating spheres of activity.

Thus Kashima-Shinryū bugei is, in a phrase, the art of hōyō-dōka, the science of acceptance and resorption in all its myriad implications. What this means for ryūha initiates is summarized in the *Ōgi* (or *Okugi*), a statement of the guiding principles or paramount teachings of the school:

> Know that the essence of Kashima-Shinryū lies not in savoring the unavailing joy of felling an enemy, of destroying evil, but in fostering noble men who strive to revere and satisfy the will of those who govern the realm. Thus it nurtures in those who practice it the will to kill one only to save ten thousand. Such an art lies in total neutrality and total impartiality. Of its own accord it maintains the state of certain life. It issues forth in limitless permutations, reaching, as a result, the epitome of form and contour.
>
> All actions exist within the unitary mind. The dictum of the unitary mind and the unitary sword must be followed.
>
> Eliminate selfishness: this is the sword of certain life. This, in turn, manifests hōyō-dōka. Certain life is certain control, is certain victory. If the heart is not pure, he who willfully attacks will only be destroyed. Destroying evil, establishing righteousness: the principle is clear. Is it [not] then worthwhile for men of spirit to come to train diligently? Thinking thus the Kashima-Shinryū first prepares the body, at the midpoint cultivates heartfelt human relationships, and arrives ultimately at realization and understanding of the fundamental principles of the Universe. This is the inner truth of the Kashima-Shinryū. As in days of old, it is the great Way of the sacred nation of Japan.

Having outlined, then, what it is that Kashima-Shinryū initiates acquire in their journeys toward shinbu and hōyō-dōka, in the next chapter I will describe the path itself, the process of training and transmission of ryūha canon.

4.
The Martial Path

The perfection of an art consists in the employment of a comprehensive system of laws, commensurate to every purpose within its
scope, but concealed from the eye of the spectator; and in the production of effects that seem to flow forth spontaneously, as though
uncontrolled by their influence, and which are equally excellent,
whether regarded individually, or in reference to the proposed result.
—JOHN MASON GOOD

Education is an admirable thing, but it is well to remember from
time to time that nothing that is worth knowing can be taught.
—OSCAR WILDE

BUGEI RYŪHA exist chiefly to propagate knowledge, but not knowledge—in the conventional Western sense—alone. In the martial and
other traditional Japanese arts, knowledge of the cerebral sort matters less than *understanding*—learning acquired by the heart rather
than by the intellect. Whether practiced as a means to mastery of
the self or simply as an expedient to success on the battlefield, classical Japanese martial art training seeks to fuse body, mind, spirit, and
weapon into something more than the sum of these parts. Kashima-
Shinryū orthodoxy thus prescribes an educational process centered
on three spheres of activity: acquiring physical and technical skills,
cultivating understanding and intuition, and polishing the spirit.

The role of the teacher in the bugei tradition is to serve as model
and guide, not as lecturer or conveyor of information, and the standard appellation for teachers of traditional arts, *"shihan,"* reflects
this role. Although commonly translated as "instructor" or "master
instructor," the term literally means something more on the order
of "master and model." Bugei teachers lead students along the path
to mastery of their arts—they do not tutor them. Issai Chozan's
early eighteenth century classic text on swordsmanship, *Neko no
myōjutsu*, concludes with an eloquent statement of this principle:

> The teacher only transmits the technique and illuminates its
> principle. To acquire its truth is within oneself. [In Zen Buddhism]

this is called self-attainment; or it may also be called mind-to-mind transmission or special transmission outside the texts. Learning in this fashion does not subvert the doctrines [of the texts], for even a teacher could not transmit [in that way]. Nor is such learning found only in the study of Zen, for in the meditations of the Confucian sages and in all of the arts, mastery lies in mind-to-mind transmission, special transmission outside the texts. Texts and doctrine merely point to what one already has within oneself but cannot see on one's own. Understanding is not bestowed by the teacher. Teaching is easy; listening to doctrines is also easy; but to find with certainty what is within oneself, to make this one's own, is difficult. [In Zen] this is called seeing one's nature. Enlightenment is an awakening from the dream of delusion; it is the same as understanding. This does not change.[1]

To say that understanding comes from within the student should not, however, imply that mastery of the martial (or other) arts mostly involves some mystical discovery of truths preexisting but buried within the self, or some magical bursting forth of the learner's inner being. Quite the contrary: Bugei instruction prescribes a gradual, developmental process in which teachers help students to internalize the key precepts of ryūha doctrine. Understanding—mastery—of these precepts comes from within, the result of the student's own efforts. But the teacher presents the precepts, and creates an environment in which the student can absorb and comprehend them, from without.[2] The overall process can be likened to teaching a child to ride a bicycle: The child does not innately know how to balance, pedal, and steer, nor will he be likely to discover how on his own. At the same time, no one can fully explain any of these skills either; one can only demonstrate them and help the child practice them until he figures out for himself which muscles are doing what at which times to make the actions possible.

Kashima-Shinryū masters maintain that those who seek enlightenment must first prepare receptacles into which knowledge has room to enter and understanding has room to develop. Before students are ready to internalize ryūha doctrine, they must first discipline their bodies; the body, as the receptacle, must first acquire the physical skills of detachment, acceptance, balance, and resorption—the corporeal side of hōyō-dōka. Accordingly, expertise in bujutsu must precede study of the other elements of budō; a student's path must begin with physical training.

Kata and Pattern Practice

If the essence of a ryūha can be found in the transmission of its ryūgi—the body of knowledge that defines it—the essence of that transmission can be found in *kata*, the oldest and still the central methodology for teaching and learning in the traditional bugei.[3] Few facets of Japanese martial art have been as consistently and ubiquitously misunderstood, even by those who practice them, as kata. Variously described as a kind of ritualized combat, exercises in aesthetic movement, a means to sharpen fundamentals such as balance and coordination, a type of moving meditation, or a form of training akin to shadowboxing, kata embraces elements of all these characterizations, but its essence is captured by none of them. Kata, in fact, defies succinct explanation.

The standard English translation of "kata" is "form" or "forms"; but while this is linguistically accurate, the nature and function of kata are better conveyed by the phrase "pattern practice." Fundamentally, kata represents a training method wherein students rehearse combinations of techniques and countertechniques, or sequences of such combinations, arranged by their teachers. In most cases, students work in pairs.* One partner is designated as the attacker or opponent, and is called the *uchitachi* (when he uses a sword), *uchite* (when he uses any other weapon), or *ukete* (when he is unarmed). The other employs the techniques the kata is designed to teach, and is called the *shitachi* (in sword training) or the *shite* (when training unarmed or with other weapons).

This sort of pattern practice provides continuity within the ryūha from generation to generation, even in the absence of written instruments for transmission. The kata practiced by a given ryūha can and do change from generation to generation—or even within the lifetime of an individual teacher—but they are normally considered to have been handed down intact by the founder or some other important figure in the school's heritage. "In order," observed Edo period commentator Fujiwara Yoshinobu, "to transmit the essence of the school *[ryūgi no honshitsu]* to later generations, one must teach faithfully, in a manner not in the slightest different from the principles *[jiri]* of the previous teachers."[4] Changes, when they occur, are

---

*Western audiences usually equate kata training with the solo exercises of Chinese, Okinawan, and Korean martial arts. But pattern practice in the Japanese bugei is fundamentally different from this sort of exercise. One important—and obvious—distinction is that kata in both traditional and modern Japanese fighting arts nearly always involve the participation of two or more people.

viewed as being superficial, adjustments to the outward form of the kata; the key elements—the marrow—of the kata do not change. By definition, more fundamental changes (when they are made intentionally and acknowledged as such) connote the branching off of a new ryūha.[5]

One of the key points to be understood about pattern practice in the traditional bugei is that it serves as the core of training and transmission. In modern cognate martial arts, such as kendō or jūdō, kata is often only one of several more or less coequal training methods, but in the traditional ryūha, pattern practice was and is the pivotal method. Many schools teach only through pattern practice. Others employ adjunct learning devices, such as sparring, but only to augment kata training—never to supplant it.

The importance of pattern practice comes from the belief that it is the most efficient vehicle for passing knowledge from teacher to student. On one level, a ryūha's kata form a living catalog of its curriculum and a syllabus for instruction. Both the essence and the sum of a ryūha's teachings—the postures, techniques, strategies, and philosophy that comprise a school's kabala—are contained in its kata. And the sequence in which students are taught the kata is usually fixed by tradition and/or by the headmaster of the school. In this way pattern practice is a means to systematize and regularize training. But the real function of kata goes far beyond this.

Learning the bugei or other traditional Japanese arts is largely a suprarational process. The most important lessons cannot be conveyed by overt explanation, they must be experienced directly; the essence of a ryūha's kabala can never be wholly extrapolated, it must be intuited from examples in which it is put into practice. David Slawson, discussing the art of gardening, describes traditional learning as taking place through an "osmosis-like process, through the senses, with little theorizing into the underlying principles."[6] His observations echo those of a late Tokugawa period commentator on the bugei:

> Theory *[narai]* is not to be taught lightly; it is to be passed on a little at a time to those who have achieved merit in practice, in order to help them understand the principles [of the art]. Theory, even if not taught, will develop spontaneously with the accumulation of correct training.[7]

To fully appreciate the function of pattern practice as a teaching and learning device, it is important to understand just what is supposed to be taught and learned, and the relationship of this knowledge to kata. The essential knowledge—the kabala—of a ryūha can be broken down into three components: *hyōhō*—or *heihō*—("strategy"), *te-no-uchi* ("skill" or "application of skill"), and *waza* ("techniques" or "tactics"). "Hyōhō" refers to something along the lines of "the essential principles of martial art," wherein "essential" is taken in its original meaning of "that which constitutes the essence." As such, "hyōhō" designates the general principles around which a ryūha's approach to combat is constructed: the rationale for choosing between defensive or offensive tactics, the angles of approach to an opponent, the striking angles and distances appropriate to various weapons, the proper mental posture to be employed in combat, the goals to be sought in combat, and similar considerations. "Te-no-uchi" constitutes the fundamental skills required for the application of hyōhō, such as timing, posture, the generation and concentration of power, and the like. "Waza" are the situationally specific applications of a ryūha's hyōhō and te-no-uchi, the particularized tactics in and through which a student is trained. Waza, te-no-uchi, and hyōhō are functionally inseparable; hyōhō is manifested in and by waza through te-no-uchi.

Kata, then, are compendiums of waza, and as such are manifestations of all three components. More importantly, they are the means by which a student learns and masters first te-no-uchi and then hyōhō. As Fujiwara Yoshinobu observed:

> Technique and principle are indivisible, like a body and its shadow; but one should emphasize the polishing of technique. The reason for this is that principle will manifest itself spontaneously in response to progress in technical training. One should emphatically stifle any impulses to verbally debate principle.[8]

In emphasizing ritualized pattern practice and minimizing analytical explanation, bugei masters blend ideas and techniques from the two educational models most familiar to medieval and early modern Japanese warriors, Confucianism and Zen.

Associating the bugei and samurai culture in general with Zen has become a time-honored habit among both Japanese and Western authors.[9] And to be sure, kata training shares elements in common with the Zen traditions of *ishin-denshin*, or "mind-to-mind-transmission" and what Victor Hori terms "teaching without teaching." The former stresses the importance of a student's own immediate experience over explicit verbal or written explanation, engaging the deeper layers of a student's mind and by-passing the intellect; the latter describes a learning tool applied in Rinzai monasteries whereby students are assigned jobs and tasks that they are expected to learn and perform expertly with little or no formal explanation. Both force the student to fully invoke his powers of observation, analysis, and imagination in order to comprehend where he is being steered. Both lead to a level of understanding beyond cognition of the specific task or lesson presented.[10]

But learning through pattern practice probably derives most directly from Confucian pedagogy and its infatuation with ritual and ritualized action. This infatuation is predicated on the conviction that man fashions the conceptual frameworks he uses to order—and thereby comprehend—the chaos of raw experience through action and practice. One might describe, explain, or even defend one's perspectives by means of analysis and rational argument, but one cannot *acquire* them in this way. Ritual is stylized action, sequentially structured experience that leads those who follow it to wisdom and understanding. Those who seek knowledge and truth, then, must be carefully guided through the right kind of experience if they are to achieve the right kind of understanding. For the early Confucians, whose principal interest was the proper ordering of the state and society, this meant habitualizing themselves to the codes of what they saw as the perfect political organization—the early Chou dynasty. For bugei students, it means ritualized duplication of the actions of past masters.[11]

In point of fact, Confucian models—particularly the Chu Hsi neo-Confucian concept of investigating the abstract through the concrete and the general through the particular, but also the Wang Yang Ming (Ōyōmei) version of neo-Confucianism's emphasis on the necessity of unifying knowledge and action—dominated all aspects of traditional samurai education, not just the bugei.[12] The central academic subjects of such an education were calligraphy and the reading of the Confucian classic texts in Chinese. Calligraphy was taught almost entirely by setting students to copy models provided by their teacher. Students would repeatedly practice brushing out characters that imitated as closely as possible those that appeared in their copybooks as the teacher moved from student to student to observe and offer corrections. Reading, too, was to be learned through what Ronald Dore describes as "parrot-like repetition."[13] After the teacher slowly read off a short passage—usually no more than four or five characters and at most half a page—from the text, students were directed to recite the passage over and over again for themselves, until they had mastered its form. Once this was achieved, the teacher would offer some general idea of the meaning of the passage, and the students would return to their practice. Such instruction formed virtually the whole of a young student's first five to seven years of training. The method showed little concern for comprehension of contents and offered little or no systematic analysis or explanation of even the principles of Chinese grammar and syntax or of the meanings of individual characters. Rather, it was expected that once acquainted with enough examples, the student would acquire the principles underlying them in gestalt-like fashion. The idea was that learning to recite texts in this manner was a necessary preparatory step to true reading. Having mastered the former, the student at length moved on to the latter, revisiting the same Confucian classics he had been struggling through for years but now with the goal of comprehending their meaning rather than just their form. Toward this end teachers offered lectures and written commentaries on the texts, but the principal pedagogical tool was still individual practice and repetition, interspaced with regular sessions in which the teacher would quiz students on difficult passages and incite them to work their way through them.[14]

In the light of this, the value medieval and early modern Japanese bugei instructors placed on kata should hardly be surprising. But the notion that "ritual formalism"—in which students imitate form without necessarily understanding content or rationale—can lead to deeper understanding and spontaneity of insight than rational instruction—in which the teacher attempts to articulate the general principles of a task and transmit these to students—is not entirely foreign to Western education either, as Victor Hori observes:

> As a graduate student in philosophy, I taught propositional logic to first- and second-year university students and noticed that the class divided into two groups, those who could solve the logic problems and those who could not. Those who could solve them started by memorizing the basic transformation formulae of propositional logic. . . . Having committed these formulae to memory, these students were thereby able to solve the logic problems because they could "just see" common factors in the equations and then cancel them out, or could "just see" logical equivalences. However, the other students, those who had not committed the transformation formulae to memory, were more or less mystified by the problems though many made serious attempts to "reason" their way through. . . . Those who had done the rote memory work had developed logical insight.[15]

Pattern practice in Japanese bugei also bears some resemblance to medieval Western methods of teaching painting and drawing, in which art students first spent years copying the works of old masters, learning to imitate them perfectly, before venturing on to original works of their own. Through this copying, they learned and absorbed the secrets and principles inherent in the masters' techniques, without consciously analyzing or extrapolating them. In like manner, kata are the "works" of a ryūha's current and past masters, the living embodiment of the school's teachings. Through their practice, a student makes these teachings a part of him and later passes them on to students of his own.

It is important, however, not to lose sight of the fact that kata are a means to mastery of a ryūha's kabala, or expressions of that kabala; they are not the kabala itself. Mastery of pattern practice is not the same as mastery of the art: A student's training *begins* with pattern practice, but it is not supposed to end there. Kata are not, for example, intended to be used as a kind of database mechanically applied to specific combat situations ("when the opponent attacks with technique 7-A, respond with countertechnique 7-A.1, unless he is left-handed, in which case..."). Rather, pattern practice is employed as a tool for teaching and learning the principles underlying the techniques that make up the kata. Once these principles have been absorbed, the tool is to be set aside.

Viewed, then, from the perspective of a student's lifetime, pattern practice is a temporary expedient in his training and development. The eventual goal is for the student to move beyond codified, technical applications to express the essential principles of the art in his own unique fashion, to transcend both the kata and the waza from which they are composed, just as art students moved beyond imitation and copying to produce works of their own.*

As he moves toward mastery of the ryūha's teachings, the bugei student's relationship with his school's kata evolves through three stages, expressed by some authorities as Preserve, Break, and Separate ("*mamoru, yabureru, hanareru,*" or "*shu-ha-ri*"). In the first stage he attempts to merge himself into the kata, to bury his individuality

---

*This concept is emphasized by many bugei ryūha in their choice of orthography for "kata." While most nonmartial traditional Japanese arts, such as *chanoyū*, *shoji*, or *ikebana*, use the character "型," most bugei schools write it with "刑" with the explanation that the former implies a rigidity and constraint inappropriate to martial training. The latter, it is argued, better represents the freedom to respond and change—albeit within a pattern—essential to success in combat.

within its confines. He is made to imitate the movements and postures of his teachers exactly, and is allowed no departure from the ordained pattern. When he has been molded to the point at which it is difficult for him to move or react in any fashion outside the framework of the kata, he is pushed on to the next stage, wherein he consciously seeks to break down this framework and step outside it. He experiments with variations on the patterns he has been taught, probing their limits and boundaries, and in the process sharpening and perfecting his grasp of the principles that underlie the forms. Only when he has accomplished this can he move on to the final stage, the stage of true mastery. Here he regains his individuality. Whereas previously he merged himself *into* the kata, he now emerges fused *with* the kabala of the ryūha. He moves freely, unrestricted by the framework of the kata, but his movements and instincts are wholly in harmony with those of the kata.[16]

Historical Problems and Criticisms of Kata and Pattern Practice

Pattern practice is a time-honored and, when properly conducted, an efficacious means of training and transmission of knowledge, but it is not without its pitfalls. It is easy to imagine that a methodology centered on imitation and rote memorization could readily degenerate into stagnation and empty formalism. The historical record indicates that this was already becoming a problem for bugei ryūha in Japan by the late seventeenth century.

Certificates of achievement and similar documents left by fifteenth- and sixteenth-century martial art masters suggest that kata had become the principal means of transmission by this time.[17] It was not, however, the only way in which warriors learned how to fight. Most samurai built on insights gleaned from pattern practice with experience in actual combat. This was, after all, the "Age of the Country at War," when participation in battles was both the goal and the motivation for martial training. A number of the most illustrious swordsmen of the age, moreover, including Tsukahara Bokuden, Kamiizumi Ise-no-kami, Miyamoto Musashi, Yagyū Muneyoshi, Yagyū Hyōgosuke, Itō Kagehisa, Morooka Ichiu, Okuyama Kyugasai, Hayashizaki Shigenobu, and Takeuchi Hisamori, are known to have traveled about the country seeking instruction and/or engaging in duels and sparring matches. This practice, known as *kaikoku shugyō, kaikoku jun'yū,* or *musha shugyō,* is

Plate 1. The main hall of the Kashima Grand Shrine (Kashima-machi, Ibaraki prefecture)

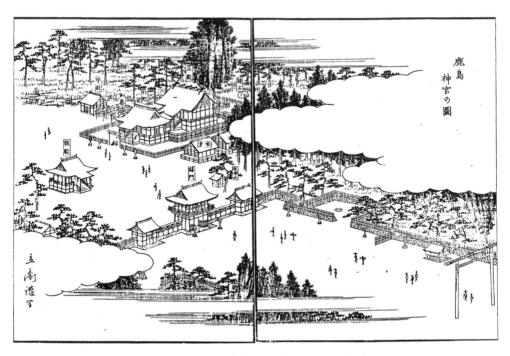

Plate 2. Nineteenth-century map of the Kashima Grand Shrine (source: *Tonegawa zushi*)

Plate 3. The grave of Matsumoto Bizen-no-kami Ki no Masamoto (Myōsenji, Shimizu City, Shizuoka prefecture)

Plate 4. The founders of the Japan Imperial Rule Association, ca. 1930. The figure standing on the *left* in the back row is Kunii Zen'ya, the eighteenth-generation headmaster of the Kashima-Shinryū. The first three figures seated in the front row *(from left to right)* are Imaizumi Teisuke, kokugaku scholar and founder of the Nihon Daigaku Imaiizumi Kenkyūjo; Ashizu Kōjirō, kokugaku scholar and hereditary attendant (gūji) of the Dazaifu Tenmangū Shrine; and Tōyama Mitsuru, well-known right-wing activist of the prewar era. The others are unidentified.

Plate 5. Kunii Zen'ya performing a *jūjutsu* technique during a demonstration at the Meiji Grand Shrine in the late 1920s

Plate 6. Seki Humitake performing in a demonstration at the Kashima Grand Shrine (June 12, 1994)

Plate 7. Kunii Zen'ya lecturing on Kashima-Shinryū history at his home, ca. 1960

Plate 8. Students at the Kunii training hall, ca. 1950. It was common at that time for students to begin training around the age of 10. The student on the right is Kunii Zen'ya's fourth son, Masakatsu.

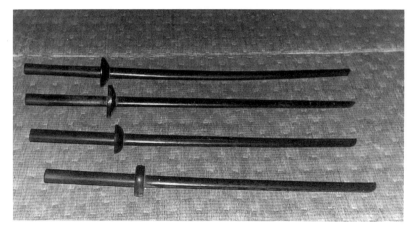

Plate 9. Wooden training swords in the collection of the Kunii family. Some of these are believed to have belonged to Tsukahara Bokuden.

Plate 10. Minamoto Yoshitsune receiving a scroll containing the secrets of swordsmanship from a tengū

Plate 11. Michael and the dragon, from Russian folklore (original painting by Andrey Isakoff). The connection of both dragons and divine flying spirits to martial affairs is not unique to Japan, as this legend illustrates. Interestingly, in this depiction, Michael holds his spear in the same manner as do Kashima-Shinryū practitioners.

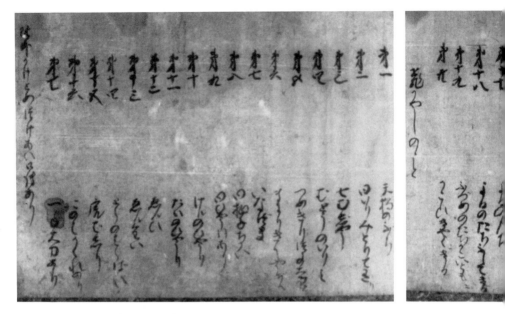

Plate 12. The *Tengu sho*

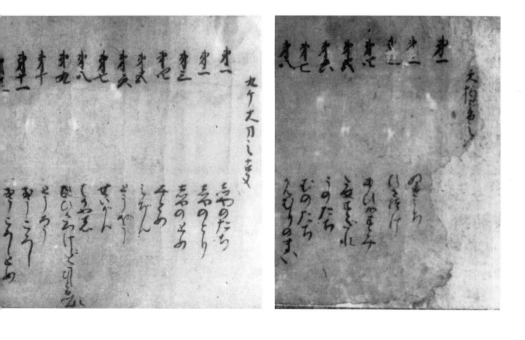

Plate 13. The *Kashima-Shinryū hyōhō denki*

Plate 14. The certificate given Seki Humitake by Kunii Zen'ya, acknowledging Seki's succession as the nineteenth headmaster of the Kashima-Shinryū (1)

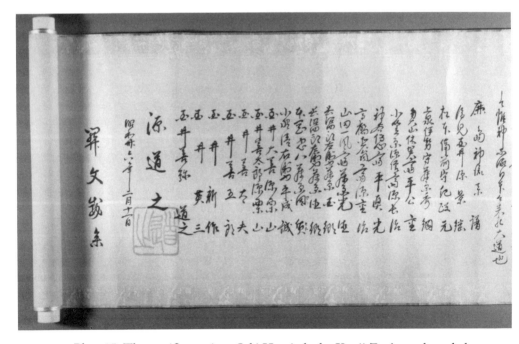

Plate 15. The certificate given Seki Humitake by Kunii Zen'ya, acknowledging Seki's succession as the nineteenth headmaster of the Kashima-Shinryū (2)

believed by many authorities to have been common among serious bugei students. Ordinarily, such students would begin their instruction with a teacher near their home, train with him until they had absorbed all they could, and then set out on the road, offering and accepting challenges from practitioners of other styles. Warriors defeated in such matches (if they survived unmaimed) often became the students of those who bested them.[18]

Training conditions altered considerably in the decades after the battle of Sekigahara. First, the new Tokugawa shogunate placed severe restrictions on the freedom of samurai to travel outside their own domains. Second, the teaching of martial art began to emerge as a profession. Adepts no longer divided their energies between training students and participation in war, as there were no longer wars in which to participate. Instead, they began to open training halls and devote themselves full time to instructing students, who paid fees for their training. And third, contests between practitioners from different schools (taryū-jiai) became frowned upon by both the government and many of the ryūha themselves.[19]

One result of these developments was a rapid proliferation of new ryūha, spurred at least in part by the disappearing need for "masters" to prove their skills in public combat.* A second was a tendency for ryūha, their kabala no longer subject to continual polishing and refinement through exposure to that of other schools, to become introverted in their training and outlook.

Under such conditions, kata came to assume an enlarged role in the teaching and learning process. For new generations of first students and then teachers who had never known combat, pattern practice became their only exposure to martial skills. As instructors slipped further and further away from battlefield and dueling experience, and as evaluation of student progress came to be based on performance in pattern practice alone, it became increasingly difficult to determine whether or not students—or even their teachers—actually understood the kata they were performing. In some

---

*Although government prohibitions on interschool contests did not eliminate the practice completely, they did provide a convenient excuse for any would-be instructor who wished to avoid such matches. Seki Humitake observes that a similar phenomenon occurred in the late twentieth century: In the early 1960s, when taryū-jiai were a common practice, there were only a handful of schools active in any public forum. Since the late 60s, when stricter Japanese government enforcement of its dueling laws put an end to taryū-jiai, the number of ryūha participating in demonstrations and the like has waxed appreciably.

schools, skill in pattern practice became an end in and of itself. Kata grew showier and more stylized, while trainees danced their way through them with little attempt to internalize anything but the outward form.

By the end of the seventeenth century, Ogyū Sorai and other self-styled experts on proper samurai behavior were already mourning the decline of the bugei and martial training. The warrior arts of ages past, they lamented, had degenerated into "flowery swordplay" *(kahō kenpō)* and gamesmanship. In the words of Fujita Tōko, an early nineteenth century commentator,

> Tests of arms with live blades ceased to be conducted. When this happened, the various houses founded their own schools and practiced only within their own ryūha. Thus . . . [training] came to be like children's play wherein one studied only kata; the arts of sword and spear could not but decline.[20]

It should be emphasized, however, that the potential problems inherent in pattern practice are just that: *potential* problems, not *inevitable* ones. Not all ryūha lapsed into kahō kenpō during the middle Tokugawa period. Some were able to keep their kata alive, practical, and in touch with their roots, their kabala in the hands of men who had genuinely mastered it. In this context Sorai seems to have drawn a distinction between the Toda-ryū and the Shintō-ryū on the one hand, and the Yagyū Shinkage-ryū and the Ittō-ryū on the other.[21] Nevertheless, a good many ryūha gradually reified methods and conventions they did not fully understand, and fossilized kata, passing on only the outward forms without fully comprehending the principles behind them. This danger may have been particularly acute for schools such as the Kashima-Shinryū under the Kunii family or the Yagyū Shinkage-ryū—in which the headship was restricted to a single family—as it was difficult to guarantee that each generation would produce a son equal to his ancestors in talent and diligence. Some schools appear to have avoided this potential pitfall more successfully than others, but in any event, by the end of the seventeenth century the shortcomings of pattern practice were provoking both commentary and responses.

In the early 1700s, several sword schools in Edo began experimenting with protective gear to allow their students to spar with one another at full speed and power without injury. This touched off a debate that continues to this day.

Proponents of sparring and the competitions that developed concomitantly argued that pattern practice alone cannot develop the seriousness of purpose, the courage, decisiveness, aggressiveness, and forbearance vital to true mastery of combat. Such skills, they said, can be fostered only by contesting with an equally serious opponent, not by dancing through kata. Pattern practice, moreover, forces students to pull their blows and slow them down, so they never develop their speed and striking power. Competition, it was argued, is also needed to teach students how to read and respond to an opponent who is actually trying to strike them.

Kata purists, on the other hand, retorted that competitive sparring does *not* produce the same state of mind as real combat and is not, therefore, any more realistic a method of training than pattern practice. Sparring also inevitably requires rules and modifications of equipment that move trainees even further away from the conditions of duels and/or the battlefield. Moreover, sparring distracts students from the mastery of the kata and encourages them to develop their own moves and techniques before they have fully absorbed those of the ryūha.

The controversy persists today, with little foreseeable prospect of resolution.[22] It is important for our purposes here to note that it represents a divergence in philosophy that transcends the label of "traditionalists versus reformers" sometimes applied to it. In the first place, the conflict is nearly 300 years old, and the "traditionalist" position only antedates the "reformist" one by a few decades. In the second, advocates of sparring maintain that their methodology is actually closer to that employed in Sengoku and early Tokugawa times than is kata-only training.* And in the third place, modern cognate martial arts schools—the true reformists—are divided over this issue: Jūdō relies exclusively on sparring to evaluate students, while aikidō tests only by means of kata, and kendō uses a combination of kata and sparring in its examinations.

In any event, one must be careful not to make too much of the quarrels surrounding pattern practice, for the disagreements are disputes of degree, not essence. All of the traditional ryūha that survive today utilize kata as their central form of training. None has abandoned it or subordinated it to other teaching techniques.

---

*Kamiizumi Ise-no-kami Hidetsuna is believed to have been the first famous swordsman to adopt the bamboo practice sword (*fukuro-shinai* or *hikihada*) in the late sixteenth century. Naganuma Shirōzaemon Kunisato, of the Jikishin-kageryū, is usually credited with introducing head and wrist protection in the 1710s.

The Kashima-Shinryū Kata

As the proverb *"Kōbō wa fude o erabazu"* ("The master calligrapher did not choose among his brushes")* suggests, a true bugei expert ought to be capable of handling weapons of almost any variety or quality. For the sake of expediency, however, Kashima-Shinryū training aims at mastering only a handful of the most practical weapons from the premodern samurai arsenal, and utilizes traditionally determined forms and sizes of these for practice.[23]

The sword serves as the core weapon of Kashima-Shinryū bujutsu; it is the first weapon students learn and becomes the point of departure for studying other arts. Sword training takes three forms: the use of the sword against opponents also armed with swords (kenjutsu), the use of the sword against other weapons (kenjutsu-tachiai), and the drawing and use of the sword against opponents who attack while one's own blade is still sheathed (battō-jutsu). Kashima-Shinryū students today learn 115 principal kata for the sword, grouped into twelve sets (seven sets of kenjutsu kata, four sets of kenjutsu-tachiai, and one set of thirty-two battō-jutsu kata), as well as several dozen variant and specialized kata taught only to advanced initiates.

Shortly after their introduction to the sword, the nucleus of the omote arts, students also begin training in jūjutsu, the core of the ura disciplines. Jūjutsu is primarily an art of fighting unarmed, but it also embraces the use of knives, iron fans, and other small weapons, as well as tasuki-dori or hōbaku-jutsu, the art of arresting and tying an opponent. Knife techniques include the use of the short sword *(wakizashi)* and daggers of various lengths. The iron fan *(tessen)* is a folding paper fan about 30 to 36 centimeters long. The outer ribs of the fan are made of the same type of tempered steel as a sword, and the paper is lacquered to strengthen it. Fans of this sort can be used folded to stab, strike, or pinch an opponent, or open to deflect rocks, darts, and other hand-thrown missiles. Under Kunii Zen'ya, Kashima-Shinryū jūjutsu was taught through 230-some kata, organized into six sets. The current headmaster has simplified and reorganized this curriculum into six sets totaling seventy-four principal kata, plus a few dozen special kata.

---

*The proverb literally refers to Kōbō Daishi, the posthumous name of Kūkai (744–835), a Buddhist priest of the Shingon sect. He was noted for his calligraphy and is thought to have invented the hiragana syllabary still used to write the Japanese language.

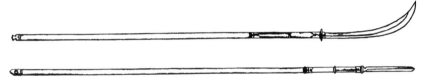

Figure 23. A medieval/early modern *naginata (top)* and a spear *(bottom)*

Once they have achieved sufficient proficiency in kenjutsu and jūjutsu, students move on to other weapons. The order and pace at which they are introduced to these other arts vary widely, depending on individual interest, aptitude, and training circumstances, but most initiates will eventually acquire at least some competence with naginata, straight spears, long and short staffs, *shuriken*, and *kusari-gama*.

The naginata (see figure 23) is a glaivelike weapon consisting of a long, sweeping blade mounted on an oval shaft. Designed initially for cutting the legs from under a horse or slashing at mounted antagonists, the weapon began as a battlefield armament for foot soldiers. It was especially popular during the late classical and early medieval periods among the *akusō* or *sōhei*, the "warrior monks" employed as hired muscle by the great Buddhist temple complexes in and around the capital.* In later medieval and early modern times, the naginata was superseded on the battlefield by the straight spear. Thereafter it was redesigned with a small, somewhat lighter blade and adopted by samurai women as their principal weapon for household defense. Twenty Kashima-Shinryū kata pit naginata against naginata, and fifteen more teach the use of the glaive against a swordsman.

Straight spears, or *yari*, versatile weapons readily wielded from horseback as well as on foot, replaced naginata as the principal battlefield pole arm during the late medieval period, and in fact became the favored weapon of the officer class. Matsumoto Bizen-no-kami Masamoto was renowned for his skill with the spear, and is credited

*"Warrior monks" is the name by which the sōhei are best known in English and is in any case less lubberly than the most common alternative, "monkish warriors." But both translations—and the Japanese originals, akusō and sōhei, as well—are misleading in that few if any of the members of these private fighting forces employed by temples had any direct involvement with the temples' religious orders. For more on sōhei, see Hirada Toshiharu, *Sōhei to bushi*; Hiyoski Shōichi, *Nihon sōhei kenkyū*; or Katsuno Ryūshin, *Sōhei*.

An excellent discussion of the naginata and its history appears in Ellis Amdur, "The Development and History of the Naginata."

with having invented a new version of the weapon with a cross-bladed head, called a *jūjiyari*. Samurai, whether mounted or on foot, normally chose spears 7 to 9 *shaku* (2.12 to 2.73 meters) long, but late medieval foot soldiers were sometimes deployed with *niken yari* of 3.64 meters or *sanken yari* of 5.45 meters.*

Many of the twenty kata for the 1.8-meter bō, or long staff, are nearly identical to kata for the spear or the naginata, but Kashima-Shinryū syllabi classify them with jūjutsu, as ura-waza, rather than with naginata-jutsu and sōjutsu, as omote-waza, principally because staffs are by design and tradition nonlethal, off-battlefield weapons. The ryūha teaches the jō, or short staff, both as a weapon for use against a sword and as a weapon to be defended against using the sword. Jōjutsu first entered the Kashima-Shinryū repertoire in this latter capacity, but Kunii Taizen later developed it as a discipline in its own right. In addition to ten kata for the 1.2-meter straight staff, three kata for the *yoseizue*, or curl-handled cane, have been included in the Kashima-Shinryū curriculum since the time of Kunii Zentarō, the thirteenth-generation shihanke.[24]

Two additional weapons also taught—albeit with decreasing frequency in recent years—are the shuriken and the kusari-gama. Shuriken are throwing darts of various forms used to attack opponents just outside of sword range. While westerners tend to associate shuriken with star-shaped devices, knife- or spike-shaped darts are more common among the classical bugei ryūha. A student adept in the use of shuriken of this sort should also be able to accurately throw anything from a short sword to chopsticks.

The kusari-gama is an odd sort of weapon developed during the late Muromachi period and consisting of a short-handled sickle attached to a long, weighted chain. Adepts use the chain to ensnare their opponent's weapons, legs, or neck and then draw them in where they can be cut with the sickle. Alternatively, the weight on the end of the chain can be used to strike and disable an opponent. Strictly speaking, the Kashima-Shinryū does not teach the use of the kusari-gama, but it does teach sword techniques for defending against the chain and sickle, making it necessary for students to be familiar with the ways in which the weapon may be used, and with its various strengths and weaknesses. Figure 24 depicts the practice kusari-gama used in Kashima-Shinryū training, which substitutes a rope of

---

*Niken yari and sanken yari refer to spears of two and three *ken*, respectively. One ken is equal to the distance between two pillars in a Japanese house—about 1.8 meters. A shaku is about one Imperial foot long.

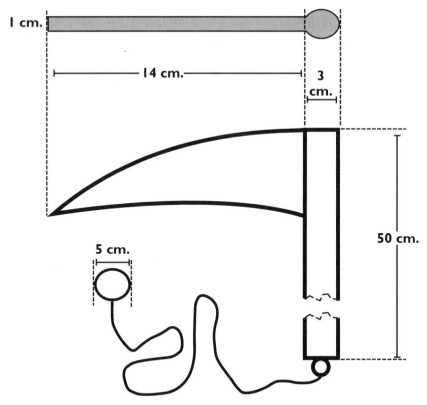

Figure 24. The Kashima-Shinryū practice *kusari-gama* (source: Seki, *Nihon budō no engen*, 38)

between 2.5 and 3.5 meters for the chain, and a stitched leather ball for the weight at the end. The sickle itself is made of wood.

Through all this, the Kashima-Shinryū claims to be unusual—perhaps even unique—in its conceptualization of kata training. Most traditional ryūha teach kata in a sequence that leads students along a path spiraling inward from the most mundane and superficial aspects of the art to the most important and profound. The innermost doctrines (*ōgi* or *okugi*) are carefully guarded secrets, imbedded in kata taught only to very advanced practitioners. The Kashima-Shinryū curriculum, however, effectively reverses the direction of this path, introducing students to all the cardinal elements of the ryūha's kabala at the outset of their training, with subsequent instruction serving only to clarify and elaborate on the earliest lessons.[25] Both the sum and the essence of Kashima-Shinryū doctrine are said to be fully realized in the first exercises a student learns: the Reiki-no-hō drill of jūjutsu and the Kihon-tachi series of kata for the sword. All other kata—for the sword, for other weapons, and for unarmed combat—are simply reiterations and alternative expressions for the same truths. Thus, while other schools limit access to their real art to a chosen few who have proven their capacity to receive it, the Kashima-Shinryū challenges initiates to improve their capacity by fully accessing lessons they have already received.

The special nature of the Kihon-tachi and the Reiki-no-hō makes them worth describing in detail, as representative illustrations of Kashima-Shinryū kata. "Kihon-tachi" literally means "basic sword strokes," but the five kata that comprise this series are more than just fundamentals broken out from more sophisticated sequences and applications. By the same token, they are also more than simple fighting techniques. The Kihon-tachi are at once fundamentals *and* practical applications. As such, while they are performed rhythmically, methodically, and precisely at greater than actual fighting distance and without concern for "authentic" speed, they are never executed by rote or in dancelike fashion, but always in a realistic frame of mind that anticipates the possibility of variations or unorthodox moves by the opponent.

Just as the whole of Kashima-Shinryū bugei are said to be found in the Kihon-tachi, the physical and physiological essence of all five kata is believed to be distilled from the first exercise in the series—the kesagiri. This fundamental cutting stroke draws its name from the *"kesa,"* a type of robe worn by Buddhist monks that leaves one shoulder bare. The kesagiri cuts diagonally, along approximately the same line as the edge of a kesa. All other Kashima-Shinryū techniques for the sword and for other weapons are described as simple variations—transformations—of the kesagiri; all unarmed techniques are explained as applications of the movements of the kesagiri without a weapon in one's hands.

To perform the kesagiri kata (illustrated in figure 25), the shitachi (the partner performing the technique for which the kata is named) and the uchitachi (the attacking partner) first face one other motionlessly, with their feet together and their swords pointed at each other's eyes. This posture, known as seigan, allows the uchitachi to set the proper practice distance. As a point of etiquette, the partners always orient themselves such that the shitachi will be moving toward the general direction of the Kashima Grand Shrine, and therefore demonstrating his art to Takemikazuchi-no-Mikoto. Both

Figure 25. *Kesagiri*

swordsmen grip their weapons firmly, but naturally, with the little fingers of their left hands overlapping the ends of the sword hilts and their right hands nearly touching the hand guards. This grip is thought to maximize the swordsmen's leverage on their weapons, as well as to prevent the hilt from becoming snared on loose sleeves or other items of clothing.

From seigan, the uchitachi steps backward with his left foot, simultaneously lowering his sword to the mugamae or otonashi-no-kamae posture, resting just above his right leg, with the tip pointed downward. His toes point outward at about 45 degrees, his front leg is bent, supporting about 70 percent of his body weight, and his rear leg is held straight. As the uchitachi assumes this posture, the shitachi moves with him, stepping forward with his right foot into the same mugamae posture. As they do this, both execute a "kiai of restoration" *(kangen no kiai)* by inhaling deeply as they make the sound "ya-a-a." When the kiai has resettled into the abdomen, they begin the technique.

The uchitachi takes another step backward, releasing the sword with his right hand and holding it in his left—about hip high—with the tip inclined slightly in and down. This posture is essentially an invitation for the shitachi to attack, and is sometimes accompanied by the command, *"sa kire!"* ("Okay, cut!"). If the uchitachi wishes, he can raise and extend his left arm a bit more so that his sword forms a target for the shitachi, about midway through and perpendicular to the path along which he will cut; this is seldom done, however, unless training with children. When he retreats, the uchitachi creates an opening into which the shitachi advances one step, simultaneously swinging his sword in a counterclockwise circle over his head. With the kiai, "ieh," the shitachi then cuts downward in a diagonal (kesagiri) path from the uchitachi's right shoulder to his left side (his blade passing a half meter or so in front of his partner). The movements of the shitachi's hands and feet must be coordinated so that the focal point of the cut is reached just as he settles into his new stance.

The uchitachi then transfers the sword to his right hand and retreats one more step, ending in a posture that is the mirror image of the previous one, with the sword angled downward to the left. Again the shitachi advances with him, swinging his sword up, around in a clockwise circle over his head, and downward, cutting diagonally from the uchitachi's left shoulder to his right side as he kiais, "tō." This left-to-right slicing action is called a reverse-kesa, or *gyaku-gesa*. The two partners then raise their swords back to the seigan position and hold this posture as they return to their starting locations.[26]

In addition to being the most fundamental, kesagiri is also perhaps the most subtle of all Kashima-Shinryū kata, for the level of interplay between the uchitachi and the shitachi is deceptive, not readily apparent to casual observers—and not always fully appreciated even by novice students practicing the exercise. Because the uchitachi performs no obvious attacks or counterattacks, one might easily assume that he serves only as a target for the shitachi's cuts, and that the shitachi could practice the exercise nearly as well alone as with a partner. Such an observation, however, misses the heart of the kata, wherein each partner fuses his movements to the other's. The two press and pull on each other, like a pair of magnets: As the uchitachi retreats, he draws the shitachi along, and as the shitachi advances, he pushes the uchitachi before him. When advanced initiates act as uchitachi for less experienced students, the uchitachi's timing tends to dominate—the uchitachi leads and guides his partner—but the higher objective is for the shitachi to take control. By stepping forward into mugamae, the shitachi presses on the uchitachi's space, forcing a reaction; the uchitachi counters simultaneously by withdrawing, while the shitachi responds *with* this action by stepping forward and performing the cut. A similar relationship between the uchitachi and the shitachi underlies all Kashima-Shinryū kata.

If the interaction of the two partners appears deceptively simple in kesagiri, in the second kata of the series, *ashibarai-ukebune* (illustrated in figure 26), it looks elusively complex. "Ashibarai" means "leg sweep," in this case a horizontal attack by the uchitachi to the shitachi's knees or shins; "ukebune," or "floating boat," refers to both the tactic the shitachi employs to stop this attack—during which the shitachi's blade rides over and clings to the uchitachi's like a boat floating on the water—and to the mental posture that makes the technique possible (see the discussion of the Axiom of the Moon on the Water in chapter 3). As in the previous technique, both partners begin from the seigan posture and kiai "ya-a-a" as they step from this into mugamae. With the kiai, "ieh," the uchitachi advances slightly with his lead (right) foot and, moving his hands in a counterclockwise circle on his right, strikes diagonally at the shitachi's neck or temple. As this happens, the shitachi swings the tip of his weapon in a counterclockwise circle on his right, and with the kiai, "ieh,"

Figure 26. *Ashibarai-ukebune*

(1)

(2)

(3)

(4)

(5)

(6)

(7)

(8)

(9)

cuts down and into his opponent's attack, stopping it dead. Both swordsmen are now momentarily stalemated (kirimusubi).

With the kiai, "ya," the uchitachi bends forward and to his right, and launches a sweeping cut (ashibarai) at the shitachi's right (forward) shin. At that instant, the shitachi bends forward from the hips and without raising his hands, swings the tip of the sword in a tight, counterclockwise circle to strike down the attacking sword as he kiais, "ieh." At this point the hilt of his sword should be just ahead and to the right of his lead (right) leg, and his blade should be perpendicular to the uchitachi's.

The instant the uchitachi's sword becomes "dead," the shitachi shifts his hands to his left and brings the tip of his sword to the uchitachi's wrist. He is now in control of his opponent's movements. The uchitachi attempts to recover by pulling his hands and sword upward to his left and retreating. The shitachi follows the movements of his opponent's hands with the tip of his sword, slowly and smoothly— moving like a "feverish snake"—bringing his weapon across the uchitachi's body into the kurai-tachi position, pushing with the tip of the weapon at the uchitachi's face, and chasing his retreating adversary. Throughout this sequence, the shitachi maintains control of the encounter. From the moment in which his leg sweep is blocked, the uchitachi can only attempt to escape, but because he is *reacting* to the shitachi, the latter remains always one move ahead. The uchitachi, moving backward, cannot outrun his advancing opponent, nor can he successfully counterattack with the shitachi's sword tip poised mere centimeters from his face. He will, then, eventually be forced to submit. As a practical application—in actual combat—the technique would end here, with the shitachi having checkmated his opponent and forced his surrender. As a kata, however, ashibarai-ukebune finishes with one additional, ritual sequence of actions: After two steps the uchitachi halts, acknowledging his defeat. He then retreats one step further, at the same time lowering his weapon and holding it in his left hand in the same manner as he did to receive kesagiri, once again inviting the shitachi to cut. The shitachi kiais, "tō," steps forward, and performs a kesagiri. Both then return to seigan, and walk back to their starting positions.[27]

Kiriwari, or "cut divider" (illustrated in figure 27), forms the third kata in the series. Once again both partners begin from the seigan position and step from there into mugamae, the uchitachi stepping backward, the shitachi stepping forward. The uchitachi then kiais, "ieh," and attempts a vertical cut (mentachi) at the shitachi's forehead.

Figure 27. *Kiriwari*

The shitachi similarly swings the tip of his weapon in a counter-clockwise circle to meet the uchitachi's sword at an angle. At the instant in which he makes contact with his opponent's blade, he kiais, "ieh," and twists his own blade sharply, cutting straight down through the uchitachi's forehead and face and continuing to his navel. When kiriwari is performed properly, the opponent's sword literally bounces off the centerline of the body (*shin*) when it meets the shitachi's blade. As in ashibarai-ukebune, the kata ends with the uchitachi retreating one step, lowering his sword, and inviting the shitachi to cut. The shitachi then steps forward and performs a kesa-giri, with the kiai, "tō."

The shitachi's technique in the fourth kata, *warizuki*, or "dividing thrust," is nearly identical to the technique he performs in kiriwari, except that he uses it against a lower, stabbing attack from the uchitachi. As before, both swordsmen begin in seigan and then step into mugamae. From mugamae, the uchitachi kiais, "ieh," and thrusts his sword at the shitachi's solar plexus. The shitachi swings his sword around in a circle to meet the incoming thrust. At the moment of contact, he rotates his wrists with a powerful snap, twisting his sword a half turn on its axis. If he does this properly, the uchitachi's sword will be batted away by the back of his (the shitachi's) own blade. If he advances slightly from his lead foot as he does this, he will be able to thrust simultaneously at the uchitachi's solar plexus. As before, the uchitachi then steps back and the shitachi finishes the technique with a kesagiri. This sequence of moves is illustrated in figure 28.[28]

In the final kata in the series, kurai-tachi, or "occupying sword" (illustrated in figure 29), the preliminary actions and the uchitachi's attack are the same as in the kiriwari kata. This time, however, the shitachi counters by swinging the tip of his sword in a counterclockwise circle on his right, cutting downward and into the uchitachi's strike to stop it cold; as he does this he kiais, "ieh." This technique is a simple modification of a kesagiri. The shitachi's hips, arms, hands, and sword move exactly as they would to perform a kesagiri, the only difference being that the shitachi does not uncock his wrists to let his sword sweep forward. Instead, he continues to hold the weapon perpendicular to his forearms so that, rather than slashing across the uchitachi's torso, his sword wedges into the uchitachi's attack, pushing it aside and ending with the tip resting a few centimeters in front and to the right of the uchitachi's left eye. As do the other kata, kurai-tachi concludes with the uchitachi stepping back to allow the shitachi to step forward and perform a kesagiri.[29]

Ryūha tradition traces the origins of the core exercise of Kashima-Shinryū jūjutsu, Reiki-no-hō ("method for emanating ki"), to the test of strength between Takemikazuchi-no-Mikoto and Tateminakata-no-Kami, deity of Shuwa, for mastery of the land (see chapter 2). Reiki-no-hō teaches initiates how to concentrate their physical and psychospiritual energy in their hands and fingertips, and how to neutralize an opponent's strength. Students learn to concentrate all their strength at a single point, while keeping the rest of their bodies completely relaxed.

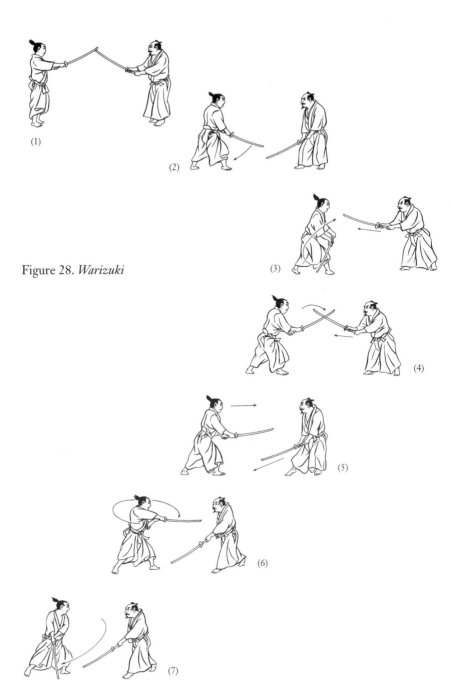

(1)

(2)

Figure 28. *Warizuki*

(3)

(4)

(5)

(6)

(7)

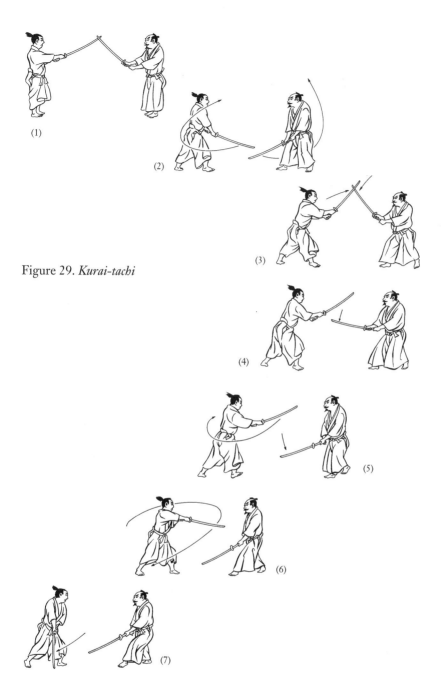

(1)

(2)

(3)

Figure 29. *Kurai-tachi*

(4)

(5)

(6)

(7)

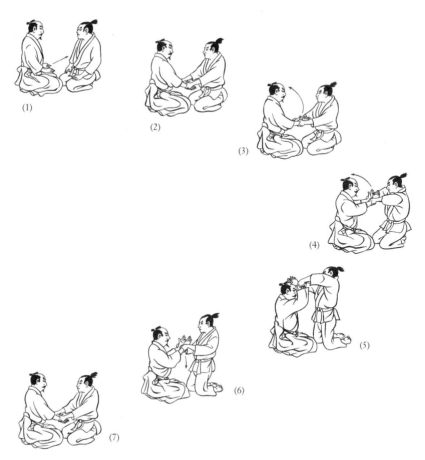

Figure 30. *Reiki-no-hō*

To perform Reiki-no-hō, the ukete and shite (the "receiving" and "performing" partners, respectively) kneel *(seiza)* facing one other, with their knees spread slightly—about two fist widths for men, and one for women. The ukete firmly and suddenly takes hold of the shite's wrists. In that instant, the shite spreads his fingers as widely as possible and, with the kiai, "ieh," allows his strength to flow into his fingertips. Next, he raises his hands until they are level with his shoulders, circling around the ukete's grip and applying his strength smoothly, with the sensation of the hands being drawn upward by the power emanating from his fingertips (see figure 30).

The effect of the shite's action is to decrease the area of his wrist grasped by the ukete. Because the total power that the ukete can apply is a function of the area held and the strength applied per unit of area, the ukete soon finds himself literally "losing his grip." In order to minimize this loss of grip and power, he must attempt, in so far as possible, to maintain the same angle of contact between his hands and the shite's wrists. He does this by spreading his elbows and rising on his knees in pace with the shite's movements. There is, however, a point beyond which this tactic ceases to be effective. As the shite continues to raise his hands to his shoulders, the ukete's grip is broken and his power neutralized. The partners then relax and return to their beginning positions. After repeating this exercise ten times, the ukete and shite switch roles; in a typical practice session, students perform three to five sets of Reiki-no-hō in each role.[30]

In Reiki-no-hō, as in kesagiri, casual observers—and even beginning students—might conclude that the ukete's principal function is to facilitate the shite's practice; but once again such an impression misses much of what is occurring in the kata, for both roles contribute essential lessons to an initiate's development. The shite learns to channel his own power and to evade the power applied against him by the ukete. If he does not do this properly, a skillful ukete can easily hold his arms immobile, and prevent him from completing the kata. At the same time, the ukete learns to focus his strength, to apply power within flexibility, and to flow with his opponent's movements. First and foremost, this means that he must hold fast to the shite's wrists with his hands while keeping the rest of his arms and body loose and relaxed. Failure to do this opens him to attack by the shite; if, for example, he attempts to hold the shite down by locking his arms and bringing his body weight to bear, the shite can use his (the ukete's) rigid arms as levers by which to push or throw him to the ground. In this respect Reiki-no-hō might be judged to be the highest form of kata, in that it simultaneously facilitates equally valuable practice for both partners.

The Kihon-tachi are performed with *bokutō*, or wooden swords, the oldest form of training weapons employed by traditional bugei ryūha. Formidable weapons in their own right, bokutō were originally adopted not for safety but for economy, wooden swords being less expensive to replace than steel ones. Bokutō are made in a wide variety of sizes, shapes, and weights, from any of several kinds of wood; nearly every ryūha has a traditional design of its own to suit the demands of its own particular training practices. Because Kashima-Shinryū kata, unlike those of modern kendō and most other classical schools, involve actually striking the training weapons

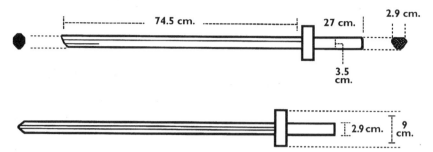

Figure 31. The Kashima-Shinryū *bokutō* (source: Seki, *Nihon budō no engen*, 36)

against one another at full speed and power, Kashima-Shinryū
bokutō are somewhat heavier than the standard wooden swords used
by kendō practitioners, but not as heavy as the deliberately oversized
"practice swing swords" *(suburitō)* utilized by some classical kenjutsu
schools to develop arm strength and striking power. A light bokutō
would break too readily in Kashima-Shinryū training, while too
heavy a weapon is thought to impair speed, slowing a trainee's movements down to the point where his timing would be adversely
affected. For similar reasons, the Kashima-Shinryū weapon is
straight, and features a heavy wooden hand guard (see figure 31 and
plate 9). While most other types of bokutō are curved slightly to better simulate a real blade, Kashima-Shinryū thinking holds that the
curvature of a Japanese sword is not so great that practicing with a
straight weapon will cause problems adjusting to a live blade; on the
other hand, a straight bokutō, in which the wood grain runs uninter-
rupted lengthwise from tip to hilt, resists breaking much better than
a curved one.

Kashima-Shinryū wooden swords, as well as the wooden training
weapons used to practice naginata, spear, and staff kata, are made
from Japanese white oak. Experiments in recent years with other
woods, such as American oaks or hickory, have failed to produce an
acceptable substitute; thus far, alternative materials have proved to
be either too heavy, too brittle, or too soft. Practice naginata are 7
shaku (2.12 meters) in length and are cut in the same shape as a real
glaive; practice spears are usually the same length and feature a
leather protective pad, about six centimeters in diameter, at the tip.

Training with hard, wooden weapons is thought to be essential in
order for the student to develop te-no-uchi, sōtai-no-shime (see
chapter 3), and other aspects of the application of power. Accordingly,
initiates of all levels use bokutō to practice the Kihon-tachi, which

are normally performed at greater than actual fighting range, and advanced initiates regularly use the wooden weapons for all sword kata. But for safety purposes, beginners and even senior students most often perform kenjutsu kata other than the Kihon-tachi with a leather-wrapped, split bamboo practice weapon called a *fukuro-shinai*.

This ancestor of the more familiar bamboo swords used in modern kendō competitions has a history almost as long as the Kashima-Shinryū itself. The first documented usage of this device was in 1563 by Kamiizumi Ise-no-kami Hidetsugu—who is generally credited with having invented it—and his student Hikida Bungorō Kagekane in their duels with Yagyū Muneyoshi.[31] While bamboo practice weapons enabled swordsmen to train and compete more realistically, with fewer injuries, they did not catch on immediately. Many ryūha continued to use only live blades or bokutō, viewing bamboo swords as tools for cowards or weaklings. Miyamoto Musashi, for example, belittled the value of training with *shinai* in the opening passages of the fourth chapter of his *Gorin no sho*. Little by little, however, one school after another began to see the advantages of the new training tool; by mid-Tokugawa times it was in widespread usage. Tominaga Kengo has identified over a dozen different orthographies applied to bamboo practice swords during the Edo period. Nearly all, however, were pronounced either "shinai" or "shinae"; the former would seem to have initially been a corruption of the latter, which apparently derives from the verb *"naeru,"* meaning "to droop"—precisely what a flexible shinai does when it strikes something.[32]

The Kashima-Shinryū fukuro-shinai (see figure 32), being completely covered in leather, looks markedly different from the modern kendō shinai, which has leather coverings at the tip and the hilt only. This leather casing serves to protect against splinters and against cuts caused by the sharp edges of the bamboo, for Kashima-Shinryū practitioners utilize no protective gear of the sort worn by kendō players. The fukuro-shinai is also considerably shorter and heavier than the kendō weapon, more closely approximating the length and weight of a real sword.

Texts and Written Transmission

Mastering the bugei is, as we have observed, mostly a suprarational process in which understanding derives principally from experience rather than explanation. Thus pattern practice, through which students intuitively assimilate their ryūha's kabala, forms the core of

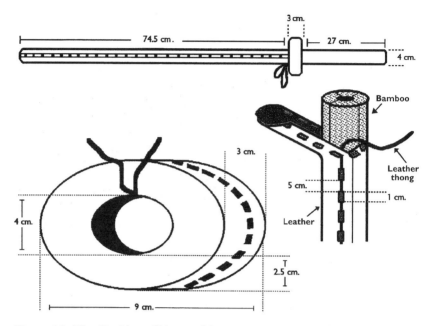

Figure 32. The Kashima-Shinryū *fukuro-shinai* (source: Seki, *Nihon budō no engen*,36–37)

traditional bugei training. But while it is true that being overly conscious of the principles underlying one's actions can hamper performance, it is also true that identifying those principles and then reabsorbing them in intuitive application can enhance that same performance. The dichotomy between intellection and intuition, which I so carefully drew in the opening section of this chapter, should not, therefore, be pushed too far. The distinction between the two processes amounts, as David Slawson asserts, to the difference between the activities of artists on the one hand and art historians and theorists on the other. But extracting and explicating the essential principles of an art is more than just the central task of the scholar; it is also the means by which the artist can reach the highest levels of mastery.[33] Integrating theory with practice—after a student has undergone sufficient training—can and does add up to more than the sum of its parts. In the bugei as in other arts, advanced initiates can therefore also benefit from direct, rational contemplation of the principles and concepts behind the kata they have learned.

In medieval Japan, the notion that theory and practice are mutually interdependent components of the path to true understanding formed a fundamental premise of esoteric Buddhism, which stressed that while exclusive study of doctrine without grounding in practice was an empty and useless exercise, ritual practice not founded on doctrinal understanding can lead only to a degeneration of the teachings and never to mastery of them.[34] Thus medieval bugei masters, many of whom were intimately involved in esoteric Buddhist practices, recognized the value of theory as well and—even as they developed pattern practice as their chief instructional methodology—augmented it with verbal teachings, or *kuden*. By the sixteenth century, some instructors were collecting their kuden into written documents called *kudensho*.

Early kudensho were terse indeed; most commonly they featured only lists *(mokuroku)* of important principles or techniques. Usually constructed in scroll form but occasionally in bound volumes, these were given to graduates from the master's tutelage, as or along with diplomas *(inka, discussed further below)* and were intended as aids to the graduates in recalling what they had already learned, rather than as teaching devices per se. But some late medieval experts also penned instructional poems and verses expounding on key concepts and even technical points for the benefit of their students and posterity. Tsukahara Bokuden's *Ikunsho* (also called *Bokuden hyakushu*) is among the earliest extant collections of this genre of pedagogical literature, which became quite fashionable in later years—John Rogers estimates there to be about a hundred known anthologies of such poetry, most of it dating from the Edo period. In early modern and modern times, instructional verses were augmented with an enormous body of prose commentary on the martial arts as ryūha headmasters, other bugei adepts, Confucian scholars, and even Buddhist priests produced tens of thousands of theoretical essays, ranging from paragraph-long annotations to book-length works. Rogers estimates that some one hundred thousand premodern documents concerning the bugei exist today in public and private collections. Among the best known are Yagyū Munenori's *Heihō kaden sho* ("Book of Family Traditions on the Military Arts"), Takuan Sōhō's *Fudōchi shinmyō roku* ("Record of Immovable Wisdom and Divine Mystery"), Miyamoto Musashi's *Gorin no sho* ("Book of Five Elements") and Issai Chozan's *Neko no myōjutsu* ("The Cat's Uncanny Skill").[35]

The Kashima-Shinryū has a rich legacy of written texts stretching from medieval inka and kudensho to early modern commentaries and instructional verses, to modern poems, articles, essays,

and books. Originals of some of these documents have been passed
from headmaster to headmaster for as many as nineteen generations; others have been copied in whole or in part and given to successful students in recognition of skills and knowledge mastered.
Sadly, many of the original documents were lost in 1965 when Kunii
Zen'ya inadvertently left them in a taxi en route to a television stu-
dio where he was to display and discuss them. Fortunately, however, copies and photographs of each of the lost texts survive for
contemporary analysis.

The oldest of these is the *Tengu sho*, purportedly the work of the
ryūha founder, Matsumoto Bizen-no-kami himself. This document
is named for the *tengu*—creatures of Japanese folklore most commonly described as humanlike, but with wings and beaks or very
long noses, and sometimes with birds' claws instead of human feet
and/or hands. Tengu inhabit the peaks and valleys of Japan's mountains and draw power from the kami nature (see chapter 3) that permeates such places; they are gifted swordsmen, having hands or
claws ideally formed for holding weapons but for little else, and
from time to time will pass on this semidivine skill to deserving
mortals. Minamoto Yoshitsune, the hero of the twelfth-century
Gempei War, was said to have been one such mortal, slipping away
at night from the temple at which he spent his youth to train with
the mountain spirits, and eventually receiving from them a scroll
revealing all the secrets of the martial arts (this event is illustrated
in plate 10). One legend relates that Yoshitsune later offered this
scroll to Takemikazuchi-no-Mikoto at the Kashima Grand Shrine,
and that it was this same document that the deity presented to
Matsumoto in the dream that inspired his formulation of the
Kashima-Shinryū.

The original text is a scroll, 17.5 centimeters long, mounted on
an old brocade and wound around a copper-colored cherry spindle
(see plate 12).[36] Like many Sengoku era kudensho produced in eastern Japan, it bears no signature or date, but is endorsed by a blood
seal embossed over the last entry. Damage to the lower part of the
beginning of the scroll obscures the characters following the heading *"tengu sho no"* ("of the Tengu's Writings") and completely hides
the name of the first technique. Sufficient traces remain of the heading to allow experts at the Shiryō hensanjo (Historiographical
Institute) of the University of Tokyo to conclude that the missing
word was probably *"shidai"* ("as follows" or "details of"), but physical evidence offers no clue to the identity of the lost technique;

extrapolation from the order and content of the rest of the scroll, however, suggests it must have been harai-tachi ("exorcising sword"—see chapter 2).[37]

In the *Tengu sho*, Matsumoto outlines the kabala of his art. As is typical of kudensho, explanation here is implicit rather than overt; the text is simply a list of forty-five terms and phrases, arranged in three groups and recorded in the native Japanese (hiragana) syllabary with minimal use of Chinese characters. The document is, moreover, uneven—almost erratic by modern conventions—in its coverage; included terms range from diffuse philosophical constructs to general principles governing sets of tactics to individual techniques, while the terminology itself ranges from the poetic and opaque ("beaded screen" or "dance of the tengu") to the mundane and concrete ("ensnaring and cutting upward" or "entering inside the strike to overturn it"). Literally translated (with the original Japanese terms in parentheses), the entire document reads as follows:

[DETAILS OF] THE TENGU'S WRITINGS

1) [Exorcising Sword] *(harai-tachi)*
2) Extracted Strike *(nukiuchi)*
3) Clinging to a Gourd *(hisatsuke)*
4) Reciprocal Mist *(aigasumi)*
5) Beaded Screen *(tamasudare)*
6) Sword of Being *(u no tachi)*
7) Sword of Nothingness *(mu no tachi)*
8) Dancing on the Crown *(kanmuri no mai)*

The Ninefold Sword *(ku ga tachi no koto)**

1) Oblique Sword *(sha no tachi)*
2) Capturing with a Diagonal *(sha no tori)*
3) Stopping with a Diagonal *(sha no tome)*
4) Conceding *(mitome)*
5) Pulverizing *(mijin)*
6) Crossing Poles *(tōbō)*
7) Directly at the Eyes *(seigan)*

*Kamiizumi Ise-no-kami used the term "*ku ga tachi*" ("the ninefold sword" or "the nine techniques") to label a list of nine tactics and principles he gathered from various ryūha. In the *Tengu sho*, however, this heading introduces a subsection consisting of twenty concepts, which suggests that the orthography Matsumoto used should not be taken in its literal meaning. It may be a pun on homophones meaning "meritorious techniques" or "eternal techniques."

8) Repeated Spirals *(hakayashi)**
9) Clinging to a Gourd and Bewitching a Person *(hisatsuke ni itashi hito enmi)*†
10) Garden Lantern *(tōrō)*
11) Intermediate Killing *(chūkoroshi)*
12) Stop by Intermediate Killing *(chūkoroshi tome)*
13) Dragon Sword *(ryūken)*
14) Cutting Opposite with a Dragon Sword *(ryūken gyaku ni kiru)*
15) Entering Opposite with a Dragon Sword *(ryūken gyaku ni iru)*
16) Extended Dragon Sword *(nobe no ryūken)*
17) Night Sword *(yoru no tachi)*
18) Night Sword Crouching and Cutting *(yoru no tachi fushite kiru)*
19) Enveloping and Striking without Closing Range *(fuzume no tachi kakoi tomo ni)*
20) Ensnaring and Cutting Upward *(kakoi gyaku ni kiru)*

On Flying Dragons (Hiryū no koto)

1) Dance of the Tengu *(tengu no mai)*
2) Entering Inside the Strike to Overturn It *(uchiirimi torite-gaeshi)*
3) Seven Warriors *(shichi musha)*
4) Entering without a Sword *(mutō no irimi)*
5) The Importance of Rising Slowly *(tsumekiritsu no daiji)*
6) Cautions on Turning and Changing Cuts *(mawari kiri yōjin)*
7) Thunderbolt *(inazuma)*
8) Discerning Inner Rhythms *(uchibyōshi chikai)*
9) The Omote and Ura of Inner Rhythm *(uchibyōshi hyōri)*
10) The Omote and Ura of the Sword *(ken no hyōri)*
11) The Omote and Ura of the Body *(tai no hyōri)*
12) Flying Swallow *(enbi)*
13) Circling Monkey *(enkai)*
14) The Bird's Roost *(tori no harabai)*
15) Running Tiger *(torabashiri)*
16) Hidden by the Tree Leaves *(ko no hagakure ari)*
17) Sword of Oneness *(ichi no tachi ari)*‡

Outside these principles are select, related verbal instructions *(kono hoka kaketome tsukeai kuden ari)*

---

*"Ha" here is an alternative reading for the character *tomoe* (巴), which denotes the spiral design found decorating Japanese shrines. "Kayashi" means to return or to repeat.

†"Hito enmi" is a pun meaning "to bewitch a person," or "one circle."

‡Ichi-no-tachi is discussed in detail in chapter 2.

Clearly a document of this sort represents little more than poetic gibberish to the uninitiated. In fact most kudensho are virtually impossible to interpret from the outside—which is, of course, exactly what the authors intended. The desire to provide students with memoranda that would jog their memories and/or further their studies needed always to be balanced with the danger of providing other potential readers with too apprehensible a textbook to one's method and secrets. In virtually every instance, bugei masters weighted this balance in favor of the latter, with the result that *Tengu sho* and other kudensho become utterly meaningless without the context provided by the oral traditions—the received interpretations—of the particular ryūha to which the text belongs. Even so armed, historians stand on less than unassailable ground as they attempt to reconstruct early texts, for oral traditions are obviously subject to evolution and revision. Moreover, as in the case of kata, ryūha tend to cloak the reality of any such change in a mythos of uncompromised bequeathal extending back to the founder, making it virtually impossible to assess the degree to which received interpretations of texts accurately reflect those intended by the authors. At the same time, insofar as ryūha like the Kashima-Shinryū look upon their task as the preservation of a flame rather than a vessel, unease over possible discrepancies between current and original meanings is largely misplaced. For as the schools themselves view it, constancy to the spirit of the founder's (and subsequent masters') teachings is far more material than maintenance of the form.

While ryūha insiders look to kudensho as catalogs of the techniques and concepts the authors considered most central to their arts, cultural historians can draw more piquant insights from the vocabulary of the texts and its relationship to the specific principles it encodes. For those seeking not to walk the martial path but simply to understand it, the engrossing questions to be asked of texts like the *Tengu sho* are, in other words, not *what* they actually say, but *how* they say it.

Some of the terminology of the *Tengu sho* makes the context of the techniques alluded to obvious, even if the specifics are left unstated. "Night Sword," for example, clearly refers to a tactic or tactics for taking an opponent unaware in darkness, but the actual technique must be explained through verbal instruction. Similarly, "Entering without a Sword" can only refer to the application of unarmed (jūjutsu) techniques against an armed opponent. Other entries, such as "Night Sword Crouching and Cutting," make even the details of the technique relatively clear.

Many terms employ expressions with particular meanings as bugei jargon, and are thus far less opaque to followers even of other ryūha than they seem to complete outsiders. *"Kasumi,"* "mist" in ordinary usage, for instance, refers in bugei terminology to an upward cutting motion, running diagonally from right to left, or to a kamae that is the mirror image of the kurai-tachi kamae (see chapter 3, figures 11 and 13); "Reciprocal Mist" (aigasumi), then, points to a series of techniques for handling a situation in which one finds oneself momentarily deadlocked with an opponent in either kasumi kamae or midway through a kasumi cut. In like manner, "Dragon Sword" (ryūken) was Matsumoto's term for *hiryūken* ("flying dragon sword"). In generic bugei usage, "hiryūken" denotes an upward diagonal cut, from left to right; in the particular application alluded to here, a swordsman draws out an opponent's attack and then avoids it by slipping to the right, dropping the tip of his blade, and then slicing upward through the opponent's wrists as he steps.

Some of the terminology, while not standardized jargon, is directly evocative. "Clinging to a Gourd," for example, means to control an opponent's weapon by clinging tenaciously to it with one's own. Physically, this is very much like trying to hold a gourd, or any buoyant object, underwater. The gourd will tend to roll out from under whatever point at which one applies pressure upon it; containing it demands continual adjustments to the direction of the pressure. Similarly, opponents will attempt to roll around one's blocks or parries; to contain this, one must freely and continuously respond with the movements. *Tōrō* in ordinary usage is a Japanese-style garden lamp; Matsumoto borrowed this image to express the principle behind the naori-taichūken technique described in chapter 3—to convey the idea that in applying this technique, one's body has no front, back, or sides, but reaches freely in all directions, like the light from the lantern.

But the imagery of some entries is rather cryptic—even if one knows the concepts it is agreed to represent. "Beaded Screen" (tamasudare) is a puzzling example of this phenomenon. A *sudare* is a hanging screen or blind composed of reeds or narrow pieces of bamboo laced together with cord; a tamasudare, in normal usage, is a sudare decorated with beads or jewels. According to received canon, Matsumoto used the term to recall the concept of ongoing motion contained within the principles of Motion and Stillness as One and Origination and Manifestation as One. Specifically, tama-sudare points to the use of spiral patterns in all movements within techniques. A sudare is rolled for storage or to open areas it is otherwise used to screen; viewed from the end when rolled, the slats form an irregular spiral with no apparent beginning or end. This may have been the allusion that Matsumoto was attempting to draw.

In any event, while *Tengu sho* was the first kudensho in the Kashima-Shinryū tradition, it was not the last. Kamiizumi Ise-no-kami Hidetsugu and most of the other figures in the shihanke lineage also left behind numerous similar documents. Within the sōke lineage, ryūha teachings were consolidated—at least by modern times—into the *Kunii-ke sōden Kashima-Shinryū menkyo kaiden mokuroku* and the *Kunii-ke sōden Kashima-Shinryū jūjutsu menkyo kaiden mokuroku*. The latter has been superseded by a reorganized jūjutsu curriculum under the current headmaster, but the former is still handed, one part at a time, to students as they advance through the ranks.

Prose essays constitute another form of pedagogical text passed on within the Kashima-Shinryū. Premodern examples of these include three histories of headmasters and/or the Kunii family: the *Kashima-Shinryū hyōhō denki* (see plate 13), a section of the *Kunii-ke sōden Kashima-Shinryū menkyo kaiden mokuroku*, and the *Kunii-ke keizu*. But inasmuch as these texts treat the ryūha's history rather than its doctrines, I will not discuss them here. All three are, however, translated in full in appendix 1.

There is, however, one surviving example of a premodern essay on Kashima-Shinryū dogma, the *Ryū no maki*, or "Dragon's Scroll."[38] Appended to the *Kashima-Shinryū hyōhō denki*, the *Ryū no maki* is one of the oldest extant documents from the shihanke lineage, although its precise origins and authorship remain uncertain.[39] The Jikishin Kageryū, which branched off from the *Kashima-Shinryū* shihanke line after Naganuma Kunisato in the early eighteenth century, maintains a nearly identical text, suggesting that the essay was probably written sometime before this split, while internal references to political ideas and social customs mark it as a product of the mid-seventeenth century or later. In any event, the inscription on the Jikishin-kageryū document identifies it as having been given to one Hagiwara Rennosuke by the twelfth-generation Jikishin-kageryū headmaster, Hayata Shintarō Fujiwara Yoshinori, on "an auspicious day in spring in the fifteenth year of Tenpō [1844]," indicating that the *Ryū no maki* dates back at least this far.* The text reads as follows:

*There is, however, a problem with the date as recorded on the Jikishin-kageryū version of the *Ryū no maki*: The Tenpō era ran from 1830 to 1843—fourteen years—there was no fifteenth year of Tenpō. This could simply be an error

The master said, "When I reflect on the qualities of the sword, [I see that] victory and defeat are found in the dual essence of Yin and Yang. Yin triumphs, and Yang retreats; or Yang triumphs, and Yin retreats. That which we call Yin and Yang are in origin a single essence. If you nurture that one essence, you will become a great man as a matter of course. The composure and dignity that exploits this aspiration is to be found in the awareness that gives vitality to living things. As the breath circulates concurrently through the tricalorium,* there is no transition or change among the gods of Heaven and Earth and the phenomena; there is only adaptation to the enemy.

"Truly, one who is able to live thus is strong and brave, but is he to be feared? The warrior's path is the origin of power and majesty. Therefore the Emperor has his jeweled sword and his court flourishes. The Son of Heaven keeps this sword with him always: When he goes forth he carries it before him, when he stops he lays it in a safe place. Even when he sleeps he does not part from it. The moral

---

resulting from ignorance on the part of Hayata as to the change in era names, or it could indicate that the document was a later compilation. The Jikishin-kageryū document is reproduced in *Nihon budō taikei* 3:306–307 and, with extensive annotation, in Ishigaki, 139–144.

The *Ōgi*, the statement of guiding principles or paramount teachings of the Kashima-Shinryū, reproduced in the conclusion to chapter 3, follows the *Ryū no maki* on the same scroll as the latter text and the *Hyōhō denki*. There is no way to conclusively determine its age or authorship, but it is written in the same style as the *Ryū no maki* and *Hyōhō denki*, suggesting that it too is of middle to late Tokugawa period origin.

*"Tricalorium" translates *sanshō* (*sanchiao* in Mandarin), one of the twelve orbs or viscera (Japanese: *zō*, Mandarin: *tsang*) conceptualized in traditional Chinese medical theory. Modern usage associates zō/tsang with the internal organs identified in Western-style anatomy, but traditional Chinese physicians conceived of them primarily in physiological—not anatomical—terms. Thus the twelve orbs define functions or effective relations of sometimes imprecisely located bodily substrata, rather than organs in the modern Western sense. The sanshō (also translated as the *"orbis tricalorii,"* the "three heated spaces," the "triple heater," or the "three caloria"), which has no equivalent in Western anatomy, regulates the circulation of all bodily fluids and energies—including the ki—through itself and all the other orbs. See Manfred Porkert, 158–162. A somewhat simplified overview of Chinese medical theory appears in Yuasa, *The Body, Self-Cultivation, and Ki-Energy,* 99–128.

Kashima-Shinryū lore identifies three anatomical points key to the functioning of the tricalorium: the *tanchū* ("upper calorium"; found at the intersection of a line connecting the nipples with the centerline of the body), the *chūkan* ("middle calorium"; also called the *suigetsu*—the solar plexus), and the *inkō* ("lower calorium"; also called the *seika tanden*, located on the body's centerline, about two centimeters below the navel). These three points (which are also referred to as the sanshō) are frequently used as targets for attack.

power of the jeweled sword flows outward and the people are liberated. How much more so should the warrior keep his sword by him night and day, revering it like a god and guarding it as he would guard his own body and mind?

"The tools of the warrior's art are claws and teeth. When one looks into the heart of things, one sees that those with teeth bite, those with claws grab, and those with stingers sting. This is not taught; it is the law of nature. The birds and the beasts are like this; what then do they who travel the path of man use? [T]eeth and claws—the sword. Men wear swords. Although they proclaim this to be distinct from using them, there are none who are completely outside the need for military readiness. Those who fail to learn this are ignorant of combat.* Even if such persons wear swords, they would have difficulty using them to fight. Would they then seek to understand?

"The old martial arts are called *hyōhō*. Warriors were made to enter this path and practice incessantly. The men of old revered the teachings of their art as they revered Heaven and Earth. They polished their spirit like the bright sun and moon."

Respectfully related, without omission.†

To one's lord one offers loyalty; to one's friends, trust and courtesy. [Knowledge of this] is [a part of] man's innate consciousness, his innermost heart. It is called Illustrious Virtue.‡

Illustrious Virtue gives rise to strength and formidability. This is called True Courage. Wisdom cannot be separated from ignorance. By nurturing this insight, the discipline of the warrior's profession is

---

*Literally, "are severed from interchange with drawn blades." Judging from the statements that precede and follow this passage, the author seems to be making a point here about the folly of seeking to avoid violence by pretending it does not exist. Confrontation and strife, he argues, are a part of the order of nature, an order from which man is not exempt.

Ishigaki (143–144) interprets the passage more prosaically, seeing it as a neo-Confucian-inspired criticism of middle Tokugawa period samurai who carried swords but could not use them. For Ishigaki, in other words, the source of the author's displeasure was the existence of persons claiming to be warriors but unable to fight.

†The Jikishin Kageryū version of this document ends here. This could indicate that the remaining passages in the Kashima-Shinryū text were added at a later date—possibly by a different author—or it could be the result of a copying error that left passages out of the Jikishin Kageryū version. The present sentence, however, suggests the former case.

‡A neo-Confucian concept especially important in the philosophy of Wang Yang Ming (Ō Yōmei, 1472–1529). It refers to the original, innate substance of the human mind, which includes an a priori knowledge of all proper virtue and of right and wrong. For Wang Yang Ming, the core of human moral activity was to be found in the effort to allow this innate knowledge to manifest itself. Some scholars prefer to translate the term as "clear consciousness."

amplified. In Japan, the realm of the sun, the martial way and the way of letters are said to be one, yet the many emphasize only the military arts. Therefore the discipline and study of our school fosters this True Courage.

Separate truth from falsehood, the shallow from the deep. Avoid discord and thus venerate kindness. Study the Five Virtues.* Through this government is made pure. Do not be lax in this even for an instant; tirelessly forge and temper your efforts toward enlightenment and accumulate merit. In ancient days it was said, "A jewel without polishing will never become useful; a man without study will never know the Way."

Respectfully related, without omission.

In addition to catalogs of techniques and principles, chronicles of the sōke and shihanke lineages, and philosophical treatises, successive Kashima-Shinryū masters have also left behind hundreds of instructional verses, or *kyūri no uta*. As I noted at the beginning of this chapter, poetry was among the earliest written tools adopted by bugei adepts to express the concepts underlying their art—Kamiizumi Ise-no-kami was, in fact, one of the pioneers of this genre. In more recent years, Kunii Zen'ya became particularly enamored with instructional verse and produced dozens of them, mostly in the classical "short verse" *(tanka)* format of thirty-one syllables. The examples that follow are representative of the genre as a whole, and have been rendered into English in the most literal way possible in order to minimize the amount of meaning lost in translation.[40]

Hitotsu!	The way of the sword:
Ken no michi	Kill not, be killed not, hesitate not;
Kiru na kiraru na okusuru na	Go forth! Return not;
Ikeyo modoru na	The way is focused
Michi wa hitosuji	*[Kashima-Shinryū kaiden mokuroku]*
Hitotsu!	The way of the sword:
Ken no michi	Toil at technique!
Waza o tsutomete	Spontaneously be apart from technique!
Onozukara	In this all the more is there technique
Waza o hanarete	[ibid.]
Waza ni koso are	

*A Confucian concept, the Five Virtues *(gojō)* consist of Justice, Politeness, Wisdom, Fidelity, and Benevolence.

Hitotsu!
Tachimukau
Yaiba no shita wa
Jigoku nare
Fumikonde miyo
Gokuraku mo ari*

Beneath the confronted sword is
    hell;
Step in!
There is also paradise
[ibid.]

Hitotsu!
Tate to mise
Yoko kiru kyo tachi
Nan no sono
Shin utsu tachi ni
Kachi wa aru nari

Appearing vertical
Cutting horizontally
Oh how much is there victory in
    the sword striking at the core!
[ibid.]

Hitotsu!
Sukui kiri kaesu
Sha no tachi
Ichi monji yaburu wa
Kashima ichi no tachi nari

Scooping, return the cut—
The diagonal cut,
Horizontal and straight, that thwarts
Is Kashima's ichi-no-tachi
[Kashima-Shinryū sōke mokuroku]

Hitotsu!
Tate yoko ya naname
Tsuki tachi-tai atari
Shin utsu tachi ni
Kachi wa aru nari

Vertical, horizontal, and diagonal
Thrust, collision of bodies and
    collision of swords;
Strike the core! In that sword
There is victory
[ibid.]

Hitotsu!
Deru to mite
Okori uchi kuru
Sono tokoro
Tai o hinarite
Sono ichi de ute

Seeming to emerge the first strike
    comes
In that instant open the body!
In that spot strike!
[ibid.]

Hitotsu!
Kachi to iu wa sen sen sen ni
Go no agete
Mata sen sen ni sengo sengo to

Victory is to initiate, lead, and change;
If countered,
It is still to initiate, respond, and change
[Kashima-Shinryū shihanke mokuroku]

---

*"Gokuraku" (極楽, "paradise") is utilized here in the same meaning as "gokui" (極意, "inner secrets").

Hitotsu!   Left and right, after and before
Migi-hidari   Are one
Ato mo saki mo   Heaven, earth and the myriad things:
Ichi shite   Same roots, one sky
Tenchi manbutsu   [ibid]
Dōkon ikkū

Hitotsu!   The empty strike cuts
Tate to mise   Upright or recumbent;
Yoko kiru kyotachi   Strike to the core!
Nan no sono shin utsu tachi ni   In this there is victory
Kachi wa aru nari   *[Kashima-Shinryū kaiden mokuroku]*

Hitotsu!   In writing; by mouth transmitted
Kaki watashi   Words in one's everyday heart;
Kuchi ni tsutauru   To hold these is true discipline
Koto no ha no   *[Kashima-Shinryū shihanke mokuroku]*
Tsune no kokoro ni
Motsu wa tanren

Hitotsu!   Mt. Tsukuba leaves and space;
Tsukuba yama   A ponderous mountain thickly grown
Ha ya ma   and yet
Shige yama   Spontaneously protecting
Shigeredomo   The silent Moon
Onozukara moru   *[Kunii ke densho]*
Shizugaya no tsuki

Hitotsu!   The hands like [the character] "ha";
Te wa "ha" no ji   The feet like [the letter] "so":
Ashi wa "so" no ji ni   Step thus and see!
fukonde miyo   In "ha" and "so"
"Ha" no ji "so" no ji ni   There is victory
Kachi wa aru nari   [Kunii Zen'ya]

Hitotsu!   Blustering wind that
Fuki kitaru kaze o   Blows and sweeps the willows
Yanagi to fuki harai ite ni   Ride it!
Norite zo   There is victory
Kachi wa aru nari   [ibid.]

Hitotsu!	The sovereign's path all the more
Sumeragi no michi koso	Truly precious and noble
Ge ni mo tōtokere	Were the teachings of one's far-
Tōtsumi oya no oshie	away parents
Nariseba	[ibid.]

Hitotsu!	The gods' guidance receiving
Ōkami no gohyōshi ukete	For one's lord take harai tachi
Kimi ga tame harai tachi tori	The journey to Kashima*
Kashima tatsu nari	[ibid.]

Hitotsu!	This body offer up to one's lord
Kono mi oba	A catalpa bow, a journey with no
Kimi ni sashigeshi	return
Azusa yumi	Here too it is pleasant
Kaeranu tabi mo	[ibid.]
Nao tanoshikere	

Hitotsu!	In motion to startle the Heavens
Hasshite wa ten o odorokasu	In stillness to startle the earth
Gyoshite wa chi o ugokasu	Truly this is shinbu
Hikkyō kore shin	For what should we lament the world?
Izukun zo konchū o nagekan ya	For the enlightened one who follows
Taigo kaigen shite tenji o kyōjuseba	the way of Heaven
Jūō keirin onozukara fukuchū ni ari	Perfect skill is spontaneously in the belly
	[ibid.]

Meditation and the Integration of Body, Mind, and Spirit

Students begin study of the traditional bugei with pattern practice, through which they intuitively absorb their ryūha's techniques and doctrines and acquire the physical skills necessary to implement them. Later, their teachers augment the lessons of the kata with verbal and written illuminations of the underlying principles. But while pattern practice and intellection are sufficient to lead students to technical virtuosity, that technical virtuosity—even at levels approaching perfection—still falls short of true mastery of the art of combat. For a warrior, unlike an athlete, cannot afford slumps, or off days, or even off moments. He cannot allow his performance to be compromised by fear, excitement, fatigue, or even by illness,

---

*This is a pun on "Kashima no tachi," "the sword of Kashima." See chapter 1.

injury, or intoxication. A single instant of imperfection can cost him his life and/or the success of his mission. True mastery of the warrior arts, therefore, must include the ability to perform at one's peak at any time, in any place, and under any circumstances.

To do this, one must be able to reach beyond the limitations normally imposed by one's body or mind, to tap into the deeper potential of what might be termed the *spirit.* Thus, very advanced students undertake a third form of training: meditation and exercises for realizing the complete integration of mental, physical, and spiritual power.

As I have observed repeatedly, warriors were already adopting methods of developing more than just neuromuscular skills and tactical savvy by late medieval times. With this step, then, the bugei became a vehicle not just to expertise in combat, but to a wider cultivation of the self—the same goal embraced by medieval religious ascetics. During the Tokugawa period the roles of motivation and process gradually reversed, and martial training came to be seen as a *means* of self-cultivation, rather than as simply an incentive for it. The bugei thereby took on a whole new identity as an elaborate form of nonreligious asceticism.

Modern observers often associate ascetic practices like meditation with mental or spiritual—as opposed to corporeal—exercise. But the medieval and early modern Japanese worldview—formed at the nexus and by the interplay of Buddhist, neo-Confucian, indigenous (Shintō) and other cosmologies—conceptualized body, mind, and spirit not as separable entities but as interpenetrating features of a single, integrated whole. In Japanese usage, "mind" (*shin* or *kokoro*) denotes the seat of both the intellect and the passions (the mind and heart of ordinary English usage), and is homologous to the spirit (*rei* or *seishin*). The body (*karada* or *shintai*) relates to the mind/heart/spirit as the omote and ura of the self.

For the bugei adept, one of the most important results of meditation training is to eliminate any perception of separation between body, mind, and spirit, which, in turn, is believed to liberate hitherto undiscovered energies and powers. Yuasa Yasao observes that humans in ordinary states of consciousness experience bodily sensations, such as pain or sensory perceptions, as being different in kind from those they label as mental states, such as thinking, imagination, and emotion. While the latter appear indigenous to the mind and the former seem to arise externally, in truth all sensations, including those we categorize as physical, are nothing more than states of mind; even "physical" sensations derive from mental calculations processing sensory input, which is why we can be fooled into experiencing pain in amputated limbs, or dry ice as hot to the touch. Meditation focuses one's consciousness inward, closing off sensory input and quieting down the "external" sensations. In so doing, it guides practitioners past the apparent dichotomy of mental and physical sensations and alerts them to the power of the mind. The mind and body cease to seem distinct. By accomplishing this state, which medieval Zen Buddhists expressed as "oneness of mind and body" *(shinshin ichinyo)* or "congealing of body and mind" *(shinshin gyōnen)*, bugei masters claim to enhance their general sense of well-being, their "physical" performance of specific tasks, and their ability to interact with other living beings.[41]

In modern psychological terms, meditation is a means of suppressing the conscious mind in order to activate and control the subconscious and the energy latent within it. In the ordinary waking state one's consciousness fixes on external objects and responses to them. Meditation exercises suspend or severely limit outside stimuli and direct the mind inward, to weaken the functioning of the conscious mind and allow the energy of the subconscious, ordinarily suppressed, to surface. In sleep this energy manifests itself as images in dreams; meditation aims to achieve this same state of freed mental energy while awake. Meditation training, in other words, fosters voluntary access to the subconscious and control of the functions—such as the emotions—that arise within it.[42]

Any tampering with the subconscious, however, carries with it a certain amount of attendant risk. Yuasa compares the meditative process to the use of vaccinations to control disease: By tapping into the energies of the subconscious, students can actually induce artificial neuroses which they may not be able to control on their own. An experienced guide or teacher is therefore needed to carefully monitor a student's psychological state and guide him past any internal demons released by the training. For this reason training alone can be dangerous, and Kashima-Shinryū lore advises against it.[43]

Kashima-Shinryū meditation exercises are adapted from the purification (chinkonhō) rituals conducted at the Kashima Grand Shrine, which seem to borrow from two sources. They combine practices adopted from esoteric Buddhism to focus the conscious mind and reach beyond it with breathing techniques and other exercises originating in Sino-Japanese medical theory and the Taoist ascetic tradition to cultivate and discipline the psychophysical life force known as ki or reiki.[44] Although these source traditions differ significantly in their immediate purposes and underlying doctrinal frameworks, the forms and content of the meditation exercises they prescribe overlap at many points and are entirely compatible. In fact, the Shugendō practices of Japanese mountain ascetics, which as I noted in chapter 2 were also an important influence on medieval and early modern bugei adepts, similarly amalgamate rituals and exercises from both sources.

Taoist ascetics focus their efforts on cultivating and renewing the "three rivers" (in Mandarin, *sanhe*; *sanka* in Japanese), or sources of power that flow through all living things: spirit (*shen*; *shin* in Japanese), procreational force (*ching*; *sei* in Japanese), and most importantly, vital force (*ch'i*; *ki* or *reiki* in Japanese). These currents are believed to weaken under the conditions of everyday life and so must be renewed through rituals in which adepts visualize and call upon various deities to reestablish contact with their bodily coordinates. Such rituals are accompanied by breathing and other exercises, the taking of certain elixirs, the use of talismans and charms, massage, esoteric sexual practices and abstinence from certain foods.[45]

Modern (Western) medicine has not yet been able to come to terms with the ki and its physiological functions; while the effects of this vital force can be detected empirically, the mechanism responsible for those effects still lies beyond current scientific explanation. Traditional Sino-Japanese medical theory posits that it flows through the body along twelve regular and eight irregular circuits or meridians that connect the head and the extremities to the various organs of the body. Although this meridian system corresponds to no vessel network recognizable to modern anatomy, Chinese physiologists mapped it in detail and identified some 350 points at which the ki tends to concentrate and which can be used for therapeutic (acupuncture, acupressure, and moxa cautery) or martial (attack point) purposes. Ki is, as we noted in chapter 3, closely associated with the breath—in fact the same Chinese ideograph used to write "ki/ch'i" is also used for "air" or "breath"—and flows in and through the body, interacting between the body and the external world in much the same way the breath does.[46]

Ki is also closely intertwined with the mind and spirit. Yuasa relates it to the domain of the subconscious, describing it as a function apprehended intuitively, a sensation of power arising from the perceptions we have of our own bodies (*shintai kankaku* or *zenshin naibu kankaku*). Ki is, therefore, best conceptualized as a phenomenon of the mind and body—of spirit and matter—as a whole. Accordingly, Yuasa views the meridian system that describes its movement and function as a mediating system transcending the borders of physiology and depth psychology.[47]

In any case, ki cannot be perceived by the ordinary consciousness; perception becomes possible only through specialized mind-body training. Taoist ascetics, traditional Sino-Japanese physicians, bugei adepts, and others who wish to learn to control and manipulate ki first learn to do so through breathing and mind-focusing exercises. The ki moves with the breath, and when it moves, it affects the activities of the mind. Thus the rhythms of breathing can be used to focus and nurture the ki, and through this to stabilize and still the mind. Meditation training is said to change the function of ki, latent in the mind-body, transforming and sublimating it to energy of a more spiritually purified state.[48] Through this adepts seek to liberate an ethereal, creative force that can be used to prolong their own lives, treat afflictions and diseases, strike at enemies, sense an opponent's movements and intentions, neutralize an adversary's blows, and dozens of other practical and sublime applications.[49]

Esoteric *(mikkyō)* Buddhism, introduced to Japan in the early ninth century by Kūkai (posthumously known as Kōbō Daishi; see footnote on page 120), maintains that all things of the world are manifestations of an underlying Buddha-nature, embodiments of the universal self that constitutes reality. The individual self is therefore an image of the universal self, and all beings have the complete Buddha-nature within them. Mikkyō meditation and related exercises, then, aim at revealing or realizing the Buddha-nature from within and without the self through concentrated activity of body, mind, and speech. Because, mikkyō adherents believe, the all-pervading activities of the Buddha's body, speech, and mind are reflected in the individual, one can become Buddha by uniting the activities of one's own body, speech, and mind with those of the Buddha. The body is brought into harmony with the Buddha-body through prescribed hand gestures or movements of the whole body (mudra), the taste of certain herbs, the smell of certain incense, the manipulation of ritual implements, and the contemplation of certain forms of art. Speech is shaped by reciting prescribed invocations (mantra or *shingon*) and chants. Mind training involves visualization of deities and symbolic forms, colors, and movements.[50]

Exoteric Buddhist meditation, such as that practiced by adherents of Zen, seeks a state of "no mind, no thought" *(munen musō)*, a void state in which the body and mind cast off all activity and all thought, and which negates all awareness of the self and the world. Esoteric Buddhism, however, views this as merely a preliminary stage that the practitioner must pass through en route to a greater awareness that affirms the self and all that exists. Rather than focusing on a passive state of "no mind, no thought," mikkyō meditation cultivates positive activity within the mind, using dozens of visualization rituals—some common, some rarely performed—all performed in conjunction with postures and vocalizations, and all based on the process of mutual empowerment *(kaji)* between the practitioner and some Buddha, deity, or saint that serves as the object of the meditation. This process, termed *"nyūga ganyū"* ("entering the self and self-entering"), involves the power of the object deity flowing into the initiate, at the same time that the initiate's power flows into the deity. In general, the practitioner first visualizes the object inside himself—absorbing it in such a way that the object becomes the subject—and then visualizes the object expanding until it envelops first himself and eventually the entire universe, making the object absorb the subject and all that the subject can experience. In conjunction with such visualization techniques, esoteric Buddhism designates certain locations on the body as points of spiritual concentration *(seishin shūchū ichi)* on which to project the symbolic images. Most often these are the heart, forehead, throat, and crown of the head, but there are many variations. The points are used differently in different practices.[51]

Neither the Kashima-Shinryū nor most other bugei ryūha are direct expressions or outgrowths of esoteric Buddhism; but many schools, including the Kashima-Shinryū, have borrowed heavily from the mikkyō tradition. It is important, therefore, not to lose sight of the fact that while the bugei purport to lead ultimately to goals similar to those of Buddhism—enlightenment and transcendence of worldly cares—they seek those goals, or at least they originally sought them, for an independent reason: to achieve proficiency in combat. And because of this, bugei adepts pursue the worldly, tangible benefits of meditation and related exercises as eagerly as the sublime objectives.

Visualization and expansion exercises, for example, have several practical applications in terms of martial art. In the case of archery and the use of other missile weapons, such as shuriken or the rowing knives, the warrior expands the target and places himself within it before releasing the arrow or throwing the missile. Thus because—

at the moment of release—there is no place that is *not* the target, the arrow or missile cannot miss its mark.* Similarly, swordsmen and other hand-to-hand fighters envision absorbing their opponents into themselves, so that their own movements become part of and control the movements of the opponents.

One of the most interesting intersections of the bugei with esoteric Buddhist doctrine serves to create an additional level of meaning for kata training by drawing out an important implication of the monistic traditional Japanese worldview in which the Kashima-Shinryū and other budō traditions developed. Mikkyō cosmologists conclude that if the eternally self-existing being of Truth pervades all phenomena, omnipresent in all levels of existence, then enlightenment must be perceptible through symbolic elements, such as certain Sanskrit syllables, mantric chants, and, most importantly to bugei students, certain postures and movements. Viewed in this light, pattern practice in the bugei can also be seen as a kind of mudric exercise, a form of spiritual cultivation in and of itself, either within or without the specific context of esoteric Buddhism.

Kashima-Shinryū doctrine, for example, does not conceptualize the world in specifically Buddhist terms, but it does assert that each and every movement in each and every Kashima-Shinryū kata fully embodies each of the Fivefold Laws, which are in turn expressions of the fundamental rhythms of the universe. When, therefore, initiates perform the movements of the kata properly, they harmonize with these primordial rhythms in much the same way that esoteric Buddhist practitioners harmonize their postures and gestures with those of the Buddha-body. Thus, Kashima-Shinryū masters maintain, the study of bujutsu through pattern practice alone should be

---

*The medieval religious and historical scholar Kitabatake Chikafusa (1293–1354) used almost exactly the same words in a passage in which he was attempting to explain the differences between esoteric (Shingon) Buddhism and the other (exoteric) schools of Buddhism, using the metaphor of weaponry:

The Master [Kūkai/Kōbō Daishi] said, "To play with the sharp sword of the One Mind is the exoteric teaching; to swing the adamantine mace of the Three Mysteries is the esoteric teaching." . . . Attempting to strike the center of the target when shooting a bow is the practice of the manifold [exoteric] schools; the conviction of our [esoteric] creed is that—East, West, South, North, along the four diagonals, up or down—there is no place that is not the target and that one makes the arrow by releasing the mind of enlightenment.

This passage appears in *Shingon naishōgi*, 230. My thanks to William Bodiford for calling it to my attention.

sufficient to guide students to "realization and understanding of the fundamental principles of the Universe."*

Nevertheless, advanced Kashima-Shinryū initiates normally augment their pattern practice with meditation training. Usually this involves visualization exercises utilizing Takemikazuchi-no-Mikoto as the object of the meditation, but this choice of methodology is one of convenience, based on the historical circumstances tying the ryūha to the Kashima Grand Shrine, not one of pedagogical or theological necessity. Trainees with deep religious convictions are free to follow the meditation forms of their own faiths, or to substitute other deities with whom they have formed strong bonds for Takemikazuchi-no-Mikoto as the object of the visualization exercises.† In fact students who experience difficulties with the methodology described below are directed to pursue exercises taken directly from esoteric Buddhism, such as "moon disk contemplation" (gachirinkan).52

Students begin by regulating their breathing, first lying down and then kneeling (seiza) or seated in a chair. Correct breathing, called abdominal, or *tanden* breathing, involves inhaling deeply— flexing the diaphragm, rather than expanding the upper chest— drawing the breath into the *seika tanden* (centered on a point located about 5 centimeters below and 3 centimeters to the interior of the navel), collecting the breath in the abdomen, and then releasing it slowly and rhythmically. The students are taught to inhale through their noses, but to imagine themselves drawing the air in through their heels, and then to exhale quietly through their mouths. The proper rhythm is sometimes termed "breathing in sevens," because

---

*The late Donn Draeger (*Classical Budo*, 52–61) also eluded to the metaphysical qualities bugei practitioners ascribe to pattern practice, when he described kata as "physical *kōan*." In this he seems to have had the right general idea, but to have been led by exaggerated perceptions of the influence of Zen on traditional warriors to explain it in terms of the wrong mechanism, drawn from a less directly related form of Buddhism.

†Yuasa Yasuo (20–21) offers an interesting secular explanation for phenomena of Japanese religious visions that accords well with contemporary Kashima-Shinryū thinking on the matter. For Yuasa, Japanese deities of all sorts have their origins in the human mind. They cannot be derived from ordinary sensible experience of the external world, and must, therefore, begin as an "autonomous power existing latently in the unconscious." When these powers are raised to consciousness, we perceive them as entities existing independently of the consciousness. When, furthermore, the images produced by the subconscious are idealized, they take the forms of deities, which are in fact "perfected stages of the ideal human spirit." Meditation focuses the consciousness on these idealized images and allows the adept to tap into the power and energies of the subconscious.

the practitioners inhale for a count of seven, retain the breath for a count of seven, and then release it for a count of seven. Students practice this exercise daily for about ten minutes a session until they are able to perform it completely without strain.

Once they have learned to control their breathing, initiates progress to visualization and ki-cultivation exercises. For the former, the initiates kneel in seiza or sit in a straight-backed Western-style chair, with their fingertips resting together on their lower abdomens, the left fingers folded around the right and the thumbtips just meeting. In this posture, the arms form a circle around the chest and abdomen, and the fingers encircle the seika tanden. Quietly "breathing in sevens," the initiate visualizes embracing a round mirror, symbolizing the boundary between the three-dimensional world of ordinary perception and the higher dimensional plane of the deities (advanced practitioners may take this exercise one step further, envisioning the mirror as reflecting Takemikazuchi-no-Mikoto in human form). Initiates who find this first step difficult are sometimes instructed to use a lighted candle as an aid in focusing their concentration, and to gradually transfer this flame to within themselves. When the image is clear and unstrained, the initiate expands it gradually in stages until it embraces first himself and then the entire universe. When the mirror can be expanded no further, the initiate slowly contracts it back to its original size, and then lets the image go.

Kashima-Shinryū adepts also utilize breathing and visualization exercises to cultivate and discipline the flow of their ki. Breathing as described above, students envision their breath—and with it, their ki—pooling in their lower abdomens. By contracting the anus upward and forward, the students form the seika tanden area into a ball, and prevent the ki from escaping. With practice, they are taught, they will begin to feel the ki rotating in the seika tanden and circulating through the ring formed by the arms, causing a burning, tingling, or vibrating sensation in the hands. At this stage, say Kashima-Shinryū masters, the students should be able to manipulate their ki in martial applications, fusing it with *(ittaika)* or overlaying it on *(noseru)* ordinary muscular strength to dramatically enhance their power. The most important exercise linking ki-cultivation practice with bujutsu application is Reiki-no-hō (pp. 131–135). To reach beyond this to still higher levels of spiritual and ki development, some very advanced initiates engage in the practice of "sun-vision contemplation" *(nissōkan)*, in which the practitioner stands facing the rising or newly risen sun, absorbing its energy and visualizing a spiritual union with it, in the manner of the esoteric Buddhist nyūga-ganyū meditation techniques discussed earlier.[53]

* * *

Teachers of the bugei and other traditional Japanese arts have long employed the notion of michi—a way or path—as a metaphor for the process students follow in their quests to master their disciplines. But the metaphor is in many respects misleading, for bugei students do not traverse a single, predetermined route to a singular terminus. Instead, they walk along a complex network of branching and intersecting roads, some leading nowhere, others to divergent havens, and still others converging toward a common destination, with each student following a unique route. A closer-fitting (albeit anachronistic) allegory might therefore liken bugei training and transmission to studying a computerized, hypertext document: Each student begins in the same place and each will eventually learn as much as he wishes and is able from the process, but the course of study is almost infinitely customizable. In any case, a skillful and attentive guide (or author-programmer in the hypertext analogy) is crucial to ensure that the student does not stray onto routes he is not yet ready to explore and to push him into new areas when he is.

The Ōgi, the statement of purpose with which I concluded the previous chapter, instructs that the Kashima-Shinryū training regimen "first prepares the body, at the midpoint cultivates heartfelt human relationships, and arrives ultimately at realization and understanding of the fundamental principles of the Universe." Accordingly, the Kashima-Shinryū's approach to self-cultivation emphasizes entering the mind and spirit through the body—training the spirit by training the body. But neither the Ōgi's schema of physical, moral, and metaphysical self-cultivation, nor the one I have outlined in this chapter (kata, theoretical instruction, and meditation), should be taken to indicate successive phases of training.

Both schema outline levels or spheres of development, spheres that interpenetrate as initiates bring into play additional aspects of their whole selves. A bugei student's involvement in each sphere is ongoing. He does not move from training the body to training the mind to training the spirit; he adds theoretical contemplation and then meditation to kata training, and embraces the moral and metaphysical implications of his art, as he becomes prepared to do so—after he has laid the groundwork necessary for entrance to the additional spheres.

Epilogue

The Sword and only the Sword raised the worthier . . . to power
upon the ruins of impotent savagery; and she carried in her
train . . . the arts and the sciences which humanize mankind.
—SIR RICHARD F. BURTON

The perfection of art is to conceal art.
—QUINTILIAN

CONCEIVED IN Japan's classical age as the servants—the "claws and
teeth" of the emperor and his court—the samurai matured into the
masters of a medieval and early modern world they themselves created. They were the architects of a political and economic order
whose legacy is still felt today. It was an order forged as much by
bow, sword, spear, and gun as by diplomacy and law. Indeed,
weapons and the arts of war defined the samurai from their nascency
in the ninth century to their abolition in the nineteenth.

Any attempt to fully comprehend the samurai without due consideration of their military skills and military training—the bugei—
is obviously futile. For, even under the warless conditions of the
eighteenth and nineteenth centuries, when the samurai had long
since evolved from battlefield warriors to sword-bearing bureaucrats and the number of true experts in the martial arts was probably not appreciably greater than it is today, it would have been as
unthinkable for a samurai to confess to complete unfamiliarity with
his swords as it would have been for one of his contemporaries in
New England to confess to total ignorance of the Bible. Nearly all
Tokugawa-period samurai had at least a nodding acquaintance with
swordsmanship; most had or feigned more, and a significant few
made it the focal point of their lives.

The bugei have a long and complex history, one befogged by
myth and legend and made further inaccessible by documentation
that was either never produced, has not survived, or was made deliberately obscure. Military training and the profession of arms in
Japan predate recorded history. The imperial state was knit together
in considerable part by war; and by the time the samurai are clearly

identifiable in historical sources, they had developed their own unique forms of weapons (particularly the bow and the sword), style of armor, tactical traditions, and training methods. Between the Heian and Sengoku eras, the samurai order and its role in Japanese society grew and evolved. Tactics, weaponry, and training evolved with them. But the most fundamental changes took place during the early modern period, when both the samurai and their bugei adapted to conditions of peace. Until then, the samurai had been warriors before all else, men whose reputations and livelihoods were made in battle, and the bugei were first and foremost arts of war. The Tokugawa-imposed peace turned most samurai into ruling aristocrats descended from warriors, with little or no firsthand knowledge of combat; and as the samurai ceased to be just fighting men, the martial arts ceased to be just methods of fighting. Thus it was that the bugei were able to survive the demise of the warrior class that created them and remain a part of Japanese culture even today.

This survival, then, offers scholars a valuable window into the samurai past, one that provides them with a clearer view than can be obtained from analysis of written evidence alone. For the classical bugei still practiced today are bits of living history that continue to propagate the beliefs and educational tools of a warrior class that otherwise disappeared over a century ago. By studying them, historians can recover much about the manner in which the samurai acquired key values, convictions, and physical abilities, as well as about the attitudes and skills themselves. A better understanding of the bugei, in other words, enriches our knowledge of late medieval and early modern warrior education and affords us new insights into samurai culture.

There is, as I noted at the outset of this study, no such thing as a "typical" or "representative" bugei, for the traditional ryūha vary widely in the specifics of their tactics, their philosophy, the vocabulary through which they express their ideas, and even their understanding of the terminology they hold in common. Nevertheless, there is enough congruity among them to make a close examination of one ryūha an efficient path to an understanding of the bugei in the abstract, as a general phenomenon of Japanese culture.

The key to forging such an understanding is to focus not on the anatomy of the ryūha under study—specific terms, tactics, or other components—but on its physiology—the interplay of the elements that comprise it. By so doing one learns, first and foremost, that the bugei were and are extraordinarily complex phenomena in which various physical, technical, psychological, and philosophical factors intertwine and interact to produce a coherent art that guides both the physical and the moral activities of those who practice it.

This intricate entanglement of tactical, corporeal, mental, and spiritual concerns speaks to the essence of the classical bugei, and yet it has been overlooked by even the best previous English-language analyses of the arts. Most focus on the tactical and the physical, a few on the philosophical and spiritual. An even smaller number discuss both tactical and spiritual concerns, but separate them as though they were opposing phenomena. (The late Donn Draeger's division of the first two volumes of his *Martial Arts and Ways of Japan* trilogy into studies of the *Classical Budō* and the *Classical Bujutsu* exemplifies and virtually reifies this separation.)

Authors like Draeger, D. T. Suzuki, Winston King, and Thomas Cleary have been intrigued by the seeming contradiction inherent in the ability of the samurai—ostensibly adherents to Buddhist and Shintō doctrines condemning warfare and killing—to celebrate these activities by raising them to the level of a high art form. But to solve this riddle, virtually all Western scholars have fallen back on the simplistic notion of an unattaching "Zen mind" that transcends and thereby transforms the act of killing. As we have seen, this idea is not entirely wrong, but it misses a critical point: In the classical bugei, proficiency in combat and spiritual enlightenment are not sequential achievements; they are interactive and interdependant developments.

The bugei, as arts of combat and war, are utterly corporeal—even visceral—in their original expression, for fighting pits body against body, flesh against flesh, and is ultimately decided by the physical domination (or the perception thereof) of one combatant over the other. And yet, even at this purely technical (bujutsu) level, mastery of the bugei—as of most traditional Japanese arts—cannot be found in physical skills alone; all the more do the bugei in their most evolved expression as life-affirming arts of self-realization (budō) transcend the merely physical.

But if the traditional bugei are more than just fighting arts, they are never less. While nearly all Japanese schools of martial art contend that the study of combat can become a vehicle toward broader goals of personal development and self-realization, only a few modern cognate arts have consciously attempted to deemphasize the practical, combative character of their disciplines. The traditional schools, like the Kashima-Shinryū, were conceived within a worldview that stresses monism and the interpenetration of all things and all actions. Budō, the martial path to self-cultivation, is workable precisely because of the indivisibility of pragmatic military, moral, and psychospiritual concerns.

Bugei terms and concepts have numerous levels of meaning. Novices normally approach them first at the level of physical combat and advance into others as their training progresses. But those who have mastered the arts conceptualize these various levels not as sequential steps, but as interpenetrating spheres—inseparable aspects of the same phenomena—to be experienced simultaneously.

As we have seen in our discussion of Kashima-Shinryū concepts and tactics, true proficiency in combat demands certain psychospiritual skills, which raise moral issues, which in turn delimit acceptable approaches to combat, which then mandate further physical and spiritual cultivation, which make otherwise impossible means of fighting feasible, and so on, in an infinite Möbius loop of determinants and reverberations.

In some respects, the relationship between the goals of budō and the methodology of bujutsu is one of deception. An ancient Buddhist allegory tells how the Buddha once tricked a lovesick monk with visions of beautiful nymphs dwelling in a certain heavenly realm. Thus inspired by the decidedly unspiritual emotion of lust, the monk redoubled his efforts in his training so that he could meet the celestial maidens. His practice, however, induced him to eschew all interest in women and sex, and he attained the highest levels of enlightenment.[1] Similarly, some bugei students are attracted from the outset by the concept of budō, while others begin training because of a perceived need for self-defense skills or a simple love of combat. Regardless of why they started, however, initiates soon realize that ultimate martial skill must take them beyond the physical into the realm of the spirit. Thus bujutsu provides the immediately perceptible goals—the motivation—needed to keep students on track toward the less tangible goals of budō.

Viewed in this way, what initially appears as an almost Orwellian paradox in Japanese martial art—the notion of creating peace, nonviolence, and spiritual harmony through mastery of the arts of violence—becomes understandable and even logical. The Kashima-Shinryū expresses the entire process whereby bujutsu leads to budō as one of discovering and acquiring hōyō-dōka in all its multiple levels. Other ryūha use different terminology, but the essence of both the concept and the path are the same for all.

APPENDIXES
Historical Texts

APPENDIX 1:
The *Kashima-Shinryū hyōhō denki*

The *Kashima-Shinryū hyōhō denki* is the oldest extant history of the Kashima-Shinryū shihanke lineage. As noted in chapter 4, the Jikishin-kageryū maintains a nearly identical document, one copy of which dates from the mid-nineteenth century. The complete text of the Kashima-Shinryū version reads as follows:

Consider now the origins of the warrior arts of Japan. [The ancient records] convey that Kashima-Shinryū began during the Age of the Gods with a mission as champion for the Imperial court. When Amaterasu Ōmikami wished her heavenly grandson [Ninigi-no-Mikoto] to descend to the central regions of the Abundant Reed Plains [Japan], she dispatched Takemikazuchi-no-Mikoto [the Kashima deity] and Futsunushi-no-Mikoto [the Katori deity] to pacify those who were not obedient to his rule. In our day we imitate this divine labor by human labor. The rule of the Heavenly Offspring is echoed in the duties of the Shōgun, while the gods of Kashima and Katori served [Ninigi-no-Mikoto] as the Deputy Shōguns [serve the Shōgun]. Eight million deities feared the majesty of these, and prostrated themselves before them. After the Kashima Deity had pursued and chastised all the malignant divinities, he was enshrined in Kashima in the province of Hitachi, becoming a martial numen worshipped throughout the ages. In later generations, all those whose names were made known in the world through feats of arms prayed to this deity. Still more did the warrior arts of our house receive his divine guidance.[1] Thus we call our art the Kashima-Shinryū. The record of how this was inherited by new generations, and of the changes of names incurred therein, is summarized below:

GENERATION I
The founder of Kashima-Shinryū was Matsumoto Bizen-no-kami Ki no Masamoto, a resident of the province of Hitachi.[2] Morning

and night he prayed before the altar of Kashima, pledging himself to the divine will. One evening in a dream he was given a single scroll, the same scroll once dedicated to the Kashima deity by Genkurō [Minamoto] Yoshitsune.[3] As it had been handed down by the gods, he called this new teaching the Shinkage ["Divine Shade," or "Abetted by the Gods"] Ryū. The subsequent help of Kunii Kagetsugu of the Minamoto clan of Hitachi also contributed greatly [to Matsumoto's enlightenment].[4]

GENERATION II

Kamiizumi Ise-no-kami, Fujiwara no Hidetsuna studied the True Way under Matsumoto, and became an expert in the arts of warfare. As a cadet branch [of the tradition originated by Matsumoto], he was daunted by the power of the first character in the name of the school [which meant "deity" or "god"], and therefore changed it to "New," [which is also pronounced "shin"].

GENERATION III

Okuyama Magojirō Taira no Kimishige, later called Kyūgasai, was of a prestigious lineage, his forebears descendents of the house of Okudaira.[5] He was the legitimate successor to Kamiizumi Ise-no-kami's school of martial art, dwelling for many years in Okuyama in Mikawa province. Day and night he attended the shrine of the tutelary deity of Okuyama, praying for guidance in the martial arts.[6] One night he received a divine oracle and changed the characters for the name of his school from Shinkage [meaning "New Shade"] to Shinkage [meaning "Silhouette of the Gods," or "Divine Shadows].[7] Thereafter he wielded his sword as if tracing the forms of shadows. He drove his students hard and became known and respected all throughout the Tōkai region.[8] There were none who could stand against his blade. Summoned from on high, he taught the inner secrets of the arts of war to Tokugawa Ieyasu, and to [Ieyasu's son] Hidetada and his brothers.[9]

GENERATION IV

Ogasawara Kinzaemon Minamoto no Nagaharu, later called Genshinsai, trained hard in the arts of the warrior. Moreover he went China and returned having learned even more marvelous arts.[10] He was the legitimate successor to Okuyama's teachings. After deliberation, he changed the name [of the school] from Shinkage to Shin-shinkage ["True New Reflections"].[11] [His skill in the arts of war] was as brilliant as the color of well-tempered, highly refined gold.

GENERATION V

Kamiya Bunzaemon-no-jō Taira no Masamitsu, later called Denshinsai, was a truly great man. He changed the name of the school from Shin-shinkage to Shinkage Jikishin ["New Shade, Upright Heart"] Ryū, teaching that heart or will must be as of the gods. He created the new name because his teachings were a new, direct guidance.

GENERATION VI

Takahashi Danjō-zaemon-no-jō Minamoto no Shigeharu was later called Jikiōsai. From the years of Kanei [1624–1644] to Genroku [1688–1704] he gathered disciples and endeavored in the arts of war. Bemoaning the proliferation of schools and the confusion of branch styles with the main line, he renamed our school the Jikishin-Seitō ["Correct Heart-True Lineage"] Ryū.

GENERATION VII

Yamada Heizaemon-no-jō Fujiwara no Mitsunori, in retirement called Ippūsai; [Takahashi] Shigeharu wrote and impressed his seal upon a document passing on the Jikishin-Seitō Ryū to Mitsunori. With unlimited humility, Mitsunori looked ahead to the future and back upon the past.[12] Accordingly he again changed the school's name, calling it the Jikishin Kageryū ["Correct Reflections of the Heart"].[13]

GENERATION VIII

Naganuma Shirōzaemon-no-jō Fujiwara no Kunisato was the third son of Mitsunori. From the age of 8 he trained in the techniques of warfare, day and night devoted to the warrior arts. Long he trained, never forsaking [his studies], until at last his diligence was vindicated. His teacher [Yamada Ippūsai] recognized this opportunity and instructed him. He built a school in the Nishikubo district of the city of Edō [now Tokyo], where his students progressed day by day. Thus by his sixtieth year his name was made known throughout Japan and he was without shame before the gods. His authentic technique beckoned disciples to him. He was the second generation of his house to serve the [Jikishin] kageryū.

GENERATION IX[14]
Naganuma Shirōzaemon-no-jō Fujiwara no Norisato, a son of Kunisato, was already skillful when he inherited the teachings of his father. He trained diligently in all of these, and was never neglectful. When he died in his thirty-sixth year, all men grieved.

GENERATION X
Motooka Chūhachi Fujiwara no Yorihito studied the arts of the warrior under Naganuma Norisato. He learned the deepest of the esoteric teachings of his art, and restored the name Kashima-Shinryū. Motooka Chūhachi was originally a disciple of Kunii Kazunobu.

GENERATION XI
Ono Seiemon Taira no Shigemasa mastered the principles of the Divine School. Following the will of Motooka Chūhachi, he passed all of this on to Kunii Taizen. After this, the post of shihanke of the Kashima-Shinryū was held by subsequent generations of the Kunii family.

GENERATION XII
Kunii Taizen Minamoto no Ritsuzan became an expert in the warrior's arts, studying their inner secrets in attendance at the Kashima Shrine in the town of Shirakawa. He originated the concept called "musōken" [discussed in chapter 2].

GENERATION XIII
Kunii Zentarō Minamoto no Ritsuzan trained in the martial skills throughout his stay in this world.

GENERATION XIV
Kunii Kyūuemon was later called Zendayu. After training Shimada Toranosuke, Takayanagi Matashirō, Sano Takenosuke, and others, he desired to teach the secret arts of the [Kashima] Shinryū to the rōnin [masterless samurai] of Mitō.[15] Thus he moved to Hitachi.

GENERATION XV
Kunii Zengorō trained in the [Kashima] Shinryū and inherited the calling of his ancestors.

GENERATION XVI
Kunii Shinsaku knew the arts of the warrior profoundly. He made his merit clear during the Satsuma Rebellion.[16]

GENERATION XVII
Kunii Eizo became the seventeenth shihanke of the Kashima-Shinryū at the age of 13.

GENERATION XVIII
Called Kunii Zen'ya Michiyuki. He inherited the Kashima-Shinryū passed down traditionally within the Kunii house. He taught at the Kashima Grand Shrine, at the Tōyama Military Academy, and other places, and founded the Nihon Kobudō Shin Kōkai, to promote the martial way. He had no equals under Heaven in the arts of the warrior and should truly be called sword-saint. Into his seventy-second year he trained day and night, but he perished on August 17, 1966, stricken with a sudden ailment of the heart. At his funeral the thunder roared incessantly, mourning the death of the sword-saint. He was laid to rest in his ancestral place, Yumoto Sekibune in Fukushima Prefecture.

GENERATION XIX
Seki Humitake.

Thus you may know at a glance of the names and procession of the One School.

APPENDIX 2:
The *Kunii-ke keizu*

The *Kunii-ke keizu*, or "Geneology of the Kunii House," constitutes the principal record of the Kashima-Shinryū sōke lineage. Compiled by Kunii Zen'ya, the eighteenth-generation sōke, it is a history, not a historical document. Nevertheless, it preserves a treasury of anecdotal information concerning the Kunii family not available in any other extant document.

GENERATION XXII (Kashima-Shinryū Generation I) Kagetsugu
Called Genpachirō; although he studied the Nenryū, his heart was not fulfilled; thus he endeavored on his own, worshiping the August Deity of Kashima and striving with all his effort in his spiritual training. At length he brought forth an art, which he called

"Kashima-Shintōryū." He later bequeathed this to Matsumoto Bizen-no-kami, and made Matsumoto the founder of the Kashima-Shinryū, while he himself served as counselor.

In the ninth month of the twelfth year of Tenmon [1543], together with Takeda Shingen, he attacked Imagawa Yoshimoto of Shizuoka and routed him. While crouching in a pine forest, waiting for the lines of the defeated troops to pass, [Matsumoto] was struck in the lower back by an arrow shot from behind him. Kagetsugu cut down his attacker and cared for [Matsumoto]. At last, on the evening of the twelfth day of the ninth month of his sixty-seventh year, Matsumoto Bizen-no-kami died. Kagetsugu buried him in the Shimizu Myōsen Temple.

In the fourth year of Eiroku [1561], he once more aided Takeda Shingen, marching forth with his kinsmen in the battle of Kawanakajima; he captured the head of the enemy general, Kasuga Tarō Morizumi. In the third year of Genki [1572], he again followed Takeda Shingen in the battle of Mikatagahara, routing the allied armies of Tokugawa Ieyasu and Oda Nobunaga, and taking the head of the enemy general, Asahina Shirō Takamasa. Later, amidst preparations to march on the capital, Takeda Shingen took ill and at length died. Later the Takeda house was destroyed. From this day forward, the power of the Tokugawa in the Kantō was extended until at length they ruled all the realm. The [Kashima]-Shinryū fell under oppression. The Kunii moved to the village of Funao in the Iwamae district of Iwaki province. Now a country samurai, Kagetsugu passed away quietly on the tenth day of the fifth month of the nineteenth year of Tenshō [1591].

GENERATION XXIII (Kashima-Shinryū Generation II) Kagekiyo Called Gengorō; he later succeeded to the name Kagetsugu. He fought with his father in the wars of the Eiroku and Genki eras, taking the head of the general, Onizuka Danjō Munetō. It is said that he was no less a master of the martial arts than his father.

GENERATION XXIV (Kashima-Shinryū Generation III) Masateru Called Yatarō; he first saw action at the battle of Mikatagahara, fighting alongside his father; he captured the head of the enemy general, Inugami Gonshirō. In the first month of the tenth year of Tenshō [1582], he took service under Oda Nobunaga. As [Nobunaga] often overlooked much when discussing political affairs and the structure of the realm, Masateru left in anger and returned home. Nobunaga later met a violent end. Following this, Masateru came to the aid of Iga Iga-no-kami, battling with Inaba Ittetsu for eight days from the seventh day of the sixth month of that same year.[17] He felled many enemy warriors, cutting his way through the enemy ranks and earning great merit. In the midst of this, Iga-no-kami was struck from his horse by a stray arrow. He was quickly surrounded by enemy troops and commanders, who took his head and attempted to carry it off. Masateru struck down these troops as well as those who came to their aid, in the process killing the enemy general, Yoshitaka. Seizing the head of Iga-no-kami, he cut an escape path out of the encirclement. He buried the head of Iga-no-kami in the woods.[18]

GENERATION XXV (Kashima-Shinryū Generation IV) Yoshitoki
Called Yagorō; a master of the spear, he went forth attached to the army of Katō Kiyomasa when, in the founding year of Bunroku [1592], Hideyoshi pacified Korea. He fought at the side of Iida Kakubei. At Ulsan, supplies ran short and the troops were forced to eat their horses. Together with Iida Kakubei, Yoshitoki broke through the siege. Carrying a sack of rice each, they then broke through again to return to their troops. This gave great courage to the troops, who sprang to their feet and rallied around Yoshitoki and Kakubei. Then, leading a cohort of brave warriors, Yoshitoki and Kakubei once more broke through the encirclement and successfully brought in supplies, again rallying the troops and enabling a great victory to be secured at last.

GENERATION XXVI (Kashima-Shinryū Generation V) Yoshimasa
Called Yajirō; in the fifth year of Keicho [1600], when Ishida Mitsunari opposed [Tokugawa Ieyasu], Yoshimasa and his father once more allied with the Satake and joined the battle at Sekigahara on Ishida's side, attached to the army of the Ukita. Father and son alike fought furiously, oblivious to the arrow wounds they both suffered. It appeared at first that the advantage lay with the Osaka [Ishida] forces but then, owing to the treachery of Kobayakawa Takakage, the tide of battle was suddenly turned.[19] Seeing that it would be difficult to reverse this and that their allies were unlikely to prevail, the father, Yoshitoki, turned to Yoshimasa.

"Escape," he said. "My wound is deep, I cannot survive this. Truly I am finished. But you are wounded only slightly, so quickly, escape! Gain first the dark of night. On Mt. Ibuki there is a mountain hut used for the gathering of medicinal plants. Find this and go there. In that place there is also money, 100 ryō."

Upon saying this, Yoshitoki resolved to die in battle and rushed at the enemy host. Yoshimasa tried to follow but, his horse wounded, he saw that it was futile. Under the cover of a ceaseless downpour of rain, he crossed several mountain streams, traveling deep into Mt. Ibuki, arriving at last at the mountain hut he sought. Cared for by friends of his father, his wounds soon healed.

At that time, Satake too came to this place. To Yoshimasa he said, "When I parted from Yoshitoki, he gave me a message for you. As I knew that you would come here, I followed. [Yoshitoki's] message was that you are to go to Toyama and [pretend to] be a seller of medicine [and thereby deceive the enemy]. You are then to return home and rebuild the Kunii house. Your father was a true warrior; his last moments were indeed splendid." He gave Yoshimasa Yoshitoki's topknot and short sword, which had been entrusted to him.

Yoshimasa gave money to his hosts, remaining in their care until the snows melted the following spring. Through the help and empathy of the master of this house, Yoshimasa traveled to Toyama with the coming of spring disguised as a medicine peddler. Obtaining a passport, he returned at last to his village, evading the eyes of the Tokugawa, who were looking for remnants of the defeated forces. He took up the life of a country squire.

GENERATION XXVII (Kashima-Shinryū Generation VI) Masaie
Called Yahachirō; he tilled the soil as a country squire but did not abandon his sword. He made it house law that the Kashima-Shinryū be handed down to only one son within the Kunii house in each generation *[isshi sōden]* and that it be transmitted to all future generations.

GENERATION XXVIII (Kashima-Shinryū Generation VII) Masauji
Called Kogorō; a country squire, he lived half as a farmer and half as a warrior, polishing his martial skills in secret. He took as a student Kanai Hanbei and through him came to know Marubashi Chūya; he taught both the military arts. Through Marubashi he met Yūi Shōsetsu, guiding and leading all of these.[20] He was active as a warrior.

Generation XXIX (Kashima-Shinryū Generation VIII) Ujie
Called Shingorō; he tilled the soil and polished his martial skills, as did his ancestors, passing his family secrets on to his son.

GENERATION XXX (Kashima-Shinryū Generation IX) Takamasa
Called Zenpachirō; as were his ancestors, he was skilled in the martial arts.

GENERATION XXXI (Kashima-Shinryū Generation X) Yoshitsugu
Called Shinpachirō; ordered to oversee the Shogunate's rice storehouse, he accepted this charge.

GENERATION XXXII (Kashima-Shinryū Generation XI) Yoshinori
Called Gentarō; he continued the Kashima-Shinryū tradition, and
oversaw the storehouse.

GENERATION XXXIII (Kashima-Shinryū Generation XII) Kazunobu
Called Banzan; while continuing the Kashima-Shinryū tradition,
and tilling the soil, he oversaw the storehouse.

GENERATION XXXIV (Kashima-Shinryū Generation XII) Taizen
Kunii Taizen Minamoto no Ritsuzan continued the Kashima-
Shinryū tradition and became an expert. He performed obeisance
at the Suwa Shrine in Shinano province.

As did his ancestors, he oversaw the storehouse. The great famine of
the Tenmei era [1781–1788][21] occurred during the time that Taizen
was engaged in this charge. Many peasants starved to death. Unable to
endure this sight, Taizen petitioned the shogunate's regional supervi-
sor to open the emergency rice stores, but this was not permitted. He
entreated again to release only enough to sustain life until the new grain
could grow, but for this too, permission was denied. Even when he himself guaranteed responsibility, the government remained unmoved.

Matters having come this far, he became convinced that he had
but one choice, and so he opened the stores himself, distributing rice
sufficient to maintain life until the new grain could be harvested. So
as to make responsibility clear, he reported his actions to the government in person, intending to commit seppuku.[22] However, owing
to the seriousness of his act, he was imprisoned while the local government awaited instructions from the shogunate. When instructions came at last, Kunii's actions were judged to be unselfish and he
was pardoned. He resigned his post and, displaying a penitent will,
abandoned his swords and devoted himself to farming. He opened a
travelers' inn, calling it Matsuya. Posing as a servant and/or as a trav-
eler, he counseled the activist warriors *[shishi]* of the realm.[23]

GENERATION XXXV (Kashima-Shinryū Generation XIII) Zentarō
He tended to his farm; in secret he trained at the sword, and supported the activists. Thus he passed through this world.

GENERATION XXXVI (Kashima-Shinryū Generation XIV) Kyūuemon
Later called Zendayu; he moved to Hitachi, in response to a secret

request by the rōnin of Mitō, where he trained shishi such as Sano Takenosuke, Seki Tetsunosuke, and Kurosawa Chūsaburō in Kashima-Shinryū swordsmanship, spearmanship, and martial strategy. He was greatly missed by these when he passed from this world.[24]

Takayanagi Matashirō, the great swordsman of the mid-nineteenth century, came bearing a letter of introduction from the Nakanishi school. He was taught the soundless combat techniques of Kashima-[Shinryū] swordsmanship. The swordmaster Shimada Toranosuke, now in his middle age, also came to him with a letter from Ōdani Shimōsa-no-kami, seeking to study the secrets of the sword.

GENERATION XXXVII (Kashima-Shinryū Generation XV) Zengorō
He was head of the Kunii house [but] divided his holdings with his younger brother, Tatsukichi.

GENERATION XXXVIII (Kashima-Shinryū Generation XVI) Shinsaku
In the tenth year of Meiji [1877], he marched forth as a soldier, striking down ten or more foes during the battle of Tawarazaka.[25] So it is recorded on the account of an old man, Karasuyakata, who marched with him.

GENERATION XXXIX (Kashima-Shinryū Generation XVII) Eizo
At the age of 13, he was separated by death from his father, when a fire broke out at the home of his neighbor, Takagi Masuji, and all was consumed by the spreading flames.

GENERATION XL (Kashima-Shinryū Generation XVIII) Zenya
Called Michiyuki.

APPENDIX 3:
The *Kashima-Shinryū menkyo kaiden mokuroku*

The greater part of Kunii Zen'ya's *Kashima-Shinryū menkyo kaiden mokuroku*, or "Certificate of Mastery of Kashima-Shinryū," is a simple listing of kata and principles, all of which have been discussed in chapters 2 and 4. The final section, entitled "Kashima-Shinryū and the Origin of Shinbu," however, is an abbreviated history of the shihanke lineage that complements the *Kashima-Shinryū hyōhō denki*:

Kashima-Shinryū and the Origin of Shinbu

Hear now of the shinbu of Japan:
In the Beginning, Izanagi and Izanami, the divine progenitors of the Imperial House, received from their Heavenly Ancestors a sacred edict to form the Mundane Realm.[26] They took up a celestial spear and with it brought forth all below the heavens. Later, Amaterasu Omikami [the goddess of the sun] bestowed upon her Imperial grandchild three sacred treasures, and decreed that he and his progeny should rule over the Mundane Realm.[27] Such was the grand origin of the sacred mission of the Imperial house.

In truth this was the fountainhead of Japan's shinbu. He who would learn the arts of war should make this his heart. Shinbu is of the will of Heaven, a manifestation of the hearts of the deities who rule over the Mundane Realm. Accordingly, it exists neither in attack nor in defense but operates of itself, the paradigm that reveals the great moral law of hōyō-dōka. Truly and clearly indomitable is Japan's shinbu; so too is the great martial path our countrymen must follow readily clear.

Kashima-Shinryū originated in Kashima-no-tachi, passed on from of old at the Kashima Grand Shrine. One thousand two hundred years ago, Kuninazu no Mahito, an official of the shrine, originated this and handed it on to the world. Gradually, however, it came to pass that Kashima-no-tachi perished.

In the middle ages, the senior advisor and leading vassal to Kashima was Matsumoto Bizen-no-kami Ki no Masamoto, a general known throughout the realm for his valor. Later he succeeded to the position of *hafuribe* of the Kashima Grand Shrine. Pursuing his deeply felt need, he strove to understand shinbu. He worshipped the Kashima Deity, seeking a divine revelation. At last through the aid of Kunii Genpachirō Kagetsugu, he arrived at a vision of the completion and perfection of the Kashima-Shinryū.

From here he passed this on to the world and gave birth to many branch styles. These were called "the seven schools of the *bandō* and eight schools of the capital."[28] In Kyūshū Marume Kurando's Taisha-ryū is well-known.[29] In Isei province was Kitabatake Tomonori, Governor of the province and called Master.[30] In the North dwelt the general of the Amako, Yamanaka Shikansuke.[31] Takeda Shingen and Takada Matabei studied first the Hōzōin school of spear fighting and later attached themselves to [Kamiizumi] Ise-no-kami, studied the spear tactics of the Kashima-Shinryū, and were called Master.[32] In Akita, there was Isobata Hanzo.[33] Takeda

[Shingen]'s great tactician, Yamamoto Kansuke, also studied Kashima-Shinryū and became expert.[34] There were other masters as well; among these were Kamiizumi Ise-no-kami Fujiwara no Hidetsuna, (upon whom Takeda Shingen later bestowed the character "Nobu" [from his own given name, Harunobu], and who was thereafter called Nobutsuna), Tsukahara Bokuden, Arima Yamato-no-kami, and others whom I have not the leisure to count. At this time Kashima was known as a great school of martial art.

In the twelfth year of Tenbun [1543], reinforcing Takeda Shingen, Kunii Kagetsugu and Matsumoto Bizen-no-kami attacked Imagawa Yoshimoto at Sunpu castle and routed him. In the fourth year of Eiroku [1561], they marched to battle at Kawanakajima, allied with Takeda Shingen.[35] Again, in the third year of Genki [1573], under Takeda Shingen as commander, Kunii clashed with the allied armies of Tokugawa and Oda at Mikatagahara, destroying them. From here Shingen made as to move on Kyoto, but amidst preparations, he was stricken ill and died.

Later, from the time the Tokugawa came to power over the Mundane Realm, the Kashima-Shinryū fell under oppression and was forced underground. Under Okuyama Kyūgasai, the Kashima-Shinryū was banned by the Tokugawa. For this reason [Kyūgasai's successor] Ogasawara Genshinsai went to China, returning after the death of Ieyasu. He received all of the mysterious teachings handed down by [Kunii] Kagetsugu and became the fourth-generation [headmaster] of the Shinkage-ryū. The fifth-generation headmaster, Kamiya Denshinsai, changed the name to Jikishin-ryū. The seventh-generation headmaster, Yamada Ippunsai, changed it from Jikishin-ryū to Jikishin-Kageryū. The tenth-generation headmaster, Motooka Chūhachi Fujiwara no Yorihito, restored the original name, Kashima-Shinryū. Ono Seiemon, [the eleventh-generation headmaster], returned the shihanke title to the Kunii house, where it was received by Kunii Taizen Minamoto no Ritsuzan; from that time to the present the Kunii house has been the true shihanke.

Know that Kashima-Shinryū delights naught in the unavailing joy of felling an enemy, of destroying evil. Rather it fosters noble men who strive to revere and satisfy the will of they who rule over the realm. Thus it nurtures in those who practice it the will to kill one only to save ten thousand. This art is *chūsei fuhen*. Of its own accord it maintains the state of certain life. It is the source of limitless permutations, reaching, as a result, the zenith of form and contour.

Motion and Stillness exist in the two sides of a single heart. One heart, one sword; this principle must be followed.

When selfishness is eliminated, for the first time the sword of certain life comes to be. This is a manifestation of hōyōdōka. Certain life is certain control, is certain victory. To attack when the heart is not pure is only to destroy oneself. Destroying evil, establishing righteousness: The principle is clear. Is it not then worthwhile for a young man to come to train diligently? Thinking thus, the Kashima-Shinryū first prepares the body, then cultivates heartfelt human relationships, and arrives ultimately at realization and understanding of the fundamental principles of the Universe. This is the secret, the inner truth of Kashima-Shinryū. As in days of old, it is the great Way of sacred Japan.

The Kashima-Shinryū lineage:

> Advisor Kunii Kagetsugu
> Matsumoto Bizen-no-kami Ki no Masamoto
> Kamiizumi Ise-no-kami Fujiwara no Hidetsuna
> Okuyama Kyūgasai Taira no Kimishige
> Ogasawara Genshinsai Minamoto no Nagaharu
> Kamiya Denshinsai Taira no Sanemitsu
> Takahashi Jikiosai Minamoto no Shigeharu
> Yamada Ippūsai Fujiwara Mitsunori
> Naganuma Shirōzaemon Fujiwara no Kunisato
> Naganuma Shirōzaemon Fujiwara no Norisato
> Motooka Chūhachi Fujiwara no Yorihito
> Ono Seiemon Taira no Shigemasa
> Kunii Taizen Minamoto no Ritsuzan
> Kunii Zentarō Minamoto no Ritsuzan
> Kunii Zendayu
> Kunii Zengorō
> Kunii Shinsaku
> Kunii Eizo
> Kunii Zen'ya Minamoto no Michiyuki

The above list shows nineteen generations, but [Kamiizumi] Ise-no-kami and [Kunii] Kagekiyo were of the same generation. Therefore [Kunii] Zen'ya is the eighteenth generation.

The wonder of martial art cannot be reached by training wholeheartedly with the body alone. One must be diligent in training the spirit as well, through devotions to the August Deity of Kashima. If one does this, he must certainly receive inspiration and will, without fail, arrive at an understanding of the ultimate truths. I have experienced this personally, and thus record it.

Kashima-Shinryū Organization

APPENDIX 4:
Constitution of the Kashima-Shinryū Federation
of Martial Sciences

ARTICLE I—GENERAL RULES AND REGULATIONS

Section I

The organization shall be called the Kashima Federation of Martial Sciences. The main office shall be under the charge of the President.

Section II

The organization shall be affiliated with the Society for the Promotion of Kashima-Shinryū (Kitamura Nishimochi, President) but shall be independent. The organization shall take as its main objective the promotion, diffusion, and advancement of Kashima-Shinryū martial art within the educational facilities of universities and the like.

Section III

In order to accomplish that objective, the following business shall be conducted:

1) Qualified persons so authorized by the organization shall be designated as Instructors and shall, upon obtaining the approval of the Council, establish branch schools and conduct martial training.
2) Correspondent to a martial event, the organization shall once annually award diplomas based on test results.
3) The organization shall publish a periodical.
4) Any other necessary business shall be conducted.

ARTICLE II—OFFICERS

Section IV

The organization shall consist of the following officers: Honorary President (2), President (1), Auditor (2), Councilors (several) and Advisors (several).

Section V

The office of the President shall be held by the shihanke of the Kashima-Shinryū. When he determines it necessary, the President can, with the approval of two-thirds or more of the Councilors, appoint a proxy President. This proxy shall take over in the event of an accident befalling the President.

The Auditor shall be elected by the Councilors.

In principle, the Councilors shall all be Instructors. However, when the President determines it necessary, he may appoint Advisors as well as members at large to that body.

Section VI

The Council shall be composed of the President, the Auditor, and the Councilors. In general, the President shall assemble the Council once annually to conduct the business of the organization set forth in the by-laws.

Section VII

The Auditor shall examine the affairs and enterprises of the organization. The results of these audits shall be reported to the Council.

Section VIII

Officers who impugn the reputation of the organization shall, upon consensus of all Council members, be expelled. In all other cases the term of office for officers shall be life. However, should an officer wish to withdraw from membership, he may resign upon receiving approval from the Council.

ARTICLE III—MEMBERS

Section IX

All members shall hold an interest in Japanese martial art and shall support the goals and opinions of the organization. Membership dues shall be 1,000 yen annually.

Section X

Persons desiring to enter into membership shall deliver a membership application form to the President. The approval of the Council is necessary.

Section XI

Members may receive their training at the branch school of their choice. Once annually they may be examined for promotion.

Section XII

Members shall prepay all dues every year. Once paid, dues shall not be returned.

Section XIII

Members shall forfeit their qualifications for the following reasons: 1) withdrawal from membership; 2) death; 3) expulsion.

Section XIV

Persons wishing to withdraw from membership must serve notice thereof.

Section XV

Members who impugn the reputation of the organization or who fail for two years to pay membership dues shall sustain a suspension of all priviledges granted under section XI. Dependent on the situation, such members shall, by vote of the Council, be expelled in the name of the President.

ARTICLE IV—RANKS AND LICENSES

Section XVI

Licenses shall be awarded from the organization headquarters for the following ranks: kirigami, shōmokuroku, shoden, chūden, okuden, kaiden, and menkyo kaiden. Tests for ranks up to and including shoden may be conducted at branch schools under the responsibility of the Instructor. Test for ranks of chūden or higher must be conducted at the headquarters.

Formal uniforms for the various ranks shall be as follows:

> kirigami: white uniform, white belt
> shōmokuroku: white uniform, black belt
> shoden: white uniform, black belt, black hakama

chūden: white uniform, black belt, black hakama
okuden: white uniform, black belt, white hakama
kaiden: white uniform, black belt, white hakama
menkyo kaiden: white uniform, white belt, white hakama

Section XVII

Testing requirements shall be as follows:

1) Kenjutsu

Rank	Kata	Other
Kirigami	Kihon tachi, Uratachi	
Shōmokuroku	Aishin kumitachi	2 tachiai
Shoden	Jissen tachigumi	5 tachiai Written test (2 questions)
Chūden	Kasen tachi	10 tachiai Written test (5 questions)
Okuden	Tsubazerai, Taoshiuchi	Thesis
Kaiden	All omote waza	Thesis

2) Jūjutsu

Kirigami	Idori, Tachiwaza	5 reiki-nage
Shōmokuroku	Nagewaza	10 reiki-nage 5 tachiai
Shoden	Kumiwaza gusokudori	10 tachiai Written test (2 questions)
Chūden	Torite gaeshi	10 tachiai Written test (5 questions)
Okuden	Ushirowaza	Thesis
Kaiden	bōjutsu	Thesis

Menkyo kaiden requires that one first obtain the rank of kaiden in both the kenjutsu and jūjutsu disciplines and then undergo an examination by thesis.

Section XVIII

For tests conducted at branch schools, the examination board shall consist of the Instructor as chief examiner and a proportionate number of assistant examiners. For tests conducted at the headquarters, the board shall consist of the *shihan* as chief examiner and at least two assistant examiners.

ARTICLE V—BRANCH SCHOOLS

Section XIX

The organization is established by the league of branch schools. In general the responsibility of operating a branch school is awarded only to those ranking kaiden or above. However, in special cases where the President deems it necessary, persons corresponding to the rank of kaiden may also be so entrusted.

ARTICLE VI—COMMENDATIONS

Section XX

Commendations shall be made to those members who have made contributions to the promotion of martial art. Candidates for such award shall be elected by the Council.

APPENDIX 5:
Constitution of the Kashima-Shinryū Federation of North America

PREAMBLE & STATEMENT OF PURPOSE

For over a millennium students of the warrior arts have sought inspiration and guidance at the Kashima Grand Shrine, on Japan's northeastern seacoast. In the mid-seventh century a Kashima shrine celebrant, the legendary Kuninazu Mabito, is said to have raised these techniques to a new level. In the late fifteenth century two warriors of extraordinary insight, Kunii Genpachirō Kagetsugu and Matsumoto Bizen-no-kami Ki no Masamoto, reformulated the Kashima martial traditions as a new school of martial art that became known as the Kashima-Shinryū.

More than five centuries after its birth, the Kashima-Shinryū remains a living martial tradition and a unique expression of Japanese thought. It is a school of martial science: a practical, wholistic system of combat encompassing nearly all the martial disciplines of traditional Japan, constituting a path to general physical, mental and spiritual well-being.

The goals of the Kashima-Shinryū are expressed in the *Kashima-Shinryū Ōgi*, its hundreds of years old statement of inner principle:

> Know that the Kashima-Shinryū delights naught in the useless joy of felling an enemy, of destroying evil. Rather, it fosters gentlemen of . . . a heart that would always kill one only to save a thousand. . . . In the beginning, prepare the body; at the midpoint, cultivate heartfelt human relationships; at the ultimate, find insight into the original principles of the Universe. This is the secret, the inner truth of the Kashima-Shinryū.

Students who would pursue these goals need careful guidance and instruction. It is to this end that we, who have been guided along our own journeys by the organization of the Kashima-Shinryū in Japan, now seek to establish a branch organization, a framework within which we may continue along the path ourselves and begin to guide others in North America and Hawaii.

Our purpose is to preserve and pass on the traditions of the Kashima-Shinryū. These traditions are, have always been, and must always be a living art, embodied in the person of the Headmaster (shihanke) of the school. We recognize both the need for a formal structure to promote and maintain the integrity of this art, and the dangers inherent in creating such a structure. For the training, and supervision of training in a living art cannot, must not, become unnecessarily rule bound. We therefore seek, insofar as possible, to maintain flexibility in the structure and operations of the organization established by this document.

ARTICLE I—GENERAL RULES AND REGULATIONS

Section 1

The organization shall be called The Kashima-Shinryū Federation of North America. The official abbreviation for this organization shall be KSR/NA.

Section 2

The organization shall be affiliated with and subject to the constitution, by-laws and authority of the Kashima-Shinryū Federation of Martial Sciences (*Kashima-Shinryū budō renmei*; hereafter cited as KSR/IN) and to the authority and directives of its Headmaster (Shihanke).

Section 3

The organization shall take as its main purpose the promotion, diffusion and advancement of Kashima-Shinryū martial art traditions (abbreviated as KSR) within North America and Hawaii, the promotion of human understanding through ethical and spiritual cultivation consistent with KSR, and the promotion of cross-cultural understanding among the peoples of North America and Hawaii, and Japan, based on a mutual appreciation of the traditional arts of Japan. Let it be explicitly noted that KSR traditions of ethical and spiritual cultivation are completely non-sectarian and non-denominational and are compatible with any religious affiliation or lack thereof. The organization shall serve as a coordinating agency for the activities of all schools and organizations wishing to teach Kashima-Shinryū martial art in North America or Hawaii. The organization shall serve as a liaison between Directors in North America and Hawaii and KSR/IN.

To accomplish these objectives, the organization shall conduct the following business:

A. Qualified persons authorized by the organization shall be designated as Directors and shall, upon obtaining the approval of the Governing Council (GC), establish affiliated training organizations (designated as "Chapters").

B. The organization shall take responsibility within North America and Hawaii for policing and certifying the credentials of all persons wishing to teach KSR. The organization shall not interfere with the day-to-day operations of the Chapters or Directors except in the case that a Chapter or Director is in violation of the constitution or by-laws of KSR/NA or of those of KSR/IN.

C. KSR/NA shall exert control over the use and franchise of the names or any logograms incorporating the names "Kashima-Shinryū," "KSR," "KSR/NA," "KSR/IN," "KSR/North America," and "KSR/International" within North America and Hawaii.

D. The organization shall conduct regular in-service training and recertification seminars for Directors. The by-laws shall establish procedures for organizing these seminars.

E. The organization shall maintain a roster of all practitioners of KSR initiated at the level of Kirikami or above.

F. The organization shall sanction and certify all awarding of ranks and diplomas to students of KSR in North America and Hawaii.

   1. The organization shall manufacture and distribute diplomas for students in North America and Hawaii who have been initiated at the levels of Kirikami, Shōmokuroku, Shoden, Chūden, or Okuden.

   2. The organization shall serve as the clearing agency for ordering and distributing diplomas for students in North America and Hawaii who have been initiated at the level of Kaiden and higher. Diplomas for ranks of Kaiden and higher shall be requested from the headquarters of KSR/IN.

G. The organization shall collect dues and/or fees as deemed necessary to maintain the operations of the organization but consistent with the character of the organization as a non-profit organization. Procedures for determining the amount and frequency of dues and fees shall be set forth in the by-laws.

H. The organization shall publish a periodical.

I. The organization shall conduct any other business necessary and relevant to its stated goals and purposes.

ARTICLE II—OFFICERS

Section 1

The officers of the organization shall be as follows: President, Vice-President, Secretary and Treasurer. All officers shall serve concurrent five year terms. The President and Vice-President shall be elected by simple majority vote of all members of the GC. The President and Vice-President shall appoint the Secretary and the Treasurer with the advice and consent of the GC.

A. The President shall be chosen from among the members of the GC. The President shall be the titular head of the organization for legal purposes and shall act as chair for all meetings of the GC.

B. The Vice-President shall be chosen from among the members of the GC. The Vice-President shall assume the duties of the President in the event that he or she is unable to perform them.

C. The Secretary shall be chosen from among all members of KSR/NA. The secretary shall be responsible for maintaining the records of the organization and any other administrative duties authorized by the GC.

D. The Treasurer shall be chosen from among all members of KSR/NA. The Treasurer shall be responsible for all financial activities of KSR/NA.

Section 2

The principal governing body of the organization shall be the Governing Council (GC). This body shall have sole authority to create and promulgate by-laws for the organization and to propose amendments to the constitution. The GC shall consist initially of the four Founding Members of the organization. When deemed appropriate and necessary, additional members of the GC may be chosen from among the senior members of the organization by two-thirds majority vote of the current members of the Council. Normally GC membership shall be restricted to members of the Okuden level or higher; however, under special circumstances, persons of Chūden level may be admitted to membership on the Council. At no time shall the membership of the Council exceed ten persons.

A. GC members may be expelled for cause by unanimous vote of all other GC members. Members expelled from KSR/IN for any reason shall be automatically expelled from the GC.

B. GC members wishing to withdraw from membership may resign with the approval of the remaining Council members.

C. In all other cases, membership on the GC shall be for life.

D. All members of the GC, including the President and Vice-President, shall have equal voting and discussion rights in Council deliberations.

E. The GC shall have the sole authority to create and promulgate by-laws as necessary to guide the operations of the organization. No legislation shall be passed without being ratified by simple majority of all members of the Council. When necessary, Council members may vote on issues by certified mail or may give written proxy to a designated representative. By-laws passed by the GC may be recalled for reconsideration by two-thirds majority of all Senior Members. Procedures for such a recall vote shall be set forth in the by-laws.

F. The GC shall have the sole authority to propose amendments to the constitution of the organization. Constitutional amendments shall require a two-thirds majority vote of all Council members and

must be ratified by a two-thirds majority of all Senior Members of
KSR/NA.

G. The GC shall not pass any by-law nor propose any amendment to
the constitution of the organization that would be in conflict with
the by-laws or constitution of KSR/IN.

H. The Headmaster (shihanke) of KSR/IN shall have veto power over
all by-laws, policies, and amendments to the constitution of
KSR/NA.

ARTICLE III—MEMBERS

Section 1

Membership of KSR/NA shall be open to anyone interested in classical Japanese martial art and supportive of the goals and opinions of
the organization regarding martial art and the teaching and practice
thereof. Membership shall not be denied because of race, creed, color,
national origin, disability, age, gender, or any consideration based on
affectional, sexual, or associational preference, or any other consideration that would deprive persons of full consideration as an individual.

Section 2

There shall be four (4) classes of membership: Members, Senior
Members, Founding Members, and Honorary Members.

A. Members shall consist of all students of KSR in North America and
Hawaii who remain in good standing with the organization and who
have been admitted at the level of Kirikami or higher. Members
shall be eligible to participate in special training seminars conducted
by the organization and to subscribe to the KSR/NA newsletter.

B. Senior Members shall consist of all members initiated at the level of
Shoden or higher. Senior Members shall have the right to petition
the GC, the right to vote on by-laws and constitutional amendments
passed by the GC, and the right to demand recalls of policy actions
by the GC. Senior Members shall not lose these rights by reason of
temporary residence outside of North America and Hawaii.

C. The Founding Members shall consist of William M. Bodiford, Karl
F. Friday, Richard J. Pietrelli, and Mark L. Taper. The Founding
Members shall serve as the initial members of the GC.

D. Honorary Members shall consist of any persons so designated by
the GC. Honorary Members shall have no special privileges, but

may, if they choose, participate in activities open to members and subscribe to the KSR/NA newsletter.

Section 3

Members, Senior Members or Founding Members who fail for two years to pay any membership dues or fees established by the by-laws shall suffer a suspension of all privileges of their membership status until said dues or fees or a portion thereof (as determined by the GC) are paid in full.

Section 4

Members of any status may suffer a suspension of membership status for cause as determined by majority vote of the GC. Such suspension shall remain in effect until the GC has determined that the transgression of the suspended member has been adequately redressed. Members of any status may be expelled from KSR/NA for cause by unanimous vote of the GC.

ARTICLE IV—CHAPTERS AND INSTRUCTION

Section 1

The organization shall certify qualified persons as Directors with the authority to teach KSR and to conduct tests and award levels of initiation in North America and Hawaii.

A. Persons petitioning for certification as Directors shall have first been initiated to the level of Okuden or higher. Under exceptional circumstances, however, several members of Shoden or Chūden levels acting collectively may be authorized by the GC to act in concert as Director and to conduct training and testing.
B. To maintain certification all Directors shall be required to attend periodic in-service training and re-certification seminars conducted by the organization. The frequency and content of such seminars and the frequency of attendance required to maintain certification, shall be set forth in the by-laws.
C. It shall be recognized that the Kashima-Shinryū is a living martial art embodied in the person of the current Headmaster (shihanke) of KSR/IN. The Headmaster may change methods of training and instruction, formats for examinations, the structure of techniques

and kata (pattern practice), and philosophy concerning application of techniques. The current Headmaster shall be the final authority in all matters of Kashima-Shinryū technique and philosophy. Instructors shall under no circumstances conduct training or testing in any way that would contravene or undermine this authority. All kata taught by instructors shall conform to those described in the *Kashima-Shinryū Shihan'yō bujutsu kyōsho* (Teaching Manual of Kashima-Shinryū Martial Science for the Use of Master Instructors) except as amended by the current Headmaster.

D. Instructors shall not teach KSR to any persons who are not members of KSR/NA or KSR/IN or members of Chapters chartered by KSR/NA or by KSR/IN without explicit permission from the GC or the Headmaster of KSR/IN.

E. Instructors shall normally teach only KSR as defined in Section 1/C above. Instructors who wish to teach other martial arts in addition to KSR shall first obtain permission from the GC or from the Headmaster of KSR/IN. Instructors who teach other martial arts in addition to KSR shall keep training and practice sessions for the other arts distinct from those in which they teach KSR and shall not teach KSR at training and practice sessions in which other martial arts are taught.

F. As per the by-laws of KSR/IN, an exception shall be made for Directors initiated at the rank of Chūden or above that wish to include instruction in techniques from schools of martial art that have branched off from the Kashima-Shinryū tradition.

Section 2

Chapters established by Directors shall be chartered and accredited by KSR/NA. In the event that a Director must be absent from an active body of students for an extended period of time, he/she may designate Acting Director(s) to carry out his/her duties in his/her absence, and shall inform the GC of this event. Acting Directors need not meet the same criteria as Directors but shall normally be students of KSR initiated at the level of Shoden or higher.

Section 3

Licenses shall be awarded from KSR/NA headquarters or through KSR/IN for the following levels: Kirikami (Pledge), Shōmokuroku (Apprentice), Shoden (First Initiation), Chūden (Middle Initiation), and Okuden (Deep Initiation). Licenses for the levels of Kaiden (Full Initiation), Menkyō kaiden (Licensed Initiate), and Shihan (Model Instructor) may be awarded only by KSR/IN.

  A. Directors initiated to the level of Okuden or higher may conduct and grade testing for initiation to levels of Chūden or lower on their own authority and may petition the President for diplomas for students who have passed the examinations.
  B. Directors initiated to the level of Chūden or lower may conduct and grade testing for initiation for up to one level lower than their own on their own authority and then petition the President for diplomas for students who have passed the examinations.
  C. All testing for initiation to the level of Okuden shall be video-taped. The tapes shall then be presented to the Headmaster (shihanke) of KSR/IN. Upon obtaining approval of the Headmaster of KSR/IN a Director may petition the President of KSR/NA to issue the appropriate certification or diploma.
  D. All testing conducted by Directors initiated only to the levels of Chūden or lower for initiation levels which they are not certified to award on their own authority shall be video-taped. The tapes shall then be presented to the members of the GC. Approval of at least two members of the Council is required in order to award the new level.
  E. Requirements and standards for testing shall be the same as those established by KSR/IN.

Section 4

  A. Persons wishing to begin the study of KSR may be accepted for training at any Chapter on the authority of Director or in his/her absence the Acting Director. Upon initiation to the level of Kirikami, they shall be admitted as members to KSR/NA and KSR/IN. All such persons shall be required to sign the oath of membership (kishōmon) designated by the Headmaster of KSR/IN.
  B. Qualified Persons seeking accreditation as Directors shall apply in writing to the GC. The Council shall review the application and act upon it as expediently as possible. Upon a two-thirds majority vote of approval by the GC applications shall be deemed approved and appropriate certification issued.
  C. The accreditation of Chapters that no longer have a qualified Director or Acting Director(s) available to guide instruction may be canceled at any time by three-fourths majority vote of the GC or by order of the current Headmaster (shihanke) of KSR/IN.

NOTES

Chapter 1: Introduction

1. Quoted in de Bary, ed., *Sources of Japanese Tradition*, 1:389.

2. Hurst, "Samurai on Wall Street," provides an entertaining account of just how far this equation of Japan with the samurai can go.

3. de Bary, *Sources*, p. 1:391.

4. Watatani Kiyoshi and Yamada Tadakichi, eds., *Bugei ryūha daijiten*, 180; "Saigo no kengō: Kashima-Shinryū dai 18 sei shihan Kunii Zen'ya shi," 85–89.

5. Some of Kunii Zen'ya's most memorable duels are recounted in Seki Humitake, *Shōwa no godai Kashima-Shinryū honden* and *Kashima-Shinryū shihan-yō bujutsu kyōsho*. The anecdotes concerning the French boxer and the Greek exorcist appear on pages 16 and 20–21 of the first volume.

6. The origins of the warrior order and the evolution of the state's military and police system are discussed in detail in Karl Friday, *Hired Swords: The Rise of Private Warrior Power in Early Japan*. See also Friday, "Valorous Butchers: The Art of War during the Golden Age of the Samurai." For information on the structure of the Heian court and the process of privatization of government, see John W. Hall, *Government and Local Power in Japan, 500–1700*, 116–128; and G. Cameron Hurst, III, "Structure of the Heian Court," or *Insei*.

7. The Gempei War, the Kamakura polity, and the establishment and structure of the Muromachi polity have all been the subject of a tremendous volume of scholarship in both Japan and the West. Excellent overviews of these topics can be found in Jeffrey P. Mass, "The Kamakura Bakufu," Ishii Susumu, "The Decline of the Kamakura Bakufu," and John W. Hall, "The Muromachi Bakufu."

8. For an overview of the atmosphere of the sixteenth century and the reunification process, see George Elison and Bardwell L. Smith, eds., *Warlords, Artists and Commoners*.

9. *The Cambridge History of Japan*, vol. 4: *Early Modern Japan*, ed. John W. Hall; *Tokugawa Japan*, ed. Chie Nakane and Shinzaburō Oishi, trans. and ed., Conrad Totman; *Studies in the Institutional History of Early Modern Japan*, ed. John W. Hall and Marius B. Jansen; and Charles J. Dunn, *Everyday Life in Imperial Japan* all offer thorough introductions to the Tokugawa period.

10. Further information on the transition from the early modern to the modern state in Japan can be found in: Conrad Totman, *The Collapse of the Tokugawa Bakufu, 1862–1868*; *The Cambridge History of Japan*, vol. 5: *The*

Nineteenth Century, ed. Marius B. Jansen; and *Japan in Transition*, ed. Marius B. Jansen and Gilbert Rozman.

11. A detailed discussion of this process appears in G. Cameron Hurst, III, *The Armed Martial Arts of Japan*, ch. 7.

12. The misleading construct of "East Asian martial arts" has been the source of considerable confusion among scholars, as well as popular audiences. See, for example, the exchange between Stewart McFarlane and John P. Keenan in the *Japanese Journal of Religious Studies* a few years back. Keenan, "Spontaneity in Western Martial Arts: A Yogācāra Critique of *Mushin* (No-Mind)," and "The Mystique of Martial Arts: A Response to Professor McFarlane"; McFarlane, "*Mushin*, Morals, and Martial Arts: A Discussion of Keenan's Yogācāra Critique," and "The Mystique of Martial Arts: A Reply to Professor Keenan's Response."

13. The first extant appearance of "bugei" was in *Shoku Nihongi* 704 6/3; of "hyōhō," in *Nihon shoki* 671 1/13.

14. Tokugawa-period authors used the terms *"gunpō"* and *"gungaku"* to indicate the meaning formerly expressed with "hyōhō." (Ishioka Hisao, *Heihōsha no seikatsu*, 10–23; Tominaga Kengō, *Kendō gohyakunen-shi*, 20–23.)

15. *Azuma kagami* 1195 8/10.

16. The term "bushidō" was rarely used until the Meiji period. In fact the word was so unusual that Nitobe Inazo, whose 1899 tract (written in English, not Japanese), *Bushidō: The Soul of Japan*, probably did more than any other single work to popularize the idea of bushidō in both Japan and the West, was able to believe that he had invented it himself! G. Cameron Hurst, III, "Death, Honor, and Loyalty," discusses this point in detail; see especially pages 512–513.

17. Tominaga, *Kendō gohyakunen shi*, 16–19; Hurst, "From Heihō to Bugei"; Hurst, *The Armed Martial Arts of Japan*, ch. 1. The Aizawa passage is quoted in Tominaga, p. 17.

18. A recent, and egregious, example is Winston L. King's *Zen and the Way of the Sword: Arming the Samurai Psyche* (New York: Oxford, 1993). This ambitious work, which purports to explain Zen Buddhism and its effects on Japanese culture, the relationship between Zen and the samurai, the history of the samurai class from its origins to its demise, the history of the sword in Japan, the history and nature of Japanese swordsmanship, samurai ethics and philosophy, and the legacy of the samurai in the twentieth century, is based almost entirely on popular sources. King's bibliography lists neither a single work in any language other than English nor a single academic monograph on pre-Tokugawa period history.

19. The perils of generalizing are vividly illustrated in a recent work by Thomas Cleary, in which he purports to elucidate *The Japanese Art of War*, but draws most of his insights from the writings of Miyamoto Musashi, Yagyū Munenori, and Takuan Sōhō. To conceptualize nearly two thousand years of history through the eyes of three men who were all contemporaries of one another would be risky under any circumstances, but Musashi, Munenori, and Takuan were all viewed as mavericks in both their own time and by later generations of bugei adepts. None of the three was widely influential until modern times. For more on Musashi and his place in Japanese history, see Hurst, "Samurai on Wall Street."

20. The fieldwork began in 1978, when I was a college senior studying in Japan. I entered the Kashima-Shinryū in September of that year and received the rank of *menkyo-kaiden* ("licensed initiate"—essentially a Ph.D. in the art; see the discussion in chapter 2) in 1987 and the designation of *shihan* ("model instructor") two years later.

Chapter 2: Heritage and Tradition

1. See Donald L. Philippi, trans., *Kojiki*, and W. G. Aston, *Nihongi: Chronicles of Japan from the Earliest Times to 697 AD*.

2. Friday, *Hired Swords*, 8–121; Friday, "Valorous Butchers"; G. Cameron Hurst, III *The Armed Martial Arts of Japan*, ch. 5.

3. *Konjaku monogatari-shū* 23.15. The timing of Norimitsu's adventure can be reckoned from *Gonki* 997 9/5, which records Norimitsu's service in the *emonfu*.

4. See, for example, *Ichijōji no kettō (The Samurai, Part II: Duel at Ichijoji Temple)*, Tōhō Productions, 1955.

5. Hurst, *The Armed Martial Arts of Japan*, ch. 2 and 8.

6. Fuller discussions of this point appear in Hurst, *The Armed Martial Arts of Japan*, ch. 3; Hurst, "From Heihō to Bugei"; and Tsumoto Yū, *Yagyū Hyōgo-suke*, vols. 1 and 2.

7. Paul L. Swanson, "*Shugendō* and the Yoshino-Kumano Pilgrimage"; Carmen Blacker, *The Catalpa Bow*; Allan Grapard, "Flying Mountains and Walkers of Emptiness"; H. Byron Earhart, *A Religious Study of the Mount Haguro Sect of Shugendō*.

8. Konishi Jin'ichi, *Michi*; Robert Eno, *The Confucian Creation of Heaven*, 64–66; Makoto Ueda, *Literary and Art Theories in Japan*. For an English-language summary of Konishi's ideas on this topic, see his *A History of Japanese Literature*, vol. 3: 139–165.

9. G. Cameron Hurst, "Ryūha in the Martial and Other Japanese Arts," p. 14.

10. Hurst, "Ryūha," 3n; Hurst, *Armed Martial Art*, ch. 8. Hurst has found that iemoto organizations were more common in domain schools, where all the students of the ryūha were from the same *han*.

11. *Kashima shi*, 460–461; *Shoku Nihongi* 758 9/8; Cornelius J. Kiley, "State and Dynasty in Archaic Yamato"; Richard Ponsonby-Fane, *The Vicissitudes of Shinto*, 156–168, 184–185.

12. Phillippi, *Kojiki*, 47.

13. Futsunushi-no-Mikoto is also known as Iwainushi-no-Mikoto at the Kasuga Grand Shrine.

14. Phillipi, *Kojiki*, 133.

15. *Kashima shi*, 490–491. The names glossed in the text as "Amenoko" and "Takamanohara" are more commonly read as "Amago" and "Takamagahara."

16. The Kashima house claimed descent from the Kammu Heishi. A detailed description of Kashima Castle appears in *Ibaraki-ken shi chūsei hen*, 347–351.

17. *Kashima jiranki*, 49; *Kashima shi*, 486; Ponsonby-Fane, *Vicissitudes*, 197; Okada Kazuo, *Kengō shidan*, 12; E. Papinot, *Historical and Geographical Dictionary of Japan*, 547.

18. *Bugei koden*, quoted in Okada, *Kengō shidan*, 21; Okada, *Kengō shidan*, 21–22.

19. *Kashima jiranki*, 53; *Kashima-shi*, 483; Nakayama Nobuna, ed., *Shinhen Hitachi kokushi*, 280–287; *Ibaraki-ken shi, chūsei hen*, vol 3: 347–355; Kunii Zen'ya, *Kunii-ke keizu*.

The *Kashima jiranki* gives no date for the battle of Takamagahara, but the text is dated "late spring, Daiei 6 (1526)" and implies that the events chronicled were very recent; the *Kashima shi* places the battle "during the Daiei era (1521–1528)"; only the *Shinhen Hitachi kokushi* gives a precise date.

The *Kunii-ke keizu* account refers to a campaign by Shingen against Imagawa Yoshimoto in 1543, but no record of this offensive appears in other extant sources. Moreover, the Takeda and the Imagawa had concluded a marriage alliance only two years earlier (*Shizuoka-ken shiryō*, vol. 1:373–374, 650–651, 726), making it highly unlikely that Shingen would have opened hostilites so soon afterward. Shingen did conduct a famous (and decisive) offensive against the Imagawa in 1568, but if the Kunii family records actually refer to this campaign, Matsumoto would have been well over 90 years old! Alternatively, the Kunii documents may have confused this 1568 campaign with an entirely different battle in which Matsumoto participated and met his end, one that may or may not have been led by Takeda Shingen.

The Matsumoto family records are discussed in Okada Kazuo, "Kashima-Katori: Kenpō to sono denryū 2, chūkō jidai sono ichi," 124–125.

20. A document entitled the *Shintōryū tetsugi no jojidai*, dated the second month, 1605, and a second document, the *Shintōryū mahijutsu*, dated the sixth, 1840, both list Matsumoto as Iizasa's student. The documents are reproduced in Imamura Yoshio et al., eds., *Nihon budō taikei*, vol. 3, 12–13, 26–27. Nakabayashi Shinji also counts Matsumoto among Iizasa's students ("Kendō shi," 48–49), as does the *Nihon chūkō bujutsu keifu ryaku*, published around 1767 (p. 121).

21. Okada Kazuo argues that Kunii must have been a *student* of Matsumoto, rather than a collaborator, inasmuch as he was some thirty years younger. The problem with this conclusion is that the Kunii family records do not give a birthdate for Kagetsugu, and, as discussed above, the birth and death dates for Matsumoto are by no means clear. Okada does not make clear on what he bases his age computation. Okada, *Kengō shidan*, 24.

22. Kaku Shōzō, "Ichi-no-tachi," discusses the contemporary Kashima-Shinryū version of ichi-no-tachi, and includes photographic illustrations.

23. Kamiizumi's first lord was Nagano Narimasa, a retainer of Uesugi Norimasa. In 1552 Hōjō Ujiyasu invaded Kōzuke, driving the Uesugi out. Norimasa fled to Echigo province and took refuge with Nagao Kagetora (who later arranged to be adopted by Norimasa and renamed himself Uesugi Kenshin). Nagano, in the meantime, took service with the Hōjō and brought Kamiizumi with him. In 1560 Nagao Kagetora drove the Hōjō back out of Kōzuke, and then enlisted both Nagano and Kamiizumi as vassals. Three years later Takeda Shingen captured Minogawa Castle. Nagano Narimasa was killed in the fighting. *Kashima-Shinryū menkyō kaiden mokuroku*; *Kashima-Shinryū hyōhō denki*; Moroda Seiji, *Kensei Kamiizumi Nobutsuna yōden*; Imamura Yoshio, "Shinkage-ryū," 51–54; Ishigaki, *Jikishin Kageryū*, 60; Ishioka Hisao et al., *Nihon no kobujutsu*, 35–39; Watatani Kiyoshi, *Nihon kengō 100 en*, 32–36.

24. The documents are reproduced in Ishigaki, *Jikishin Kageryū*, 61. For a capsule biography of Marume, see Watatani, *Nihon kengō*, 52–54. The

orthography used in the 1567 document employs the same character later adopted by Kamiizumi's student Okuyama Kyūgasai Kimishige—see below.

25. Quoted in Ōmori, *Bujutsu densho*, 15. Some scholars believe *"Chūkonenryū"* to be an equivalent term for *"Chūkoryū,"* which refers to Kashima-based martial traditions.

26. Biographical information on Aisu Ikōsai Hisatada can be found in Watatani Kiyoshi, *Nihon kengō*, 29–31; Okada, *Kengō shidan*, 66–83; Ishioka et al., *Nihon no kobujutsu*, 31–34; and Moroda, *Kensei*, 124–133.

27. Okada, *Kengō shidan*, 30.

28. The length of training required by ryūha at various times in their history is discussed in John M. Rogers, "Shoden in Japanese Swordsmanship," 4; the diploma is reproduced in Imamura Yoshio, ed., *Shiryō Yagyū Shinkage-ryū*, vol. 1:239.

29. Nakabayashi Shinji, "Kendō shi," 51–54.

30. Excellent discussions of *katsujin-ken* and *setsunin-tō* appear in Iwai Tsukuo, *Kobujutsu tankyū*, 25–27; and Tsumoto Yū, *Yagyū Hyōgosuke*, vol. 3:30. Kamiizumi himself did not explain either term in any extant text, but his student, Yagyū Munenori and his heirs in both the Edo and Owari branches of the Yagyū Shinkage-ryū commented on them—and on Kamiizumi's emphasis on *katsujin-ken*—extensively. See Ōmori, *Bujutsu densho*, 11–46.

Virtually all English-language discussions of these concepts and translations of Japanese commentaries on them have missed the vital distinction between the literal meanings of the terms and their application in bugei jargon. See, for example, Yagyū Munenori (Hiroaki Sato, tr.), *The Sword and the Mind*, 50n, 55–56, 81n; Miyamoto Musashi (Thomas Cleary, tr.), *The Book of Five Rings*, 65, 86; or Donn Draegar and Gordon Warner, *Japanese Swordsmanship*, 74, 96.

31. Diploma given to Yagyū Muneyoshi, dated the fifth month, 1566. Quoted in Ōmori, *Bujutsu densho*, 15.

32. Okuyama first drew Ieyasu's attention by distinguishing himself in the service of Okudaira Sadataka, during the battle of Anekawa (1570), which pitted Tokugawa Ieyasu and Oda Nobunaga against Asakura Yoshishige and Asai Nagamasa, in Ōmi province. His service to Ieyasu began in 1574 at Ieyasu's castle in Okuyama. Ishigaki, *Jikishin Kageryū*, 68–69; Watatani, *Nihon kengō*, 51.

33. *Kashima-Shinryū hyōhō denki;* Ishigaki, *Jikishin Kageryū*, 14, 72–74; Okada, *Kengō shidan*, 25–26.

As noted in the text, the Yagyū Shinkage-ryū was founded by Yagyū Muneyoshi of Yamato province. His son Munenori and his progeny became hereditary fencing instructors to the Tokugawa shōguns, while his grandson Toshiyoshi founded a rival branch in Owari.

34. *Kashima-Shinryū hyōhō denki;* Ishigaki, *Jikishin Kageryū*, 14, 75–78; Watatani, *Kengō shidan*, 148–149.

35. Kamiya's first post was in the Edo mansion of Tsuchiya Tajima-no-kami Kazunao, the daimyō of Tsuchiura (in present-day Ibaraki prefecture). In 1665 he left Tsuchiya to become the fencing instructor for Nagai Iga-no-kami Naoyasu of Takatsuki domain in Kyushu, but he later resigned this post as well. *Kashima-Shinryū hyōhō denki;* Ishigaki, *Jikishin Kageryū*, 14–15, 78–80.

36. *Kashima-Shinryū hyōhō denki;* Ishigaki, *Jikishin Kageryū*, 80–82.

37. *Kashima-Shinryū hyōhō denki;* Nakabayashi, "Kendō shi," 75, 86–87; Ishigaki, *Jikishin Kageryū,* 82–85. Hurst, *The Armed Martial Arts of Japan,* ch. 4 and 7, offers a detailed discussion of the origins and development of sport kendō.

38. *Kashima-Shinryū hyōhō denki;* Ishigaki, *Jikishin Kageryū,* 84–87.

39. Friday, *Hired Swords,* 88–93; Oboroya Hisashi, *Seiwa genji,* 21–27. Yorinobu (968–1048) was one of the premier warriors of the Heian period (794–1185). The twelfth-century tale collection *Konjaku monogatarishū* contains a half dozen or so stories featuring him as protagonist: See William R. Wilson, "Way of the Bow and Arrow: The Japanese Warrior in the Konjaku Monogatari"; and Kobayashi Hiroko, *The Human Comedy of Heian Japan: A Study of the Secular Stories in the 12th Century Collection of Tales, Konjaku Monogatarishu,* 115–119.

40. The *Kunii-ke keizu* lists Yoshimasa as the fourth son of Yorinobu and describes him as having been governor of Hitachi, but both points are probably in error. The *Sonpi bunmyaku* (vol. 3:211) records him as Yorinobu's fifth son, a point reinforced by his nickname, "Gorō," which literally means "fifth son." Hitachi was one of three provinces (the others being Kōzuke and Kazusa) in which the governorships were reserved during the Heian period as sinecures for imperial princes. Such royal governors inevitably remained in the capital; to serve as assistant governor was therefore tantamount to being governor; for this same reason many public and private records confuse the two titles (on this point see Takeuchi Rizō, *Bushi no tōjō,* 14). Unfortunately, no extant records corroborate Yoshimasa's tenure in either post; in fact, there seem to be no contemporaneous sources attesting to who occupied either post between 1031 and 1094 (see Nakayama Nobuna, *Shinhen Hitachi kokushi,* 459). The Kunii family and their activities in Hitachi during the Heian and Kamakura periods are discussed in *Ibaraki-ken shi, chūseihen,* vol. 3:46–47, 108–109, 115–121.

A *hō* was a special form of landholding that, while still under the jurisdiction of the provincial government and therefore not yet a completely private estate *(shōen),* was managed by officers outside the provincial and district office chains of command. The tax revenues from landholdings of this sort were earmarked for the upkeep of local religious institutions or for imperial relatives. For more information, see Nagahara Keiji, *Shōen;* in English, see Nagahara, "Land Ownership Under the Shoen-Kokugaryo System," or Peter Arnesen, "The Struggle for Lordship in Late Heian Japan." Overviews of the history of the Yoshida Shrine and Kunii-hō appear in Takeuchi Rizō, ed., *Kadokawa Nihon chimei daijiten* vol. 8: 977–978, 372–373.

41. The *Kunii-ke keizu* relates that Kunii Takayoshi fled to Shirakawa under pressure from the Ashikaga shogunate, which would place the move in the 1330s or 1340s. Takayoshi apparently earned Ashikaga Takauji's wrath by siding with the Southern Court, and was forced to move to Shirakawa, a center of Southern Court loyalism. Unfortunately, the only record of Takayoshi's activities (the *Kunii-ke keizu*) is not reliable on the matter. It describes Takayoshi as allying with Kitabatake Akiie to protect Emperor Chōkei in Hitachi from an attacking army under Takauji, and further relates how Takayoshi provided naval forces to escort the emperor to Hachinohe, in Mutsu province. The problem with this is that Chōkei was emperor from 1368–1383,

but Kitabatake Akiie died in the battle of Sakai-no-Ura, in 1338. Akiie did escort Prince Yoshinaga, the future Emperor Murakami, to Mutsu in 1336, but the campaigns in Hitachi were waged by his younger brother Akinobu between 1338 and 1344. The *Kunii-ke keizu*, moreover, describes Takayoshi as a twelfth-generation descendant of Yoshimasa, while the *Sonpi bunmyaku* (vol 3:211–212) records him as a ninth-generation descendant.

The only clear documentary reference to the Kunii family in Mutsu in the fourteenth century is a shogunal order of 1397 ordering one Kunii Waka-no-kami chastized for his involvement in a local conflict against the shogunate (*Sōma monjo* doc. 131, Ashikaga Ujimitsu gunsei saisokujō an). There are, however, some twenty-one documents relating to a house called Kunii, albeit written with different characters, who had holdings in Iwaki-gun (Mutsu) from 1292 or earlier and who fought for the Southern Court (*Fukushima-ken shi*, vol. 7, *Kodai chūsei shiryō*, 208–214; vol. 1, *Genshi kodai chūsei tsūshi*, 629–631). This may or may not have been the same family as the Kashima-Shinryū sōke house.

42. Kunii family documents record Kagetsugu's participation in the fourth battle of Kawanakajima in 1561, in the battle of Mikatagahara in 1573, and in other campaigns, and credit him with taking the heads of several enemy commanders.

Kawanakajima, near the border of Shinano and Echigo provinces, was the site of five battles between Takeda Shingen (1521–1573) of Kai province and Uesugi Kenshin (1530–1578) of Echigo, two of the greatest daimyō of their age. The first three battles—in 1553, 1555, and 1557—and the last—in 1564—were relatively minor skirmishes, but the fourth, in 1561, ranks as one of the bloodiest battles in Japanese history.

The battle of Mikatagahara pitted Takeda Shingen against the allied forces of Oda Nobunaga and Tokugawa Ieyasu. While resulting in a rout of the Oda-Tokugawa forces, it was not decisive: Ieyasu and his troops escaped to his castle at Hamamatsu and Shingen elected to withdraw and continue later. Shingen, however, died the following spring, shortly after resuming the campaign.

The *Kunii-ke keizu* also places Kagetsugu and Matsumoto with Shingen in a battle (in which Matsumoto was purportedly killed) against Imagawa Yoshimoto in 1543. As I noted earlier, however, there seems to be no other record of this battle ever having taken place.

Unless otherwise noted, the source here and below for information on the Kunii family is the *Kunii-ke keizu*.

43. *Kunii-ke keizu*; Stephen R. Turnbull, *The Samurai: A Military History*, 228–230.

44. This story is recorded in Seki Humitake, *Shōwa no godai Kashima-Shinryū honden*, 2–3, which cites (unspecified) court records from Sendai.

45. *Kunii-ke keizu*; *Kashima-Shinryū hyōhō denki*; Seki Humitake and Takei Yoshinori, inscription on tombstone erected in Kunii family burial plot, Shōzōin Temple, Kansenazuyado, Yūmoto-chō, Iwaki City, Fukushima prefecture; Watatani and Yamada, eds., *Bugei ryūha daijiten*, 180. Morikawa Tetsurō, "Muteki kengō o tazunete," 330–341.

46. Seki Humitake and Takei Yoshinori, inscription on tombstone erected in Kunii family burial plot, Shōzōin Temple, Kansenazuyado, Yūmoto-chō, Iwaki City, Fukushima prefecture.

47. Seki, *Shōwa no godai*, 49.

48. Personal letter from Seki Humitake dated July 21, 1995.

49. Ōmori, *Bujutsu densho*, identifies at least eight surviving diplomas from Kamiizumi in a chart inserted between pages 16 and 17. Imamura et al., *Nihon budō taikei* vol. 1:16–17 offers a similar list.

50. Tominaga, *Kendō gohyakunen-shi*, 409–415.

51. Hurst, "Ryūha," 17 (1995).

52. Extensive discussions of kishōmon and the ryūha initiation process can be found in Tominaga, *Kendō gohyakunen-shi*, 404–409; Ishioka, *Heihōsha no seikatsu*, 40–68; and Hurst, *Armed Martial Arts*, ch. 8.

53. For background on the Kamakura judicial system, see Jeffrey Mass, *Development of Kamakura Rule*.

54. Ishioka, *Heihōsha no seikatsu*, 40–41, 68. Tominaga, *Kendō gohyakunen-shi*, 405, lists several notables for whom surviving examples of kishōmon have been found, including Oda Nobunaga's son Nobutada, Toyotomi Hideyoshi's adopted heir Hidetsugu, Tokugawa Ieyasu, and his son Hidetada and grandson Ietsuna, the second and fourth shōguns.

55. Examples of kishōmon from various ryūha are reproduced in Ishioka, *Heihōsha no seikatsu*, 42–67. An English translation of a kishōmon from an archery school appears in Ronald Dore, *Education in Tokugawa Japan*, 149–150.

56. Tominaga, *Kendō gohyakunen-shi*, 406.

57. The Jikishin Kageryū document is quoted in Tominaga, *Kendō gohykunen-shi*, 407–408. The Kashima-Shinryū document is quoted in Seki Humitake, *Nihon budō no engen: Kashima-Shinryū*, 14.

58. The Jikishin Kageryū version of the document reads: "Being most grateful for permission to become a student of the Jikishin-Kageryū"; the rest of the text is identical to the Kashima-Shinryū version, except for the final clause, as noted below.

59. From this point forward, the Kashima-Shinryū document differs from the Jikishin Kageryū one; the latter invokes a longer, more elaborate list of divine punishments.

60. Kunii Zen'ya's "Rules for Entrance into the Kashima-Shinryū" are reproduced in Seki, *Nihon budō no engen*, 14.

61. For the original of the constitution for the Kashima-Shinryū Federation of Martial Sciences, see Seki, *Nihon budō no engen*, 16–18.

Chapter 3: The Philosophy and Science of Combat

1. Kunii Zen'ya, "Imaizumi Sensei no oshie o sōki shite," *Kōdō hatsuyō*, 18–22.

2. Kuroda Toshio, "Shintō in the History of Japanese Religion"; Allan Grapard, "Japan's Ignored Cultural Revolution"; Grapard, *The Protocol of the Gods*. Kuroda notes (page 6) that during the period in which the term "shintō" first came into use in Japan (the late seventh and early eighth centuries), it was being employed in China as a variant label for Taoism.

3. Joseph Kitagawa, *On Understanding Japanese Religion*, 139; italics in the original. Pages 139–173 of this volume offer an excellent concise treatment of the vicissitudes of Shintō and its interaction with imported religious traditions.

4. Kitagawa, *On Understanding*, 36, 44–48, 70–71.

5. Following a tradition established in the eighteenth century by Hirayama Gyōzō (who in turn adopted the term from the *Shui hu chuan*, a Ming dynasty Chinese text), Japanese authorities commonly speak of the "Eighteen Forms of Bugei" (bugei jūhappan). This list varies somewhat from author to author, but it typically includes the following arts: the bow, the spear, the sword, sword-drawing, the knife, the *jutte* (a kind of truncheon used by police during the Edo period), shuriken, the naginata, the gun, the staff, the *kusari-gama* (sickle and chain), grappling, binding or tying, horsemanship, swimming, and espionage. (Sasama Yoshihiko, *Zusetsu Nihon budō jiten*, 605–606.)

The Kashima-Shinryū no longer teaches archery, horsemanship, swimming, gunnery, or espionage; it uses the kusari-gama only to teach techniques for defending against it with the sword; and it never taught specialized techniques for the jutte (although many techniques for knives or folding fans lend themselves to the jutte as well).

6. Seki, *Nihon budō no engen*, 35; Jeffrey Dann, *"Kendō" in Japanese Martial Culture*, 260–267, also provides an excellent discussion of *bu* and its connotations in Japan.

7. Niimura Izuru, ed., *Kōjien*, 156. *Neko no myōjutsu* is reproduced in Watanabe Ichirō, ed., *Budō no meicho*, 10–15. The phrase "shinbu ni shite fusetsu" appears on page 13. See D. T. Suzuku, *Zen and Japanese Culture*, 428–435 for an English translation of the entire text.

8. Reproduced in Seki, *Nihon budō no engen*, 13.

9. Seki, *Nihon budō no engen*, 28–29.

10. *Kunii-ke sōden Kashima-Shinryū menkyo kaiden mokuroku*; a partial translation of this document appears in appendix 3.

11. Seki, *Nihon budō no engen*, 30.

12. Seki, *Nihon budō no engen*, 19.

13. Wing-tsit Chan, *A Source Book in Chinese Philosophy*, 245.

14. Seki, *Nihon budō no engen*, 22.

15. Seki, *Nihon budō no engen*, 19–20.

16. Jill Purce, *The Mystic Spiral: Journey of the Soul*, offers an interesting discussion of the spiral as both an example and a nearly universal symbol of natural movement.

17. *Kunii-ke sōden Kashima-Shinryū jūjutsu menkyo kaiden mokuroku*; Seki, *Nihon budō no engen*, 22–23. Yagyū Shinkage-ryū documents, such as the *Shinkage-ryū hyōhō mokuroku* (reproduced in Imamura Yoshio et al., eds., *Nihon budō taikei*, 1:43–60) record the term *"sankakuen-no-tachi"* in a coded orthography that uses a Buddhist term, *"sangaku,"* that refers to the three learnings, or three stages, in one's progress toward enlightenment.

18. Seki, *Nihon budō no engen*, 21–22.

19. The *Kunii-ke sōden Kashima-Shinryū jūjutsu menkyo kaiden mokuroku*; Kunii Zen'ya, "Imaizumi Sensei no oshie o sōki shite."

The eight deities of the diagram are the guardians and protectors of the emperor and his realm, listed as the *Mikannaki no matsuru kami hachiza* in the *Engi shiki*, a fifty-volume collection of regulations for proper imperial court procedures published during the Engi era (901–923) on the orders of Emperor Daigo (r. 897–930) and later revised and expanded by Matsudaira Naritake in 1818. In *Shintei zōhō kokushi taikei* (Tokyo: Yoshikawa kōbunkan, 1937) vol. 26, 180.

20. Seki, *Nihon budō no engen*, 21–23.

21. *Kunii-ke sōden Kashima-Shinryū menkyo kaiden mokuroku* and *Jikishin seitō ichiryū hyōhō mokuroku* (see below).

The fifteen constructs the documents have in common are *aigamae, aishin, aijaku, metsuke, shikake, te-no-uchi, tome-sandan, tai-atari, tachi-atari, kiriotoshi, gimmi, kiate, gontaiyū, sōtai-no-shime,* and *tatazu-no-kachi.* The Jikishin Kageryū's interpretation of what the Kashima-Shinryū certificate lists as applied constructs is laid out in the *Jikishin Kageryū kata mokuroku denkai*, a commentary on the *Jikishin Kageryū chūden mokuroku*, a nineteenth-century abbreviated version of the *Jikishin seitō ichiryū hyōhō mokuroku*. The *Jikishin seitō ichiryū hyōhō mokuroku*, *Jikishin Kageryū kata mokuroku denkai*, and the *Jikishin Kageryū chūden mokuroku* are reproduced in Imamura Yoshio et al., eds., *Nihon budō taikei*, vol. 3: 300–302, 321–326, and 314–318, respectively. Ishigaki 183–249 contains a contemporary annotation of the Jikishin Kageryū's version of the constructs.

22. Seki, *Nihon budō no engen*, 29.

23. Seki, *Nihon budō no engen*, 27.

24. Yuasa Yasuo offers a detailed English-language discussion of the concept of ki and its application to the bugei and other physical activities in *The Body, Self-Cultivation, and Ki-Energy*. A brief but illuminating discussion of ki as the term is used in modern Japanese culture and by Japanese religions appears in Helen Hardacre, *Kuroizumikyō*, 20–21.

The phenomenon of ki and Kashima-Shinryū methods for cultivating and controlling it are discussed further in chapter 4.

25. Seki, *Nihon budō no engen*, 29.

26. E. J. Harrison, *The Fighting Spirit of Japan*, 129–130, following Kumashiro Hikotaro, *Kiaijutsu* (publication data unknown).

27. Seki, *Nihon budō no engen*, 28.

28. Akagawa Imao, "Reitai kaihatsu o motomete."

29. Seki, *Nihon budō no engen*, 28.

30. The *Jikishin Kageryū kata mokuroku denkai* describes the same todome techniques for gyoi uchi, teki-uchi, and ishu uchi (Imamura et al., *Nihon budō taikei* vol. 3: 323–324). Ishigaki (226) also discusses todome sandan, based on a Jikishin Kageryū text he identifies as the *Gokui kaiden sho*. This document names the three contexts for killing as "loyalty [to one's lord]" *(chū)*, "filial piety" *(kō)*, and "fidelity [to one's friends]" *(shin)* and reverses the procedures prescribed for todome in the cases of gyoi uchi and teki-uchi.

31. Seki Humitake, *Kashima-Shinryū shihan-yō bujutsu kyōsho*, 83.

32. Seki, *Nihon budō no engen*, 27.

33. Seki, *Nihon budō no engen*, 29.

34. Seki, *Nihon budō no engen*, 29.

35. Seki, *Nihon budō no engen*, 23, 27.

36. Seki, *Nihon budō no engen*, 27.

Chapter 4: The Martial Path

1. Issai Chozan, *Neko no myōjutsu*, reproduced in Watanabe Ichirō, ed., *Budō no meicho*, 15.

2. G. Victor Sōgen Hori discusses at considerable length the notion of "Development" versus "Self-Discovery" (his terms) as it applies to Rinzai Zen Buddhist training in "Teaching and Learning in the Rinzai Zen Monastery."

3. The following discussion of kata is elaborated from Karl Friday, "Kabala in Motion."

4. Fujiwara Yoshinobu, *Menhyōhō no ki*, quoted in Nakabayashi Shinji, "Kenjutsu Keiko no ikkōsatsu," 161–162.

The date of publication of Yoshinobu's text is unknown, but it is believed to have been written in the late Edo period. The ryūha discussed is one from the Shinkage-ryū tradition, transmitted within the Nabeshima family.

5. cf. Tomiki Kenji, *Budō ron*, 42–56, 60.

6. David Slawson, *Secret Teachings in the Art of Japanese Gardens: Design Principles and Aesthetic Values*, 54.

7. Fujiwara Yoshinobu, *Menhyōhō no ki*, quoted in Nakabayashi, "Kenjutsu Keiko," 165.

8. Fujiwara Yoshinobu, *Menhyōhō no ki*, quoted in Nakabayashi, "Kenjutsu Keiko," 166.

9. Eugen Herrigel, *Zen in the Art of Archery*, and D. T. Suzuki, *Zen and Japanese Culture*, 87–214, are perhaps the two authors most responsible for creating the association of the bugei with Zen. Most subsequent works on the bugei seem to have accepted this association rather uncritically, discussing at length the nature of Zen and why it ought to have appealed to the samurai, but never questioning whether or not it actually *did* have a widespread influence on the bugei prior to modern times. Thus studies like Donn F. Draeger, *Classical Budō*, and Oscar Ratti and Adele Westbrook, *Secrets of the Samurai*—both standard volumes on the shelves of martial arts aficionados—exemplify this epistomological blind spot, while two more recent books, Thomas Cleary, *The Japanese Art of War*, and Winston L. King, *Zen and the Way of the Sword*, virtually reify it, depicting Zen as the heart and soul of samurai martial culture.

Far better perspectives on the intersection of Zen with samurai traditions are provided in E. J. Harrison, *Fighting Spirit*, 140–152; Martin Collcutt, *Five Mountains: The Rinzai Zen Monastic Institution in Medieval Japan*; and G. Cameron Hurst, *The Armed Martial Arts of Japan*. John P. Keenan, "Spontaneity in Western Martial Arts: A Yogācāra Critique of *Mushin* (No Mind)"; Stewart McFarlane, "*Mushin*, Morals, and Martial Arts: A Discussion of Keenan's Yogācāra Critique"; Keenan, "The Mystique of Martial Arts: A Response to Professor McFarlane"; and McFarlane, "The Mystique of Martial Arts: A Reply to Response Professor Keenan's Response" offer a lively debate over the role of Zen and other Buddhist and non-Buddhist Eastern religious traditions in Asian martial art.

10. Hori, 11–12, provides a thorough discussion of "teaching without teaching." For a general discussion of Zen teaching philosophy and the notion of mind-to-mind-transmission, see Chang Chung-yuan, *Original Teachings of Buddhism, Selected from The Transmission of the Lamp*, 85–87.

11. Robert Eno, *The Confucian Creation of Heaven: Philosophy and the Defense of Ritual Mastery*, offers an insightful and provocative discussion of the meaning of ritual in early Confucianism. See especially pages 6–13 and 68–69.

12. For a general introduction to neo-Confucianism, see Fung Yu-lan, *A Short History of Chinese Philosophy*, 266–318.

13. Ronald Dore, *Education in Tokugawa Japan*, 127.

14. Dore, 124–152.

15. Hori, 5–7. Pattern practice and drill are also the key to the highly successful Kumon and Suzuki programs for teaching academic and musical skills in contemporary Japan. Nancy Ukai's "Kumon Approach to Teaching and Learning" is an enlightening discussion of the former.

16. Jeffrey Dann, "Kendō in Japanese Martial Culture," 237–244, offers an alternative analysis of shu-ha-ri as the process is conceptualized in modern kendō. Donn Draeger, *Classical Budo*, 41–65, breaks the learning process into four stages—*gyō, shugyō, jutsu* and *dō*—illustrating them by analogy to the process of mastering touch typing.

17. Examples of such documents are reproduced in Imamura Yoshio et al., eds., *Nihon budō taikei*, vol. 1: 14, 20–21; vol. 2: 402–403, 439–462; vol. 3: 12–13; and Seki Humitake, *Nihon budō no engen: Kashima-Shinryū*, 30–32.

18. Kurogi Toshiharu, "Budō ryūha no seiritsu to shūgendō"; Tominaga Kengo, *Kendō gohyakunen-shi*, 50–51, 63–69; Ishioka Hisao, Wakada Kazuo, and Katō Hiroshi, *Nihon no kobujutsu*, 15–18; Nakabayashi Shinji, "Kendō shi," in *Nihon budō taikei*, vol. 10, 40–42; Ishioka Hisao, *Heihōsha no seikatsu*, 69–76. Tominaga asserts that musha shugyō served a double purpose, helping a warrior both to hone his martial skills and to attract the attention and interest of potential employers. Ishioka observes that it also provided a cover for various espionage and intelligence-gathering activities. Accounts of specific musha shugyō adventures can be found in Inagaki Motō, *Kengō no meishōbu 100 wa*; Kobe Shinjūrō, *Nihon kengōdan*; Okada Kazuo, *Kengō shidan*; Watatani Kiyoshi, *Nihon kengō 100 en*; and Sugawara Makoto, *Lives of Master Swordsmen*.

19. The conventional wisdom among the Japanese authorities on this topic attributes the decline of taryū-jiai and musha shugyō to prohibition edicts issued in the mid-seventeenth century by the shogunate and quickly echoed by the lords of numerous domains and by many of the ryūha themselves (see, for example, Ishioka et al., *Nihon no kobujutsu*, 20; Nakabayashi, 72–74; or Tominaga, 272–275). A word of caution on this point is in order, however: The bans on taryū-jiai are mentioned by most studies of the subject, but we have been unable to identify the specific dates for the bans or to locate a primary source confirming them. Moreover, neither taryū-jiai nor musha shugyō disappeared completely, as the numerous accounts of celebrated duels during the middle and late Tokugawa period attest. In fact, Tominaga (273) quotes two documents from the late seventeenth century—one issued by the government of Tsuyama domain in Mimasaka province and the other by a bugei school (the Asayama Ichiden-ryū)—that both imply a general prohibition on taryū-jiai to have existed but also outline circumstances under which such contests were to be permitted. This is further evidence that duels and matches were still occurring, even if with restrictions.

20. Quoted in Ishioka et al., *Nihon no kobujutsu*, 20.

21. See the passage quoted in Ishioka et al., *Nihon no kobujutsu*, 21.

22. For recent discussions of this issue, see Nakabayashi Shinji, "Kenjutsu Keiko no ikkōsatsu"; Yoshitani Osamu, "Kenjutsu kata no kōzō to kinō ni kansuru kenkyū"; Tomiki Kenji, *Budō ron*, 5–9, 13–25, 52–101; or Iwai Tsukuo, *Kobujutsu tankyū*, 58–67, 88–107.

23. Seki, *Nihon budō no engen*, 35.

24. Seki, *Kashima-Shinryū shihan-yō*, 20, 102–105.

25. Matsushita Keishi, "Korai no waza," 26–27.

26. Seki, *Nihon budō no engen*, 40–41. See also, Kaku Shōzō, "Kesagiri."

27. Seki, *Nihon budō no engen*, 41–43; see also Kaku, "Ashibarai-ukebune."

28. Seki, *Nihon budō no engen*, 43–44.

29. Seki, *Nihon budō no engen*, 44–45; see also Kaku, "Kurai-tachi."

30. Seki, *Nihon budō no engen*, 104; see also Matsushita, "Sōgō bujutsu."

31. The duel between Kamiizumi Ise-no-Kami Hidetsugu and Yagyū Muneyoshi is discussed in detail by Inagaki Motō, *Kengō meishōbu hyakuwa*, 26–31. An English language account of the same contest appears in Sugawara Makoto, *Lives of Master Swordsmen*, 96–99.

32. Tominaga, *Kendō gohyaku-nen-shi*, 447–450. Miyamoto Musashi, *Gorin no sho*, in Imamura et al., *Nihon budō taikei*, 2:72.

33. Slawson, 55.

34. Yamasaki, *Shingon: Japanese Esoteric Buddhism*, 35–36. Tominaga, *Kendō gohyakunen-shi*, 418, observes that esoteric Buddhism's stress on secretive transmission only to the initiated also influenced bugei masters in their choices of vocabulary for expressing concepts, and in their design of rituals surrounding the transmission process.

35. John M. Rogers, "Shoden in Japanese Swordsmanship," 1, 8. Further discussion of instructional verses, and examples thereof, can be found in Ishioka, *Heihōsha no seikatsu*, 77–92; and Imamura, *Budō ka enshū*, vols. 1–2.

Ikunsho is dated 1571 and is reproduced in Imamura et al., *Nihon budō taikei*, 3:58–66.

Watanabe, *Budō no meicho*, contains annotated transcriptions of forty-one traditional texts, while the ten volumes of the *Nihon budō taikei* include transcriptions and commentary on dozens more. Ōmori, *Budō densho no kenkyū*, is a collection of analytical essays on important bugei texts.

Modern Japanese translations of the *Heihō kaden sho*, *Fudōchi shinmyō roku*, *Gorin no sho*, *Tengu geijutsuron*, and other texts appear in Yoshida Yutaka, *Budō hitsudensho*. Famous martial art essays and volumes translated into English include: D. T. Suzuki, *Zen and Japanese Culture*, which contains translations of *Taiaki* (166–168), *Neko no myōjutsu* (428–435), and partial translations of *Fudōchi shinmyōroku* (94–108, 111–112) and *Mujūshinken* (170–180); *A Book of Five Rings*, tr., Victor Harris, a translation of *Gorin no sho*; *The Book of Five Rings*, tr., Nihon Services Corporation, a more recent translation of the same work; Takuan Sōhō, *The Unfettered Mind*, which contains translations of *Fudōchi shinmyōroku* (17–44), *Taiaki* (77–92), and *Reirōshū* (45–75); Yagyū Munenori, *The Sword and the Mind* (tr., Hiroaki Sato), which contains translations of *Fudōchi shinmyōroku* (110–120), *Heihō kaden sho* (21–110), and *Taiaki* (123–125); Betty J. Fitzgerald, *Zen and Confucius in the Art of Swordsmanship*, a translation of *Tengu geijutsu ron*, from Reinhard Kammer's 1969 German translation, *Die Kunst der Bergdämonen*; and Miyamoto Musashi, *The Book of Five Rings*, tr., Thomas Cleary, a translation of *Gorin no sho* (5–62) that also includes a translation of *Heihō kaden sho* (63–111). Trevor Leggett, *Zen and the Ways*, contains partial translations of *Tengu geijutsu ron* (182–201), *Heihō kaden sho* (158–64), *Ittōsai sensei kenpō sho* (169–173), several instructional verses from the Hōzōin-ryū (165–168), and a text from the Shin-no-Shintō-ryū (174–180); Sugawara Makoto, *Lives of Master Swordsmen*, 217–239, offers yet another translation of *Fudōchi shinmyō roku*.

36. The *Tengu sho* was among the documents lost in 1965.

37. Seki, *Nihon budō no engen*, 32–33.

38. The Kashima-Shinryū version of *Ryū no maki* is transcribed in Seki, *Nihon budō no engen*, 5–6.

39. No documents from Kamiizumi Ise-no-kami Hidetsuna to Okuyama Kyugasai Kimishige, his successor within the Kashima-Shinryū shihanke lineage, survive, and for this reason I have chosen not to translate any of Kamiizumi's writings here. But at least nine kudensho and inka (all consisting of simple lists in the style of the*Tengu sho*) given to other senior disciples are extant, as are a handful of more effusive texts by these disciples and their students, making it possible for analysts to draw at least some conclusions about Kamiizumi's martial philosophy and tactics. The lengthiest of this latter group are those produced by the members of the Yagyū Shinkage-ryū lineage, including a text called the *Yūkansho* purportedly written by Kamiizumi himself (reproduced in Imamura et al., *Nihon budō taikei* 1:254–267). This document is, however, unsigned, undated, and written in an identical hand and on paper and mountings identical to that of a second document, the *Himonshū*, also unsigned but listing as its authors Kamiizumi, Yagyū Muneyoshi, Yagyū Munenori, and Yagyū Mitsuyoshi (Jūbei), suggesting that it was either a later copy of a document signed by Kamiizumi or perhaps the work of one or more later swordsmen in the Yagyū Shinkage-ryū lineage. In any case, Kashima-Shinryū masters have not recognized the text as belonging to the Kashima-Shinryū tradition.

For more on Kamiizumi and his writings, see Ōmori, 11–46 and *Nihon budō takei*, 1:12–17.

40. The verses translated below appear in Seki, *Nihon budō no engen*,33–34.

41. Yuasa, 21–23.

42. Yuasa, 15–16.

43. Yuasa, 17–20. Yuasa argues that meditation and psychotherapy utilize essentially the same psychological mechanism, the resolution of the conscious and subconscious minds. But whereas psychotherapy seeks to restore to a normal state a patient experiencing problems arising from conflicts between his conscious and his subconscious, meditation seeks to strengthen and enhance the function of an otherwise healthy subject, raising his mind to levels above the normal state. He offers further discussion of pathological and hallucinatory states that can be encountered in the course of meditation (pages 90–97).

44. Shintō purification rituals are discussed in Tanaka Jigohei, *Chinkonhō no jisshū*.

45. The Taoist religion, China's oldest and most highly developed indigenous theology, emerged between the second and fourth centuries CE, combining elements of local spirit cults, China's ancient state religion, alchemic practices, and immortality cults with a reformulation of the ideas expressed in the classics of the Eastern Chou (770–256 BCE) era, the *Tao te ching*, and the *Chuang-tzu*. For an overview of the Taoist religion, see Daniel Overmeyer, "Chinese Religion," 265–267, 272–275, 279–281. Daniel P. Reid, *The Tao of*

Health, Sex, and Longevity, offers a detailed discussion of Taoist exercises for cultivating the Three Rivers. The philosophy of religious Taoism is highlighted in *Vitality, Energy, Spirit: A Taoist Sourcebook,* tr. and ed. by Thomas Cleary. Yuasa, 69–128, and Waysun Liao, *T'ai Chi Classics,* 3–85, provide in-depth treatments of Taoist methods for regulating and controlling the *ch'i/ki.*

46. Yuasa, 100–109.

47. Yuasa, 76, 117–118; *shintai kankaku* and *zenshin naibu kankaku,* rendered "coenesthesis" in English translation, are discussed on pages 37–65.

48. Yuasa, 76–79.

49. Ki training, called *"kikō"* in Japanese or *"ch'igung"* in Chinese, has become a minor industry in Japan, and more recently in the United States as well. Interested applicants can enroll in any of several dozen commercial schools and clinics operated by reiki "masters" and "grandmasters" whose curricula promise to endow students with amazing psychophysical powers. One such master, in Honolulu, reports the ability to heal injuries by laying on of hands, and even recounts an experience in which she healed her cat with treatments projected from miles away. See Joan Tully, "So What Does It Do?"

50. Allan Grapard, "Flying Mountains and Walkers of Emptiness"; Yamasaki Taikō, *Shingon,* 61–62, 106–107.

51. Yamasaki, 119, 152–169, 182–215. Yuasa (21) describes the meditation practices of esoteric Buddhism as techniques for "artificially creating visual images through the active imagination."

52. Gachirinkan, and the closely related practice of *ajikan,* are discussed in Yamasaki, 190–215. Kashima-Shinryū meditation and breathing exercises are discussed in Seki, *Nihon budō no engen,* 127–129.

53. Seki Humitake, "Bujutsu to ki."

Epilogue

1. This anecdote appears in McFarlane, *"Mushin,* Morals, and Martial Arts," 408.

Appendixes

1. The phrase "our house" is a literal rendition of *"waga ie,"* but its precise meaning is unclear. It cannot refer to any specific biological family—such as the Kunii house—since it also appears in the Jikishin Kageryū version of this document. The Jikishin Kageryū—or, more formally, the Kashima Shinden Jikishin Kageryū—claims the same lineage as the Kashima-Shinryū through the first nine generations, and its version of the *Hyōhō denki* is nearly identical to the Kashima-Shinryū version for the first seven generations. Neither document, however, makes reference to the ryūha as belonging to any one biological lineage prior to the twelfth generation, when the Kashima-Shinryū version records the succession of Kunii Taizen. The Jikishin Kageryū version of the *Hyōhō denki* is reproduced in Ishigaki, *Jikishin Kageryū,* 44–46.

2. The Jikishin Kageryū version of this document calls the founder "Sugimoto Bizen-no-kami Ki no Masamoto." This is probably the result of an error in the transcription of the character "matsu" at some point in the past when the text was copied: Virtually all historians agree on "Matsumoto" as the correct surname. The "Sugimoto" surname appears in copies of the document

dating as far back as 1844 (Ishigaki, *Jikishin-kageryū*, 55), so the error must have occurred prior to this point.

3. 1159–1189; the great hero of the Gempei Wars of 1180–1185, out of which Japan's first military government, the Kamakura shogunate, was born. Yoshitsune has become one of Japan's best-loved heroes. He had a falling out with his elder brother, Yoritomo, the founder of the shogunate, shortly after the Gempei fighting ended and was hunted down and killed by Yoritomo.

4. This last sentence does not appear in the Jikishin Kageryū version of the text.

5. The Okudaira had once been vassals of the Takeda. In 1573 they left this service to join Ieyasu.

An alternative interpretation for this passage is offered by Imamura Yoshio in *Nihon budō taikei*, vol. 3:304: Imamura's reading would translate as, "His ancestors were a branch of the Taira [Heike]." This reading, which splits the "oku" from "taira" and appends it to the previous character ("sen," or "forebears") is, however, somewhat problematic in that I have been unable to find the term *"senoku"* in any dictionary. Ishigaki (67) reads it as I have translated it.

6. The original term rendered here as "guidance" is *"shinryō,"* a Buddhist term meaning the aid of a deity toward salvation.

7. The character read as "kage" in Matsumoto's original orthography for the school was intended to convey that the school was a direct transmission from the deity of the Kashima Shrine. In its Japanese reading *(kage)*, it carries the meaning of indebtedness for favors granted, and of invisible backing and support. But in its Chinese reading (*in* or *on*—*yin* in Mandarin Chinese), it has connotations of negativity and darkness. Kamiizumi retained this character, but changed the first character from the one used by Matsumoto—meaning "divine" or "deity"—to one that meant "new." This passage relates that Okuyama then restored the original "shin" (i.e., "divine") but changed the character for "kage" to one without the negative connotations of the original character. The new character—read *"ei"* in its Sino-Japanese reading—means "reflection," "figure," "light," or "tracings," in addition to its literal meaning of "shadow."

8. The Tōkai region consists of the eastern Pacific seaboard provinces of Japan—i.e., Ise, Iga, Shima, Owari, Mikawa, Tōtōmi, Suruga, Kai, Izu, Sagami, Awa, Kazusa, Shimōsa, Hitachi, and Musashi.

9. Hidetada (1579–1632) was the the second shōgun, and the third son of Ieyasu.

10. The word "moreover" does not appear in the Jikishin Kageryū version of the document.

11. Ishigaki, *Jikishin-kageryū*, (14) suggests that the name change was to distinguish Ogasawara's school from that of the Yagyūs.

12. Ishigaki (80–81) suggests that this indicates concern that the Shinkage had been dropped and thus the school might no longer be readily connected with the original tradition.

13. The new name carried something of a pun. Literally meaning "direct reflections (or shadows) of the heart," it was also a homophone for "correct (or directly transmitted) Shinkage-ryū."

14. From this point forward, the Kashima-Shinryū version of the document is completely different from the Jikishin Kageryū version.

15. Sano Takenosuke was a retainer of the Mitō domain and a famous loyalist of the Meiji restoration. Mitō was a domain in eastern Japan consisting principally of what is now Ibaraki prefecture. From the time of Mitō Mitsukuni (1638–1700), Mitō City—the domain capital—became famous as a center of scholarly and martial learning, emphasizing the native heritage of Japan over the Chinese tradition.

16. The Satsuma Rebellion marked the apotheosis of the samurai class. In 1877 some 30,000 ex-samurai, led by Saigō Takamori, began a rebellion that took the new national government six months and 40,000 troops to put down. The rebels are traditionally perceived as having been alarmed over the pace of social change in general and the abolition of many of the privileges of the samurai class in particular. The government victory was a victory of a modern-trained, modern-equipped peasant conscript army over an army of traditional warriors and signalled the end of the age of the samurai.

17. Inaba (1516–1588) was known as one of the "Three-Man Crowd of Minō," along with Ujiie Hitachi-no-kami and Andō Iga-no-kami. A formidable general, he served first the Tozaki, then the Saitō, then Nobunaga, and finally Hideyoshi.

18. Heads, particularly those of ranking warriors, were a standard trophy collected by samurai in battle. They were normally presented to one's superiors as proof of one's accomplishments during the fighting, in the expectation of a reward. Victorious commanders often publicly displayed the heads of vanquished enemies. To prevent this sort of dishonor, Masateru took his lord's head himself and buried it where the enemy would not be able to find it.

19. Kobayakawa defected to the forces of Tokugawa Ieyasu according to a prearranged plan, thus assuring the victory of the Eastern faction.

20. Marubashi (??–1651), a samurai of Yamagata in northern Japan, and Yūi (??–1651), the son of a dyer who had raised himself to samurai rank and earned a reputation as an expert in the military arts, were involved in a plot against the shōgun, Iemitsu, in 1651. They were arrested; Yūi committed suicide and Marubashi was crucified. Kanai Hanbei (1619?–1651) was also a member of Yūi's band; he committed suicide after the rebellion failed.

21. A catastrophic, nationwide famine lasting from 1783–1787. It was part of a long series of natural disasters.

22. Ritual suicide, the final avenue open to a samurai to atone for a wrong; also called *hara-kiri*.

23. *Shishi* were anti-shogunal activists in the 1850s and 1860s. The use of the term for warriors of the early eighteenth century is anachronistic.

24. Sano and Kurosawa were famous swordsmen and anti-bakufu activists of the Mitō domain.

25. A violent battle of the Satsuma Rebellion. In seventeen days of hard fighting, casualties reached over 4,000 for both sides.

26. "Mundane Realm" translates *"tenka"*; literally meaning "all below the heavens," the term was used by early modern Shintō and neo-Confucian political philosophers to refer to the whole of Japan, as opposed to the individual (and semiautonomous) domains of the late medieval and early modern "daimyō."

27. The "three sacred treasures" refer to the Imperial Regalia: a mirror, sword, and jewel.

28. The "*bandō*," literally "East of the Barrier," refers to eastern Japan—principally the provinces of Sagami, Musashi, Kazusa, Shimōsa, Hitachi, Kōzuke, Shimotsuke, and Mutsu, although Dewa and Awa are sometimes included as well. The capital specifically indicates the imperial capital city of Kyoto, but when juxtaposed against the bandō in this manner refers, by extension, to the whole of western Japan.

29. A student of Kamiizumi Hidetsuna, Kurando began studying the sword at the age of 10, after an experience at age 8—in which he captured a robber in his storehouse—convinced him of the need to learn the weapon.

30. Tomonori (1528–1576) was a daimyō and seventh-generation governor of Ise. Defeated by Oda Nobunaga in 1569, he accepted vassalage under him. In 1576 he fell ill, and was later murdered by his own samurai.

31. A general of the Sengoku period and a vassal of the Amako family.

32. Takada (1590–1671) was an expert with the spear and the founder of the Takada-ryū, a branch of the Hōsōin-ryū. He fought on the Toyotomi side during the summer seige of Osaka castle (one account says he did so on orders from Ieyasu) and also distinguished himself in the Shimabara Rebellion of 1637–1638. He taught sōjutsu first at a private dōjō in Edo and then as personal instructor to several daimyō. In 1651 he performed a demonstration for Shōgun Iemitsu.

33. A student of Kamiizumi Hidetsuna and the founder of the Kitan-ryū.

34. One of Shingen's top commanders, Kansuke is thought to have been killed in battle at Kawanakajima in 1561, at the age of 69.

35. The date of this battle is probably in error. Kawanakajima was the site of most of the Takeda/Uesugi battles, the last of which was fought in 1564.

BIBLIOGRAPHY

Primary Sources

Engi shiki. Shintei zōhō kokushi taikei. Tokyo: Yoshikawa kōbunkan, 1937.
Fukushima-ken shi. Vol. 7 of *Kodai-chūsei shiryō.* Compiled by Fukushima-ken. Fukushima, 1966.
Gekken sōdan. In *Shinhen bujutsu sōsho (zen),* ed. Budōsho kangyōkai, 187–242. Tokoyo: Jibutsu Ōraisha, 1968.
Honchō bugei shōden. In *Shinhen bujutsu sōsho (zen), ed.* Budōsho kangyōkai, 5–108. Tokyo: Jinbutsu Ōraisha, 1968.
Ibaraki-ken shi chūseihen, vol. 3. Compiled by Ibaraki-ken. Ibaraki-ken, 1986.
Ibaraki-ken shiryō, chūsei hen. Compiled by Ibaraki-ken shi hensan chūsei shi bukai. 2 vols. Mito, Ibaraki-ken, 1970.
Imamura Yoshio, Nakabayashi Shinji, Ishioka Hisamu, Oimatsu Shin'ichi, and Fujikawa Seikatsu, eds. *Nihon budō taikei.* 10 vols. Tokyo: Dōshōsha, 1982.
Kashima jiranki. Vol. 21 of *Gunsho ruijū, kassen-bu.* Edited by Hanawa Hōkinoichi. Tokyo: Shoku gunsho ruijū kanseikai, 1931.
Kashima shi. Vol. 22 of *Shintō taikei, jinjahen.* Tokyo: Seikōsha, 1984.
Kashima-Shinryū hyōhō denki. Kunii family private collection.
Kashima-Shinryū ōgi. Kunii family private collection.
Kitabatake Chikafusa. *Shingon naishōgi.* Vol. 83 of Nihon koten bungaku taikei. Tokyo: Iwanami shoten, 1964: 226–240.
Konjaku monogatari-shū. 5 vols. Nihon koten bungaku zenshū. Tokyo: Shōgakkan, 1971.
Kunii-ke sōden Kashima-Shinryū jūjutsu menkyo kaiden mokuroku. Kunii family private collection.
Kunii-ke sōden Kashima-Shinryū menkyo kaiden mokuroku. Kunii family private collection.
Mutsuwaki. Gunsho ruijū. Tokyo: Shoku gunsho ruijū kanseikai, 1941.
Nihon chūkō bujutsu keifu ryaku. In *Shinhen bujutsu sōsho (zen),* ed. Budōsho kangyōkai, 109–142. Tokyo: Jinbutsu Ōraisha, 1968.
Nihon shoki. 2 vols. Shintei zōhō kokushi taikei. Tokyo: Yoshikawa kōbunkan, 1985.
Ryū no maki. Kunii family private collection.
Shingon naishōgi. Vol. 83 *(Kana hōgo)* of *Iwanami Nihon koten bungaku taikei.* Tokyo: Iwanami shoten, 1964: 226–240.
Shinhen Hitachi kokushi. Compiled by Nakayama Nobuna. 2 vols. Mito, Ibarakiken, 189–1901.
Shin sarugakki. Vol. 8 of Nihon shisō taikei. Tokyo: Iwanami shoten, 1986.
Shinsen bujutsu ryūso roku. In *Shinhen bujutsu sōsho (zen),* ed. Budōsho kangyōkai, 143–185. Tokyo: Jinbutsu Ōraisha, 1968.
Shizuoka-ken shiryō. Compiled by Shizuoka-ken. 5 vols. Shizuoka-ken, 1932–1941.

Shoku Nihongi. 2 vols. Shintei zōhō kokushi taikei. Tokyo: Yoshikawa kōbunkan, 1986.

Sōma monjo. Compiled by Toyoda Takeshi and Tashiro Osamu (Zoku Gunsho ruijū kanseikai, *Shiryō sanshū, komonjo hen*). Toyko, 1979.

Sonpi bunmyaku. 5 vols. Shintei zōhō kokushi taikei. Tokyo: Yoshikawa kōbunkan, 1983.

Tengu sho. Kunii family private collection.

Watanabe Ichirō, ed. *Budō no meicho.* Tokyo: Tōkyō kopii shuppanbu, 1979.

Secondary Sources

Akagawa Imao. "Reitai kaihatsu o motomete (7)." *Shinrei kenkyū* 29:3 (March 1975): 20–24.

———. *Shinshin no kiseki.* Tokyo: Tama shuppan, 1978.

Amdur, Ellis. "The History and Development of the Naginata." *The Journal of Asian Martial Arts* 4:1 (1995): 32–49.

Anderson, L. J. *Japanese Armour.* New York: Lionel Leventhal, 1968.

Arnesen, Peter J. "The Struggle for Lordship in Late Heian Japan: The Case of Aki." *Journal of Japanese Studies* 10:1 (1984): 101–141.

Asakura Kōtarō. "Kashima-Shinryū: Ki nokagaku." *Gekken kendō nihon* 4 (1991): 63–66.

Aston, W. G. *Nihongi: Chronicles of Japan from the Earliest Times to 697 ad.* 1896. Reprint. Rutland, VT: Tuttle, 1972 .

Blacker, Carmen. *The Catalpa Bow: A Study of Shamanistic Practices in Japan.* 1975. Reprint. London: Allen and Unwin, 1986.

Bottomly, I., and A. P. Hopson. *Arms and Armour of the Samurai: The History of Weaponry in Ancient Japan.* New York: Crescent Books, 1988.

Chan, Wing-tsit. *A Source Book in Chinese Philosophy.* Princeton, NJ: Princeton University Press, 1963.

Chang Chung-yuan. *Original Teachings of Buddhism, Selected from The Transmission of the Lamp.* New York: Pantheon, 1969.

Cleary, Thomas. *The Japanese Art of War.* Boston, MA: Shambala, 1991.

Cleary, Thomas, trans. and ed. *Vitality, Energy, Spirit: A Taoist Sourcebook.* Boston, MA: Shambala, 1991.

Collcutt, Martin. *Five Mountains: The Rinzai Zen Monastic Institution in Medieval Japan.* Cambridge, MA: Harvard University Press, 1981.

Craig, Darrell. *Iai: The Art of Drawing the Sword.* 1981. Reprint. Rutland, VT: Tuttle, 1988.

Daniel, Charles. *Kenjutsu: The Art of Japanese Swordsmanship.* Burbank, CA: Unique Publications, 1991.

Dann, Jeffrey. "*Kendo* in Japanese Martial Culture: Swordsmanship as Self-Cultivation." (Ph.D. dissertation, University of Washington, 1978.) Ann Arbor, MI: University Microfilms, 1978.

de Bary, Theodore, ed. *Sources of Japanese Tradition.* 2 vols. 1958. Reprint. New York: Columbia University Press, 1964.

Deshimaru Taisen. *The Zen Way to the Martial Arts.* New York: Dutton, 1982.

Dore, Ronald P. *Education in Tokugawa Japan.* Berkeley: University of California Press, 1965.

Draeger, Donn F. *Classical Budo.* Vol. 2 of *The Martial Arts and Ways of Japan.* New York: Weatherhill, 1973.

———. *Classical Bujutsu.* Vol. 1 of *The Martial Arts and Ways of Japan.* New York: Weatherhill, 1973.

———. *Modern Bujutsu and Budo.* Vol. 3 of *The Martial Arts and Ways of Japan.* New York: Weatherhill, 1974.

Draeger, Donn F., and Gordon Warner. *Japanese Swordsmanship: Technique and Practice.* New York: Weatherhill, 1982.

Draeger, Donn F., and Robert W. Smith. *Comprehensive Asian Fighting Arts.* 1969. Reprint. Tokyo: Kodansha, 1980.

Dunn, Charles J. *Everyday Life in Imperial Japan.* New York: Putnam, 1969.

Earhart, H. Byron. *A Religious Study of the Mount Haguro Sect of Shugendō: An Example of Japanese Mountain Religion.* Monumenta Nipponica Monograph. Tokyo: Sophia University Press, 1970.

Elison, George, and Bardwell L. Smith, eds. *Warlords, Artists, and Commoners: Japan in the 16th Century.* Honolulu: University of Hawai'i Press, 1981.

Eno, Robert. *The Confucian Creation of Heaven: Philosophy and the Defense of Ritual Mastery.* Albany, NY: State University of New York Press, 1990.

Finn, Michael. *Martial Arts: A Complete Illustrated History.* Woodstock, NY: Overlook, 1988.

Fitzgerald, Betty J. *Zen and Confucius in the Art of Swordsmanship.* London: Routledge and Keagan Paul, 1987.

Frederic, Louis. *A Dictionary of the Martial Arts.* Rutland, VT: Tuttle, 1991.

Friday, Karl. *Hired Swords: The Rise of Private Warrior Power in Early Japan.* Stanford, CA: Stanford University Press, 1992.

———. "Kabala in Motion: Kata and Pattern Practice in the Traditional Bugei." Los Angeles, CA: Annual Meeting of the Association for Asian Studies, 1993.

———. "Kabala in Motion: Kata and Pattern Practice in the Traditional Bugei." *Journal of Asian Martial Arts* 4:4 (1995): 27–39.

———. *Mononofu: The Warrior of Heian Japan.* Master's Thesis. University of Kansas, 1983.

———. "Teeth and Claws: Provincial Warriors and the Heian Court." *Monumenta Nipponica* 43:2 (1988): 153–185.

———. "Valorous Butchers: The Art of War during the Golden Age of the Samurai." *Japan Forum* 5 (April 1993): 1–19.

Fujimoto Masayuki. "Bugu to rekishi II." *Rekishi to chiri* 421 (1990): 58–72.

———. "Bugu to rekishi I." *Rekishi to chiri* 418 (1990): 40–52.

Fung Yu-lan. *A Short History of Chinese Philosophy.* New York: Free Press, 1948.

Futaki Ken'ichi, Irie Kōhei and Katō Hiroshi, eds. *Budō.* Tokyo: Tōkyōdō, 1994.

Grapard, Allan. "Flying Mountains and Walkers of Emptiness: Toward a Definition of Sacred Space in Japanese Religions." *History of Religions* 20 (February 1982): 195–221.

———. "Japan's Ignored Cultural Revolution: The Separation of Shinto and Buddhist Divinities (Shimbutsu Bunri) in Meiji and a Case Study, Tōnomine." *History of Religions* 23:3 (1984): 240–265.

———. "Patriarchs of Heian Buddhism: Kūkai and Saichō." In *Great Historical Figures of Japan*, ed. Murakami Hyoe and Thomas J. Harper, 39–48. Tokyo: Japan Culture Institute, 1978.

————. *The Protocol of the Gods: A Study of the Kasuga Cult in Japanese History.* Berkeley, CA: University of California Press, 1992.

Grossinger, Richard, and Lindy Hough, eds. *Nuclear Strategy and the Code of the Warrior: Faces of Mars and Shiva in the Crisis of Human Survival.* Berkeley: North Atlantic, 1984.

Hall, John W., ed. *Early Modern Japan.* Vol. 4. of *The Cambridge History of Japan.* New York: Cambridge University Press, 1991.

————. "Feudalism in Japan: A Reassessment." In *Studies in the Institutional History of Early Modern Japan,* ed. John W. Hall and Marius B. Jansen, 15–55. 1962. Reprint. Princeton, NJ: Princeton University Press, 1977.

————. "Foundations of the Modern Japanese Daimyō." In *Studies in the Institutional History of Early Modern Japan,* ed. John W. Hall and Marius B. Jansen, 65–79. 1961. Reprint. Princeton, NJ: Princeton University Press, 1968.

————. *Government and Local Power in Japan 500–1700: A Study Based on Bizen Province.* Princeton, NJ: Princeton University Press, 1966.

————. "Japanese History: New Dimensions of Approach and Understanding." In *Washington Service Center for Teachers of History.* 1961.

————. *Japan: From Prehistory to Modern Times.* Tokyo: Tuttle; 1971.

————. "Japan's 16th Century Revolution." In *Warlords, Artists, and Commoners,* ed. George Elison and Bardwell L. Smith, 7–21. Honolulu: University of Hawai'i Press, 1981.

————. "The Muromachi Bakufu." In *Medieval Japan,* ed. Kozo Yamamura, 175–230. *The Cambridge History of Japan,* vol. 3. New York: Cambridge University Press, 1990.

Hall, John W., and Marius B. Jansen. *Studies in the Institutional History of Early Modern Japan.* Princeton, NJ: Princeton University Press, 1968.

Hall, John W., Nagahara Keiji, and Yamamura Kozo, eds. *Japan Before Tokugawa: Political Consolidation and Economic Growth, 1500–1650.* Princeton, NJ: Princeton University Press, 1981.

Hall, John W., and Toyoda Takeshi, eds. *Japan in the Muromachi Age.* Berkeley: University of California Press, 1977.

Hardacre, Helen. *Kurozumikyō and the New Religions of Japan.* Princeton, NJ: Princeton University Press, 1986.

Harrison, E. J. *The Fighting Spirit of Japan: The Esoteric Study of the Martial Arts and Way of Life in Japan.* London: Foulsham, 1955.

Heckler, Richard Strozzi, ed. *Aikido and the New Warrior* Berkeley: North Atlantic, 1985.

Herrigel, Eugen. *Zen in the Art of Archery.* New York: Pantheon, 1953.

Hesselink, Reinier H. "The Warrior's Prayer: Tokugawa Yoshimune Revives the Yabusame Ceremony." Los Angeles, CA: Annual Meeting of the Association for Asian Studies, 1993.

————. "The Warrior's Prayer: Tokugawa Yoshimune Revives the Yabusame Ceremony." *Journal of Asian Martial Arts* 4:4 (1995): 40–49.

Hirada Toshiharu. *Sōhei to bushi.* Tokyo: Nihon kyōbunsha, 1965.

Hiraoka Sadaumi. "Sōhei ni tsuite." In *Nihon shakai keizaishi kenkyū,* 547–582. Tokyo, 1967.

Hiyoshi Shōichi. *Nihon sōhei kenkyū.* Tokyo: Kokushokan gyōkai, 1972.

Hori, G. Victor Sōgen. "Teaching and Learning in the Rinzai Zen Monastery." *Journal of Japanese Studies* 20:1 (1994): 25–32.

Hurst, G. Cameron, III. *The Armed Martial Arts of Japan*. New Haven, Conn.: Yale University Press, forthcoming.

———. "Death, Honor, and Loyalty: The Bushidō Ideal." *Philosophy East and West* 40 (1990).

———. "Development of Insei: A Problem in Japanese History and Historiography." In *Medieval Japan: Essays in Institutional History*, ed. John W. Hall and Jeffrey P. Mass, 60–90. New Haven, CT: Yale University Press, 1974.

———. "An Emperor Who Reigned as Well as Ruled: Temmu Tennō." In *Great Historical Figures of Japan*, ed. Murakami Hyoe and Thomas J. Harper, 16–27. Tokyo: Japan Culture Institute, 1978.

———. "From Heihō to Bugei: The Emergence of Martial Arts in Tokugawa Japan." *Journal of Asian Martial Arts* 2:4 (1993): 40–51.

———. *Insei: Abdicated Sovereigns in the Politics of Late Heian Japan 1086–1185*. New York: Columbia University Press, 1976.

———. "Ryūha in the Martial and Other Japanese Arts." Los Angeles, CA: Annual Meeting of the Association for Asian Studies, 1993.

———. "Ryūha in the Martial and Other Japanese Arts." *Journal of Asian Martial Arts* 4:4 (1995): 12–25.

———. "Sumurai on Wall Street: Miyamoto Musashi and the Search for Success." *UFSI Reports* 44 (1982).

———. "Structure of the Heian Court: Some Thoughts on Familial Authority." In *Medieval Japan: Essays in Institutional History*, ed. John W. Hall and Jeffrey P. Mass, 39–59. New Haven, CT: Yale University Press, 1974.

Hyams, Joe. *Zen in the Martial Arts*. New York: Tarcher, 1979.

Imamura Yoshio. *Budō ka enshū*. 2 vols. Tokyo: Daiichi shobō, 1989.

———. *(19 seiki ni okeru) Nihon taiiku nokenkyū*. Tokyo: Fumeidō, 1967.

———. *Shiryō Yagyū Shinkage-ryū*. Tokyo: Jinbutsu ōraisha, 1967.

Inagaki Motō. *Kengō meishōbu hyaku wa*. Tokyo: Tatsukaze shobō, 1982.

Ishigaki Yasuzō. *Kashima Shinden Jikishin Kageryūgokui denkai*. Tokyo: Shingisha, 1992.

Ishii Susumu. "The Decline of the Kamakura Bakufu." Trans. Jeffrey P. Mass and Hitomi Tonomura from vol. 3 of *The Cambridge History of Japan: Medieval Japan*, ed. Kozo Yamamura, 128–174. New York: Cambridge University Press, 1990.

———. "The Decline of the Kamakura Bakufu." In *Medieval Japan*, ed. Kozo Yamamura, 128–174. *The Cambridge History of Japan*, vol. 3. New York: Cambridge University Press, 1990.

Ishikawa Kazuo. "Bu no kami: Kashima, Katori." *Gekken kendō Nihon* 3 (1991): 68–72.

Ishioka Hisao. *Heihōsha no seikatsu*. Tokyo: Yūsan kakaku, 1981.

Ishioka Hisao, Wakada Kazuo, and Katō Hiroshi. *Nihon no kobujutsu*. Tokyo: Shinjinbutsu ōraisha, 1980.

Iwai Tsukuo. *Kobujutsu tankyū*. Tokyo: Airyūdō, 1991.

Jansen, Marius B., ed. *The Nineteenth Century*. Vol. 5 of *The Cambridge History of Japan*. New York: Cambridge University Press, 1989.

Jansen, Marius B., and Gilbert Rozman, eds. *Japan in Transition: From Tokugawa to Meiji*. Princeton, NJ: Princeton University Press, 1986.

Kaku Shōzō. "Ashibarai ukebune." *Gekken kendō Nihon* 11 (1991): 71–73.

———. "Enpi-ken." *Gekken kendō Nihon* 2 (1992): 63–65.

———. "Ichi-no-tachi." *Gekken kendō Nihon* 1 (1992): 71–73.

———. "Kesagiri." *Gekken kendō Nihon* 10 (1991): 71–73.

———. "Kurai-tachi." *Gekken kendō Nihon* 12 (1991): 79–81.

———. "Tsukite-dori." *Gekken kendō Nihon* 3 (1992): 79–81.

Katsuno Ryūshin. *Sōhei*. Tokyo: Tōbundō, 1955.

Keenan, John P. "The Mystique of Martial Arts: A Response to Professor McFarlane." *Japanese Journal of Religious Studies* 17:4 (1990): 421–432.

———. "Spontaneity in Western Martial Arts: A Yogācāra Critique of *Mushin* (No-Mind)." *Japanese Journal of Religious Studies* 16:4 (1989): 285–298.

Kensei Tsukahara Bokuden seitan gohyaku nensai kinen jitsugyō iinkai, ed. *Kensei Tsukahara Bokuden seitan gohyaku nensai kinenshi*. Ibaraki, Japan: Ishizaki insatsusho, 1989.

Kiley, Cornelius J. "State and Dynasty in Archaic Yamato." *Journal of Japanese Studies* 3:1 (1973): 25–49.

King, Winston L. *Zen and the Way of the Sword: Arming the Warrior Psyche*. New York: Oxford University Press, 1993.

Kitagawa, Joseph. *On Understanding Japanese Religion*. Princeton, NJ: Princeton University Press, 1987.

Knutsen, Roald M. *Japanese Polearms*. London: Holland Press, 1963.

Kobayashi Hiroko. *The Human Comedy of Heian Japan: A Study of the Secular Stories in the 12th Century Collection of Tales, Konjaku Monogatarishu*. Tokyo: Centre for East Asian Cultural Studies, 1979.

Kobe Shinjūrō. *Nihon kengōdan*. Tokyo: Mainichi shinbunsha, 1984.

Konishi Jin'ichi. *The High Middle Ages*. Ed. Earl Miner, trans. Aileen Gatten and Mark Harbison. Vol. 3 of *A History of Japanese Literature*. Princeton, NJ: Princeton University Press, 1991.

———. *Michi: Chūsei no rinen*. Vol. 3 of *Nihon koten*. Tokyo: Kodansha gendai shinso, 1975.

Kōno Yoshinori. *Bujutsu o gataru: Shintai o tōshiteno "manabi" no genten*. Saitama: Sōshinsha, 1987.

Kunii Zen'ya. "Imaizumi Sensei no oshie o sōki shite." *Kōdō hatsuyō* 135 (1958): 18–22.

———. *Kunii-ke keizu*. Kunii family private collection.

Kuroda Toshio. "Shintō in the History of Japanese Religion." *Journal of Japanese Studies* 7:1 (1981): 1–20.

Kurogi Toshiharu. "Budō ryūha no seiritsu to shūgendō." *Saga-dai kyōiku gakubu kenkyū ronbunshū* 15 (1967): 159–193.

Leggett, Trevor. *Zen and the Ways*. Boulder, CO: Shambala, 1978.

Liao, Waysun. *T'ai Chi Classics*. 1977. Reprint. Boston, MA, and London: Shambala, 1990.

Lishka, Dennis. "Zen and the Creative Process: The 'Kendō-Zen' Thought of the Rinzai Master Takuan." *Japanese Journal of Religious Studies* 5:2–3 (1978): 139–158.

Lowry, Dave. *Autumn Lightning: The Education of an American Samurai*. Boston, MA: Shambala, 1985.

Majima Isao. *Zenkoku shohan kengō jinmei jiten.* Tokyo: Shinjinbutsu Ōraisha, 1996.

Mass, Jeffrey. *Development of Kamakura Rule 1180–1250: A History with Documents.* Stanford: Stanford University Press, 1979.

———. "The Early Bakufu and Feudalism." In *Court and Bakufu in Medieval Japan: Essays in Kamakura History,* ed. John W. Hall and Jeffrey P. Mass, 123–142. New Haven, CT: Yale University Press, 1982.

———. "The Kamakura Bakufu." In *Medieval Japan,* ed. Kozo Yamamura, 46–88. *The Cambridge History of Japan,* vol. 3. New York: Cambridge University Press, 1990.

———. *Lordship and Inheritance in Early Medieval Japan: A Study of the Kamakura Sōryō System.* Stanford: Stanford University Press, 1989.

———. "Translation and Pre-1600 History." *Journal of Japanese Studies* 6:1 (1980): 61–88.

———. *Warrior Government in Medieval Japan: A Study of the Kamakura Bakufu, Shugo and Jitō.* New Haven, CT: Yale University Press, 1974.

Mass, Jeffrey, ed. *Court and Bakufu in Japan: Essays in Kamakura History.* New Haven, CT: Yale University Press, 1982.

Matsushita Keishi. "Korai no waza o kagakuteki ni, gōriteki ni shidō: Kashima-Shinryū." *Gekken kendō Nihon* 8 (1992): 26–29.

———. "Sōgō bujutsu: Kashima-Shinryū." *Gekken kendō Nihon* (1992): 17.

McFarlane, Stewart. "*Mushin,* Morals, and Martial Arts: A Discussion of Keenan's Yogācāra Critique." *Japanese Journal of Religious Studies* 17:4 (1990): 397–420.

———. "The Mystique of Martial Arts: A Reply to Professor Keenan's Response." *Japanese Journal of Religious Studies* 18:4 (1991): 355–368.

McGuinness, Diane, ed. *Dominance, Aggression and War.* New York: Paragon, 1987.

Minami Tsugumasa. *Budō to wa nani ka.* Tokyo: San'ichi shobō, 1977.

Minouchi Sōichi. *Budō tanrenjutsu: tairyoku zukurino kūden to hippō.* Tokyo: Tsuru shobō, 1973.

Miyamoto Musashi. *A Book of Five Rings.* Trans. Victor Harris. Woodstock, NY: Overlook, 1974.

———. *The Book of Five Rings.* Trans. Thomas Cleary. Boston, MA, and London: Shambala, 1993.

———. *The Book of Five Rings (Gorin No Sho).* New York: Bantam, 1982.

———. *Gorin no sho.* Prepared by Ōkōchi Shōji. Tokyo: Kyōikusha, 1980.

Morikawa Tetsurō. "Muteki kengō o tazunete." *Kengō retsudenshū* 68 (1961): 330–341.

Morisawa, Jackson, S. *The Secret of the Target.* 1984. Reprint. New York and London: Routledge, 1988.

Moroda Seiji. *Hōshinryū sasagaki: jitsuroku engen sōdō.* Vol. 1 of *Kōzuke kenjutsu shi.* Tokyo: Kangodō, 1979.

———. *Kensei Kamiizumi Nobutsuna yōden.* Vol. 2 of *Kōzuke kenjutsu shi.* Tokyo: Kangodō, 1984.

Moyer, K. E. *Violence and Aggression.* New York: Paragon, 1987.

Nagahara Keiji. "Land Ownership Under the Shoen-Kokugaryo System." *Journal of Japanese Studies* 1:2 (1975): 269–296.

————. *Shōen.* Wakai seidai to kataru Nihon no rekishi. Tokyo: Hyōronsha, 1978.

Nakabayashi Shinji. "Kendō shi." In *Nihon budō taikei,* Imamura Yoshio et al., 29–132. Tokyo: Dōshōsha, 1982.

————. "Kenjutsu Keiko no ikkōsatsu." In *Budō ronkō,* 160–168. Ibaraki, Japan: Nakabayashi Shinji sensei isakushū kangyōkai, 1988.

————. "Nihon kobudō ni okeru shintairon." *Risō* 604 (1983): 106–115.

Nakane Chie, and Shinzaburō Ōishi, *Tokugawa Japan.* Trans. and ed. Conrad Totman. Tokyo: University of Tokyo Press, 1990.

Nakayama Nobuna, ed. *Shinpen Hitachi kokushi.* Tokyo: Miyazaki Hōonkai, 1970.

Nakazato Sukeyama. *Nihon bujutsu shinmyōki.* Tokyo: Shimazu shobō, 1994.

Nandō Tsugumasa. *Budō to wa nanika?* Tokyo: San'ichi Shoten, 1977.

Nelson, Randy F., ed. *The Overlook Martial Arts Reader: An Anthology of Historical and Philosophical Writings.* Woodstock, NY: Overlook, 1989.

Niimura Izuru, ed. *Kōjien.* Tokyo: Iwanami Shoten, 1955.

Oboroya Hisashi. *Seiwa genji.* Tokyo: Kyoikusha, 1984.

Ogasawara Harunobu et al. "Budō no ryūha (iemoto seido) ni tsuite." *Taiiku no kagaku* 17:11 (1967): 656–661.

Okada Kazuo. "Kashima-Katori: Kenpō to sono denryū 2, chūkō jidai sono ichi." *Gekkan budō* (October 1977).

————. *Kengō shidan.* Tokyo: Shinjinbutsu ōraisha, 1984.

Ōmori Nobumasa. *Bujutsu densho no kenkyū.* Tokyo: Chijinkan, 1991.

Otake Risuke. *The Deity and the Sword: Katori Shinto Ryu.* Trans. Donn F. Draeger. 3 vols. Tokyo: Minato Research and Publishing, 1977.

Ouwehand, Cornelius. *Namazu-e and Their Themes.* Leiden: Brill, 1964.

Overmeyer, Daniel L. "Chinese Religion." In *The Religious Traditions of Asia,* ed. Joseph M. Kitagawa, 257–304. 1987. Reprint. New York: Macmillan, 1989.

Ozawa Aijirō. *Ōkoku kendōshi.* Tokyo: Tanaka Seikōdō, 1944.

Papinot, E. *Historical and Geographical Dictionary of Japan.* 1910. Reprint. Rutland, VT: Tuttle, 1972.

Parulski, George R. *Sword of the Samurai: The Classical Art of Japanese Swordsmanship.* Boulder, CO: Paladin Press, 1985.

Perrin, Noel. *Giving Up the Gun: Japan's Reversion to the Sword, 1543–1877.* Boulder, CO: Shambala, 1979.

Philippi, Donald L., trans. *Kojiki.* Tokyo: Tokyo University Press, 1968.

Ponsonby-Fane, Richard. *The Vicissitudes of Shinto.* Kyoto: Ponsonby-Fane Memorial Society, 1963.

Porkert, Manfred. *The Theoretical Foundations of Chinese Medicine: Systems of Correspondence.* Cambridge, MA: MIT Press, 1974.

Purce, Jill. *The Mystic Spiral: Journey of the Soul.* New York: Avon, 1974.

Ratti, Oscar, and Adele Westbrook. *Secrets of the Samurai: A Survey of the Martial Arts of Feudal Japan.* Rutland, VT: Tuttle, 1974.

Reid, Daniel P. *The Tao of Health, Sex, & Longevity: a Practical Guide to the Ancient Way.* New York: Simon & Schuster, 1979.

Rielly, Robin L. *Japan's Complete Fighting System: Shin Kage Ryu.* Rutland, VT: Tuttle, 1989.

Robinson, H. Russell. *Japanese Arms and Armor.* New York: Crown, 1969.
Rogers, John M. "Arts of War in Times of Peace: Archery in the Honchō Bugei Shōden." *Monumenta Nipponica* 45:3 (1990): 253–284.
———. "Arts of War in Times of Peace: Swordsmanship in the Honchō Bugei Shōden, Chapter 5." *Monumenta Nipponica* 45:4 (1990): 413–447.
———. "Arts of War in Times of Peace: Swordsmanship in the Honchō Bugei Shōden, Chapter 6." *Monumenta Nipponica* 46:2 (1990): 173–202.
———. "Shoden in Japanese Swordsmanship." Los Angeles, CA: Annual Meeting, Association for Asian Studies, 1993.
"Saigo no kengō: Kashima-Shinryū dai 18 sei shihan Kunii Zen'ya shi." *Rekishi dokuhon* (November 1960): 85–89.
Sasama Yoshihiko. *Nihon kōchū-bugu jiten.* Tokyo: Kashiwa shobō, 1981.
———. *Zusetsu Nihon budō jiten.* Tokyo: Kashiwa shobō, 1982.
Sasama Yoshihiko, Takayanagi Kaneyoshi, Momose Akiharu, Uchida Ryūya, Sone Taeko, Taniguchi Takuhisa, and Murai Sanae. *Bushi no seikatsu.* Vol. 3. Tokyo, Kashiwa Shobō, 1982.
Sasmori, Junzo, and Gordon Warner. *This is Kendo: The Art of Japanese Fencing.* Rutland, VT: Tuttle, 1989.
Sato Kanzan. *The Japanese Sword.* Tokyo: Kodansha, 1983.
Seki Humitake. "Bujutsu to Ki." Unpublished paper. Privately printed, 1993.
———. *Kashima-Shinryū shihan-yō bujutsu kyōsho.* Unpublished manuscript. Privately printed, 1990.
———. *Nihon budō no engen: Kashima-Shinryū.* Tokyo: Kyōrin shoin, 1976.
———. *Shōwa no godai Kashima-Shinryū honden: bujutsu gokui gugen no koto.* Unpublished manuscript. Privately printed, 1991.
Slawson, David. *Secret Teachings in the Art of Japanese Gardens: Design Principles and Aesthetic Values.* New York: Kodansha International, 1987.
Stevens, John. *The Sword of No-Sword: The Life of Master Warrior Tesshu.* Boston, MA: Shambala, 1984.
Sugawara Makoto. *Lives of Master Swordsmen.* Tokyo: The East, 1985.
———. "Ronkosho: The Dream of the Bushi." *East* 15:7–8 (1979): 65–70.
Suzuki, D. T. *Zen and Japanese Culture.* 1959. Reprint. Princeton, NJ: Princeton University Press, 1973.
Suzuki Susumu. *Nihon kassenshi hyakubanashi.* Tokyo: Tatsukaze shobō, 1982.
Swanson, Paul L. "Shugendō and the Yoshino-Kumano Pilgrimage: An Example of Mountain Pilgrimage." *Monumenta Nipponica* 36:1 (1981): 55–79.
Takahashi Tomio. *Bushidō no rekishi.* 3 vols. Tokyo: Shin Jinbutsu ōraisha, 1986.
Takayanagi Mitsutoshi, and Suzuki Tōru. *Nihon kassenshi.* Tokyo: Gakugei Shorin, 1968.
Takeda Ryūichi. "Kendō ni okeru 'sen' ni kansuru ikkōsatsu." In *Nihon budōgaku kenkyū,* ed. Watanabe Ichirō kyōjū taikan kinenkai, Japanese, 457–462. Tokyo: Shimazu shobō, 1988.
Takeuchi Rizō, ed. *Bushi no tōjō.* Nihon no rekishi. Tokyo: Chūō kōronsha, 1965.
———. *Kadokawa Nihon chimmei daijiten.* 47 vols. Tokyo: Kadokawa Shoten, 1978–1990.
Takuan Sōhō. *The Unfettered Mind: Writings of the Zen Master to the Sword Master.* Trans. William Scott Wilson. Tokyo: Kodansha International, 1986.

Tanaka Fumon. *Koryū kenjutsu.* Tokyo: Airyūdō, 1994.

Tanaka Jigohei. *Chinkonbō no jisshū.* Tokyo: Kasumigaseki shobō, 1972.

Tanaka Mamoru. "Kinsei kenjutsu denshō ni miru 'kamae' no kōsatsu." In *Nihon budōgaku kenkyū,* ed. Watanabe Ichirō kyōjū taikan kinenkai, 67–90. Tokyo: Shimazu shobō, 1988.

Tō Minoru. *Kashima jingū.* Tokyo: Gakuseisha, 1968.

Tomiki Kenji. *Budō ron.* Tokyo: Daishūkan shoten, 1991.

Tominaga Kengo. *Kendō gohyakunen-shi.* Tokyo:Hyakusen shobō, 1971.

Totman, Conrad. *The Collapse of the Tokugawa Bakufu, 1862–1868.* Honolulu: University of Hawai'i Press, 1980.

———. *Japan Before Perry: A Short History.* Berkeley: University of California Press, 1981.

———. *Politics in the Tokugawa Bakufu.* Cambridge, MA: Harvard University Press, 1967.

Tsumoto Yū. "Kobudō o tazuneru 1 and 2." *Bungei shunshū* 61:11–12 (1983): 202–219; 446–461.

———. *Yagyū Hyōgosuke.* 3 vols. Tokyo: Mainichi shinbunsha, 1986.

Tully, Joan. "So What Does It Do?" *Ohohia* (April-June 1995): 14–15.

Turnbull, Stephen R. *Battles of the Samurai.* London: Arms and Armour Press, 1987.

———. *The Lone Samurai and the Martial Arts.* London: Arms and Armour Press, 1990.

———. *The Samurai: A Military History.* New York: Macmillan, 1976.

———. *Samurai Armies, 1550–1615.* London: Osprey, 1979.

Ueda Makoto. *Literary and Art Theories in Japan.* Cleveland, OH: Western Reserve University Press, 1967.

Ukai, Nancy. "The Kumon Approach to Teaching and Learning." *Journal of Japanese Studies* 20:1 (1994): 87–113.

Varley, H. Paul. "Samurai in School: Ryuha in Traditional Japanese Martial Arts." *Journal of Asian Martial Arts* 4:4 (1995): 10–11.

Watatani Kiyoshi. *Nihon kengō 100 en.* Tokyo: Akita shoten, 1971.

Watatani Kiyoshi, and Yamada Tadachika, eds. *Bugei ryūha daijiten.* Tokyo: Nihon kopii shuppanbu, 1978.

Wilson, William R. "Way of the Bow and Arrow: The Japanese Warrior in the Kojaku Monogatari." *Monumenta Nipponica* 28:1–4 (1973): 177–233.

Wilson, William Scott, ed. *Ideals of the Samurai: Writings of Japanese Warriors.* Burbank, CA: Ohara, 1982.

Yagyū Munenori. *The Sword and the Mind.* Trans. Hiroaki Sato. Woodstock, NY: Overlook, 1986.

"Yagyū-Shinkage School of Swordsmanship: The Great Yagyū Swordsmen." *East* 12:1 (1976): 54–61.

Yamamura Kozo, ed. *Medieval Japan.* Vol. 3 of *The Cambridge History of Japan.* New York: Cambridge University Press, 1989.

Yamasaki Taikō. *Shingon: Japanese Esoteric Buddhism.* Trans. Richard Peterson and Cynthia Peterson. Ed. Morimoto Yasuyoshi and David Kidd. Boston, MA, and London: Shambala, 1988.

Yasuda Motohisa. *Senran.* Tokyo: Kintō Shuppansha, 1984.

Yasuda Motohisa, ed. *Bakumatsu ishin no sōran.* Senran Nihonshi. Tokyo: Daiichi hōgen, 1988.

————. *Gekokujō no makuake.* Senran Nihonshi. Tokyo: Daiichi hōgen, 1988.

————. *Nanbokuchō no nairan.* Senran Nihonshi. Tokyo: Daiichi hōgen, 1988.

————. *Sengoku no gunyū (kinai • tōgoku).* Senran Nihonshi. Tokyo: Daiichi hōgen, 1988.

————. *Sengoku no gunyū (saigoku • okuwa).* Senran Nihonshi. Tokyo: Daiichi hōgen, 1988.

————. *Tenka fubu.* Senran Nihonshi. Tokyo: Daiichi hōgen, 1988.

————. *Tenkajin e no michi.* Senran Nihonshi. Tokyo: Daiichi hōgen, 1988.

————. *Yūsha no jōken.* Senran Nihonshi. Tokyo: Daiichi hōgen, 1988.

Yoshida Yutaka. *Budō hitsudensho.* Tokyo: Tokuma shoten, 1968.

Yoshitani Osamu. "Kenjutsu kata no kōzō to kinō ni kansuru kenkyū." In *Nihon Budōgaku Kenkyū*, ed. Watanabe Ichirō kyōju taikan kinenkai, Japanese, 114–129. Tokyo: Shimazu shobō, 1988.

Yuasa Yasuo. *The Body, Self-Cultivation, and Ki-Energy.* Trans. Shigenori Nagatomo and Monte S. Hull. Albany, NY: State University of New York Press, 1993.

Yumoto, John M. *The Samurai Sword: A Handbook.* Rutland, VT: Tuttle, 1959.

INDEX

About the Authors

Karl F. Friday, an associate professor of Japanese history at the University of Georgia, is a specialist in premodern military and institutional history. His publications in this field include *Hired Swords: the Rise of Private Warrior Power in Early Japan* (Stanford University Press, 1992), "Valorous Butchers: the Art of War During the Golden Age of the Samurai" (*Japan Forum*, 1993), "Bushidō or Bull? A Medieval Historian's Perspective on the Imperial Army and the Japanese Warrior Tradition" (*The History Teacher*, 1994), and the forthcoming "Pushing Beyond the Pale: the Yamoto Conquest of the Emishi and Northern Japan." In addition, he has studied samurai and other combative arts extensively in Japan and Korea, and holds a *shihan/menkyo kaiden* ranking from the Kashima-Shinryū, as well as black-belt ranks in several other arts.

Seki Humitake is the nineteenth-generation headmaster *(shihanke)* of the Kashima-Shinryū and a professor of the Institute of Biological Sciences at the University of Tsukuba. In addition to seven books and more than one hundred articles on marine microbiology, he has authored a book and numerous articles on Kashima-Shinryū martial art, including *Nihon budō no engen: Kashima-Shinryū* (Kyōrin shōin, 1976).